W9-AHF-846

$\mathcal{T}ime\ of\ \mathcal{Y}our\ \mathcal{L}ife$

WHY ALMOST EVERYTHING GETS BETTER AFTER FIFTY

Jane Glenn Haas

SEVEN LOCKS PRESS

Santa Ana, California
Minneapolis, Minnesota
Washington, D.C.

Seven Locks Press
P.O. Box 25689
Santa Ana, CA 92799
(800) 354-5348

Individual Sales. This book is available through most bookstores or can be ordered directly from Seven Locks Press at the address above.

Quantity Sales. Special discounts are available on quantity purchases by corporations, associations, and others. For details, contact the "Special Sales Department" at the publisher's address above.

Printed in the United States of America

Library of Congress Cataloging-in-Publication Data
Haas, Jane Glenn, 1937–
    Time of you life: why almost everything gets better after fifty / Jane Glenn Haas
       p. cm.
    ISBN 0-929765-84-2
    1. Aged--United States. 2. Aging--United States 3. Haas, Jane, Glenn, 1937–
4. Aged women--United States--Biography. I. Title.

HQ1064.U5 H15 2000   00-063563
305.26'0973--dc21

Front and back cover photographs ©Bruce C. Strong, courtesy of the photographer
Cover and Interior Design by Sparrow Advertising & Design

Dedication

To my patient husband, Bob

Contents

Foreword
XV

Prologue
XIX

Part 1—I'm Not Really Old—This Is Just a Disguise

WHAT A RELIEF TO FINALLY HIT THE BIG 6-0
3

MIRROR, MIRROR, PLASTIC SURGERY
5

MIRROR, MIRROR, COSMETIC SURGERY
1 1

READ MY LIPS (AND CHIN, CROW'S FEET, EARLOBES . . .)
1 7

MIRROR, MIRROR, COSMETIC SURGERY: ONE YEAR AFTER A FACELIFT
20

THEY'RE ALL YOU HAVE TO STAND ON
24

Part 2—The Big "C" Hits Me

LIFE THROWS A PUNCH
29

ANOTHER LUMP, ANOTHER BOUT OF FEAR AND HOPE
34

EMOTIONS RUN HIGH SUNDAY IN NEWPORT BEACH
37

FOUR YEARS OF FREEDOM FROM BREAST CANCER? GIVE A CHEER!
40

EVEN DOCTORS COME TO BELIEVE: FAITH CAN HEAL BODY AND SOUL
42

WRITER'S EXPERIENCE WITH BREAST CANCER CHANGED HER LIFE
44

Part 3—We Say They're Seniors— They Say, "I'm Old"

HELP EXPOSE A TRAGIC SECRET: ELDER ABUSE
49

GRANNY IN STIR: SENIOR EQUALITY CUTS BOTH WAYS
52

POWERFUL ROLE FOR SENIORS: GUARDIAN ANGEL
55

JUST BEING THERE IS WHAT IS NEEDED DURING PERSONAL CRISIS
57

"HARD-BOILED, THICK-SKINNED," TODAY'S
SENIORS ARE "SURVIVORS"
59

DOMESTIC VIOLENCE IS PROBLEM OF OLD
AS WELL AS YOUNG WOMEN
61

WITHHOLDING VISITATION? JUST STOP IT!
63

THERE ARE TIMES FOR A HAPPY FACE, TIMES
FOR REALISTIC OUTLOOK
65

WHERE IS RELIEF FOR CAREGIVERS?
67

Part 4—Don't Ever Call ME a "Senior Citizen"

THE "GIRL" AT 71
73

ATTITUDE, ENTHUSIASM, ENERGY SEPARATE AGING FROM THE OLD
77

MEN TAKING A "FIRMATIVE" ACTION ON SKIN CARE
79

DOES MATURITY MAKE YOU RIGID? ONLY IN THE CONDENSED EDITION
81

IMAGES AND STEREOTYPES OF GROWING OLDER
83

KEEPING FIT IN OLD AGE IS OUR RESPONSIBILITY
85

SENIORS TODAY GET YOUNGER AS THEY AGE
87

KEEP ON GROWING IF YOU WANT TO SLOW THE DEMISE OF MIDLIFE
89

AGING NATURALLY
91

STEPS THAT LEAD TO BEING MORE ACTIVE
97

AVOID FOLLY OF TRYING TO DENY AGING
99

Part 5—Women—The 21st Century Gender

WOMEN NEEDN'T GET WORKED UP OVER RETIREMENT
103

WOMEN FINALLY ARE GETTING THE TREATMENT THEY DESERVE
105

RETIREMENT MIGHT NOT MEET EXPECTATIONS
107

WOMEN IN THE "INVISIBLE ZONE" WON'T ACCEPT SOCIETY'S DECREE
109

DAUGHTERS HAVE FULL RANGE OF OPTIONS FOR LIFE OPEN TO THEM
111

CHALLENGES STILL TO BE OVERCOME
113

Part 6—Ah, the People I've Known

A GOOD ATTITUDE HELPS TO MAKE A GOOD SPORT
119

CREATURE COMFORTS UNNEEDED BY SOME ADVENTURESOME SOULS
121

STILL LOOKING AHEAD AT 108
123

LET CREDIT ROLL FOR ENTERTAINMENT FIGURES WHO
CARE FOR THEIR ELDERS
126

LEARNING TO BALANCE CONTROL, SURRENDER
128

CELEBRATING A CENTURY OF LIVING—HE AND
HIS BREATH STILL STRONG
130

COUPLES FIND RETIRING CAN BE A TRICKY TIME
133

WAR FILM'S A WINDOW TO DAD'S EXPERIENCE
135

WE HAVE A LOT TO LEARN FROM JENNIE, 109
138

FRIENDSHIP WITH AN OLDER WOMAN ALLAYS FEARS OF AGING
141

Part 7—And the Books They've Written

NOTABLE "LATE BLOOMERS" CAN PROVIDE INSPIRATION FOR OTHERS
145

TALENT IS MORE THAN BAKING GREAT CUPCAKES
147

TOGETHERNESS MAY PROVE TO BE WAVE OF
FUTURE FOR GENERATIONS
149

RETIRING CAREER WOMEN ARE MAKING IT UP AS THEY GO ALONG
151

WEATHERING BUMPS OF MARRIAGE TAKES DEDICATION, COMPROMISE
153

BALANCE IS THE KEY TO SHAPING THE NEW AMERICAN RETIREMENT
155

PERVASIVE SENSE OF HOSTILITY IS FOUND IN ALL WALKS OF LIFE
157

SOMETHING CRABBY THIS WAY COMES
159

RETIREMENT BRINGS NEW SET OF MARITAL CHALLENGES
163

Part 8—Everyone's a Hero to Someone

WHEN THE KEYS ARE GONE, WHO DRIVES GRANDDAD?
167

BOOKMARK FROM THE PAST IS A BENCHMARK OF LIFE'S CHANGE
169

THE SANDWICH GENERATION
171

MOST HEROES AREN'T CELEBRITIES BUT DO THEIR WORK UNNOTICED
175

OUR EVERYDAY HEROES ARE EVERYWHERE
177

AMID GLENN'S AGE-DEFYING FLIGHT, A GENDER BARRIER FALLS
180

Part 9—What It Was, What It Is, What It Will Be

PRIME TIME HEIRLOOMS LOSING THEIR SENTIMENTAL VALUE
185

DUMP "STUFF" NOW AND START ENJOYING LIFE
187

REMEMBER, IT'S WHAT YOU HAVE BECOME THAT COUNTS
189

Part 10—There Are Friends, and Then There Are FRIENDS

NAMES CHANGE, AND FINDING OLD FRIENDS BECOMES DIFFICULT
193

WHY DO SOME FRIENDSHIPS AGE GRACEFULLY
WHILE OTHERS DON'T?
195

CELEBRATING FRIENDSHIPS IS ESSENTIAL
197

Part 11—Family, Family Everywhere

BABY STEPS TAKE STRIDES TO HEAL A RIFT
201

MOM, AFTER VOWING BETTER LIFE FOR CHILD, SEES
HER MOVE TO SIMPLER LIFE
203

GENERATIONS ALL LEARN FROM ONE ANOTHER
205

LOVE AND CONCERN HELP MIKE COME TO GRIPS WITH CHANGES
207

A LIFETIME OF GRUDGES IN A GUNNYSACK
209

GRANDPARENTS, LIKE PARENTS, AREN'T ALL ALIKE
211

EXPERTS IN ELDERCARE CAN EASE BURDEN
213

A DIFFERENT WAY TO LOOK AT RACE IN U.S.
215

HAPPIEST PLACE ON EARTH FOR KIDS, MAYBE
217

RECORDING FAMILY MEMORIES HELPS STEM LONELINESS OF AGING
219

HER EX REAPS WHAT HE SOWS WITH CHILDREN
221

A MENDED FAMILY RIFT BRINGS JOY
223

Part 12—Modern Motherhood

BEING A GRANDMA IS GREAT, BUT BEING A NEW MOM AT 50 ISN'T
227

NEVER TOO OLD?
229

MOTHERS AND DAUGHTERS: THE TIE THAT BINDS RELATIONSHIPS
236

YOUR KIDS GROW UP TO BE THEMSELVES
242

Part 13—Boomers in Prime Time?

BOOMERS JUST CAN'T STOP TALKING ABOUT
THEIR G-G-G-GENERATION
247

LOW RATE OF CHILDBEARING HAS CONSEQUENCES
FOR THE BOOMERS
249

BASICS NO LONGER COME NATURALLY
251

FOR BOOMERS, RETIREMENT SOON MAY BECOME
JUST A FOND DREAM
253

JOB SENIORITY JUST BECAME YOUR LIABILITY
255

BABY BOOMERS MOBILIZE FOR LIFE'S NEXT PHASE: AGING
258

AARP? AARTH! SOMETIME AROUND A BOOMER'S 50TH BIRTHDAY, IT
COMES LIKE A CALLING CARD FROM THE GRIM REAPER
263

Part 14—Sex—What Else Is There to Say?

SEPARATE BEDS DOESN'T MEAN SEPARATE LIVES
271

COUPLES CAN RE-IGNITE SPARK FROM THE PAST
273

VIAGRA AND THE MACHO MAN: A WOMAN'S VIEW
275

CHEMISTRY KEEPS THOSE OLD BEAUS FROM FADING AWAY
277

BEING REALISTIC MAY BRING THE ROMANCE BACK
279

ROMANCE IS ELUSIVE FOR MANY BOOMERS
281

SEX AFTER MENOPAUSE: WOMEN LIVE BY THEIR OWN ASSUMPTIONS
284

MIDLIFE CALLS FOR RENEGOTIATING RELATIONSHIPS
286

IT'S NEVER TOO LATE TO HAVE FRANK TALK ABOUT GOOD SEX
288

Part 15—No-Geezer, Over-50, Light-Verse Contests

WINNERS OF THE FIRST NO-GEEZER, OVER-50,
LIGHT-VERSE CONTEST
293

LONG LIFE SHORT VERSE
299

Part 16—And Other Stuff

HEY, RUDE GUY IN LAS VEGAS—TAKE BACK A LITTLE OF YOUR OWN
309

FICTIONAL BRAND-NAME PEOPLE PERSONIFY OUR EVERYDAY REALITY
311

LOVING PET BECOMES A BALM FOR LONELINESS—AT ANY AGE
313

STEREOTYPES HAVE GROWN TOO OLD TO USE
315

SOME WORDS OF ADVICE FOR THE CLASS OF '98
317

BAD NEWS—WE'RE LIVING A LOT LONGER
319

GRADUATION IS KNOWLEDGE, ON THE WAY TO GREATNESS
321

Part 17—In the End

CHOOSING DEATH IS EASY; ALL YOU NEED IS NOBILITY
325

WHEN DOES A GOOD DAUGHTER SAY GOODBYE?
327

SEND OFF LOVED ONES WITH A PERSONAL TOUCH
329

DEATH IS LESS TERRIFYING IF WE DON'T HAVE TO FACE IT ALONE
331

PEOPLE'S WISHES FOR THEIR FINAL FAREWELL
AS VARIED AS THEY ARE
333

RULING SHUTS A DOOR FOR TERMINALLY ILL
335

Epilogue
337

Author's Note
339

I do not think there was a time in my life before I hit my mid-40s when I did not fear getting old.

I had my first aging crisis when I was 10 and I saw the film *Beach Blanket Bingo* with Annette Funicello and Frankie Avalon. They were in Southern California—the sun, the beach and the freedom of teenage youth. I was in Chicago—brown skies, ice and my grandmother living in the apartment upstairs from us, stomping across the floor in her orthopedic shoes. Even if I could dream big enough to imagine the day I could escape to the beach and dance with Moon Doggie, I knew no dream could ever be gargantuan enough to come up against reality. Eventually I would end up like my grandmother—old, alone and watching *The Perry Como Show.*

Middle age—that haze my parents seemed to live in—looked like the waiting room. My parents were waiting to forget they were once young and hoping to avoid ever getting too old. Psychologically armed with this outlook on aging, I began to make my way in the world.

Fourteen years later I was living in Los Angeles. I was 24. I wasn't stressed out daily about getting old because I had no evidence it would ever happen to me. Everybody was young. Los Angeles was not the place to get old. If it was, somebody would have done it already. I lived about 40 feet from the beach. I was married to a surfer. I was a baby boomer, and if that failed me, I lived in the plastic surgery and liposuction capital of the universe. Gravity could not keep me down for long.

Over the following years I wrote 18 books for children and spoke to about a hundred thousand kids in schools across the country. In looking back, I realize several of my books had heroines who were grandmothers or older women. I was subconsciously inspiring children to respect the elderly in case one day I became old. Being around children, I got to witness my own childhood again and see ageism at its earliest roots. Age to kids was hell: you had to do what adults said since most of them were at least three times your size. But age was also power. Instead of asking in social situations, "What do you do?" kids ask, "How old are you?" They reply, "I'm seven." "I'm seven and a half." The older you got, the better—unless you turned older than Shaquille O'Neal, in which case you were becoming a relic.

While I hung out with kids, I divorced the surfer, buried my grandmother, watched my mother die of Parkinson's disease and cancer, moved back and forth from Los Angeles to New York, got orthotics and tried everything short of plastic surgery to deny I was aging. I hit a brick wall with my work and never wanted to write again. I questioned the meaning of my life and then, true to good baby boomer course, burned out.

A few years later, I decided to adopt an elderly person through a volunteer program for seniors that helped me begin my ascent from the walk of the middle-aged dead. I chose a woman named Adele. She was 94, blind, totally alone, completely independent, smart as a whip, loving and physically strong, and although 50 years my senior, she was, in many ways, spiritually younger than me. She changed my ideas about aging and my life forever. I wrote *Am I Old Yet?* about our friendship, and because of that book, I was invited to be interviewed by Jane Glenn Haas.

Meeting Jane was like meeting the Indiana (Anna) Jones of aging. She has tackled many aging adventures, she's cool, she looks great, she's 60, she's outwitted and outlived danger and she's a quiet hero about it. "I had a facelift," she told me at lunch like she was asking me to pass the salt. I was a little taken aback because she looked so natural compared to the hundreds of people with facelifts I had seen. I didn't have a clue it was surgery. I guess that's what it looks like when a person is really "in her skin." And that's what Jane Haas is in body and in words. It is a privilege and humbling experience to introduce her book.

The book starts with "What a Relief to Hit the Big 6-0." What a relief to hear someone say what a relief it is! "Limits," she writes, "what limits? Make dust or eat dust." That's her philosophy. This book makes dust. From the articles about Jane's breast cancer surgery to the elective facelift, I was intrigued with the courage and detail in which Jane lays it all out step by step, cut by cut, one physical and emotional discovery after the next. What is particularly wonderful about these pieces is that they are thorough and include facts, figures and resources.

I loved reading about the breast cancer survivor ceremonies and the healing power of prayer in all aspects of our lives. In the article "Powerful Role for Seniors: Guardian Angel," I laughed out loud when Jane related her experience of meeting her spirit guide: "Howard is your spirit guide. He was a scribe in Greece. He'll be with you until he works out his karma. Say hello to Howard." I too have gone through many a search for psychic and spirit guides. I found one in my 94-year-old friend Adele. I have found it in the words of many other elderly people I have met these past few years who do not think of themselves as old. Jane includes several wonderful poems from the delightful "Winners of the First No-Geezer, Over-50, Light Verse Contest." And my winner, please:

> The question I'm asked:
> "Do you still have sex?"
> And I never mind to say,
> "Being now as we're both seventy-two
> "It's only once a day."

I am still shy of 50; it appears I am a long way from retiring but close to facing the realities of old age and illness since my father now has Alzheimer's. I am now less fearful, more inspired, and it is because of facing the issues of aging and learning from those who have gone before me.

Jane Haas lives what she knows. Life at every age is to be celebrated. This book is a celebration of aging. I do not have to end up like my grandmother. *Time of Your Life* can be your real-world and spiritual guide. Read it and grow young!

Leah Komaiko
Los Angeles, August 2000

Prologue

To me, old age is always 15 years older than I am.
—BERNARD BARUCH

I got my first case of crinkly-wrinklies 10 years ago when the *Orange County Register* editors suggested I accept a new beat. They wanted me to write about a topic new to American journalism. They called it "the elderly."

Fact: I was a couple of years on the dark side of 50. True: I had suggested that the editors consider the demographics of an aging society and the impact on local business.

But *elderly!* I thought I was middle-aged. Elderly people are old!

We compromised. We renamed my new beat "aging issues."

Oh, good, I thought. Now I get to age in public, an unladylike Godiva of Gerontology.

In fact, that's what I've done—in print and on television. Some of the results are in this book, a compilation of my best articles and columns on everyone's "aging issues," including some of my own.

I know now that age is as much in our minds as in our creaky joints. Hopefully, most of you will find out this is the best stage of life, a time when you can indulge yourself, a chance to do the things you put off during your "responsible" years.

Sure, at 63 my knees ache and my shoulders suffer from years of "writer's hunch." I've had breast cancer. I've watched a friend die, comforted by family and hospice care. I've also seen my three children marry and I'm enjoying three exceptional grandsons. What's more, I've repackaged myself with the help of plastic surgery. More than a thousand women have called, e-mailed or faxed me to talk about my facelift since I wrote about it two years ago.

Aging is no excuse to stop setting goals—whether they're planting a garden, writing your memoirs, even finding new romance. The aging of America—the aging of the world—is a 21st-century phenomenon. No one knows how society will change by midcentury, when a quarter of the world population will be 65 or older. Already, two-thirds of all the people to reach that birthday are alive today. And suiting up for the Big Six-O and beyond are 76 million boomers. Try telling them they're "elderly" at 65!

Few newspapers and magazines, even fewer radio and television stations, have the vision to explore the impact of aging on a community. The support of my newspaper, the *Orange County Register*, and its editor, Tonnie Katz, has allowed me to flourish in this new arena; my deputy editor, Robin Doussard, has let me explore the opportunities in television, in magazine writing and on the Internet; while my topic editor, Cathy Armstrong, has made it all work for me.

Together, we have told stories that have made a difference in people's lives. There is no higher accolade for journalists than that simple fact: we made a difference.

My articles also have twice been nominated for a Pulitzer Prize and have won the American Medical Writers' Rose Kushner Award for breast cancer reporting, the American Society on Aging's regional media award 2000 and the American Society of Aesthetic Plastic Surgeons' media award 2000. Even the American Motorcyclist Association named me a "Most Valued Person."

Two valued people in my life deserve recognition here: Claudia Suzanne, editorial consultant *extraordinaire* who made organizational sense out of this pile of work, and Lynne Lawrence, my good friend who listened to it all.

I'm having the time of my life. You see, almost everything does get better after 50.

Part 1—I'm Not Really Old—This Is Just a Disguise

WELCOME TO YOUR MIDDLE AGES! FINALLY, YOU GET PERMISSION TO BE
A LITTLE SELFISH AND PUT YOURSELF FIRST. CELEBRATE!
CREATE YOUR OWN RENAISSANCE BECAUSE THESE
ARE THE BEST YEARS OF YOUR LIFE.

Monday, May 12, 1997

I'm a zero again. A really big zero.

By the end of the week, I will have lived 60 years. A guy at the gym heard me mention the date and cracked, "That's the day you'll be 'old.'" I was so startled I dropped a 10-pound barbell. (Sorry about your toe, Sam.)

Old? Mature? In your dreams. Like, one day I'm qualifying for the Indy 500 and the next day it's the slow lane?

Okay, so the knees won't do much StairMaster. So the treadmill's set at a 15-minute mile, level 3. At least I'm staying ahead of the pack.

Being 60 honestly is a relief. Instead of tilting at the tail end of an era—an aging midlifer—I'm a novice in another. Call me "new old"—or "Old Lite," as a colleague says. A from-the-bottle Goldilocks, I get to test fresh options for the last third of my life.

I've found the bed that's too hard: "The essence of life is declining," is the way poet Stephen Levine told me he felt approaching 60.

And the bed that's too soft: "Old age is ridiculous!" Studs Terkel once shouted at me. The Chicago author likes to talk about a friend who always orders double martinis because "At our age, who knows when or where we'll have our next?"

And maybe, the bed that's just right: Gloria Steinem said 60 heralded a future of "full, glorious, alive-in-the-moment, don't-give-a-damn yet caring-for-everything sense of the right now" years.

"Age is exciting," she told me.

But so is youth. So is middle age. So what's the deal about 60? And what's this talk about age as a big loss, anyway? In each stage of life, we balance wins and losses. Marriage or independence? Children or career? Climb the hill or coast into the valley? If 60 starts the age-stage, here is my "Old Lite" balance sheet:

- My children have married and started their own lives. I've won less responsibility, more time to flourish.
- I'm lucky to be married to my best friend, a man who treats me like an adult.
- Yes, I wear glasses. But I also can afford better theater tickets so I sit closer to the stage and see just fine.
- Of course, I have days when the bed's too hard. Catch me then and hear me whine those "September Song" lines about "the days trickle down to a precious few . . ."
- Thankfully, the wine still tastes fresh most of the time.

What's gained by living 60 years? Depends on what you needed to learn, I guess. Living 60 years doesn't guarantee insight. "Wisdom doesn't automatically come with old age," Abigail Van Buren says. "Nothing does—except wrinkles."

Ah, a big splash of reality from Dear Abby. But I don't have wrinkles—just tiny character lines. And hurrah for events that force us to look inside ourselves.

"Birthdays are punctuation marks in our lives," Malcolm Boyd says. "Pride in birthdays is the healthiest way of dealing with them." The "You and I" columnist for *Modern Maturity* magazine, Boyd has the credentials to speak about life. He's a poet, priest, author, civil-rights worker, gay activist and the author of 24 books. This pride is a good thing, certainly better than the attitude of the boss who once told me, "At some point, all of us bump up against limits."

Limits? What limits? You want to hear a little of my 60-year wisdom? Make dust. Or eat dust.

MIRROR, MIRROR, PLASTIC SURGERY

She Swore She Would Never Get a Facelift. Later, She Rethought That. Then She Inherited a Little Money . . .

Sunday, January 10, 1999

Let's start with the money because without it there's nothing more to say: I'm having a facelift because my Uncle Mike refused to spend money on quality care for himself in the last years of his life.

He bought cheap TV dinners and went without a new hearing aid. "I'm leaving my money to you kids," said my uncle, who was 91, a bachelor with five nieces and a nephew.

Now I'm spending one-third of the money he left me on something I can live without.

I'm part of a trend, a giant transfer of wealth from the frugal depression generation through their I-will-never-grow-old heirs to the plastic surgeons and other appearance enhancers of America.

One of my friends sold an antique Harley motorcycle she inherited from her father to pay for breast enlargements because "What he couldn't give me naturally he can give me artificially." Another friend has stopped saving for her own retirement since inheriting a substantial amount from her parents. Instead, she is spending her extra money on having her teeth straightened and "improved." "Freshening" my appearance, I decided, is not vanity. It's a business decision, a boost to self-esteem and confidence.

Confess: you tamper with God's handiwork every day. You wear stylish clothes. You color your hair, apply makeup, stuff your torso into body-slimming underwear. You take vitamins and hormone supplements, have surgery to fix your eyesight.

Men do the same. Yes, some even wear "slimmers." And they want more than youthful good looks. Bob Dole, on national television, said men are entitled to Viagra to restore their "vigor."

I just want to get rid of jowls.

DESIRE BEFORE MONEY

When I was "young" and my skin was "elastic" (i.e., younger than 50), I used to snicker at people who had facelifts. "Not for me," I said. "If I had that kind of money, I'd take a trip somewhere exotic, like Egypt."

Well, I went to Egypt last year for my 60th birthday.

I went there looking old and tired. A small breast cancer four years earlier was estrogen-positive, a pathology that means no more hormone-replacement therapy. Without artificial estrogen, my body started to age. Fat pads rearranged themselves. Newton's law of gravity took over.

I began to look like photos of long-dead relatives. My great-grandfather Patrick Glynn, for example, an Irishman with meaty arms crossed in front of his barrel chest and his chin tucked into his thick, bull neck. My German grandmother Madeline Geck, skinny and saggy.

The Irish and German genes were dragging me down.

Gazing into the bathroom mirror, I would pull up on the skin around my temples, stretching my cheeks taut and searching for a glimmer of the girl who used to be me. Admit it. You've done it, too.

Then a colleague got a facelift half-price (don't ask details!) and a good friend began egging me about how I looked each week hosting a cable television show. "Get a facelift," she advised.

Well, I thought, it doesn't hurt to find out what one costs.

Here is what I found out: the number of cosmetic procedures tracked by the American Society of Plastic and Reconstructive Surgeons increased by at least 50 percent between 1992 and 1997. New York leads us in buttock lifts (109 to 42), but, overall, California is the most altered state. In 1996, almost 13,000 California women paid plastic surgeons an estimated $58.4 million ($4,547 each) just for facelifts. Eyelid surgeries add another $3,049 each. Prices tend to be negotiable.

And surgeon fees don't include hospital and anesthesia costs.

Little wonder plastic surgeons mean it when they call California the Golden State.

Your Face in Whose Hands?

Insurance companies rarely pay for cosmetic procedures. You're laying out your own bucks to recapture lost youth. So watch out! You've already bought into a fantasy industry that advertises itself in slick magazines with testimonials for "European" treatments (whatever they are) and "affordable" surgery (whatever that is).

Where to start looking for a plastic surgeon? I knew enough to avoid "cosmetic surgeons," who may or may not have any extensive training or experience. I knew I wanted a Board-Certified Plastic Surgeon.

For recommendations, I asked people who really know the details.

I talked to facial aestheticians and hair stylists. I also talked to nurses and other medical specialists. And I looked at women I know who'd had facelifts. Of course, I have another advantage. A colleague at the *Register* has done extensive reporting on liposuction fatalities. She steered me from surgeons with excessive lawsuits.

Still, I ended up in some scary situations: waiting in medical offices that look like Beverly Hills hair salons or petite Florentine palaces; talking with surgeons who "morphed" me on their computer simulators to show me how terrific I could look if every inch was pulled and lifted; consulting with a surgeon who wanted to do my procedure—he estimated it could take at least five hours—while in a "twilight sleep" in his office instead of being under full, physician-administered anesthesia in a hospital outpatient setting.

In retrospect, shopping before I could afford the procedure, giving myself more than a year to think about it, turned out to be wise. I finally chose to have a reasonable amount of work done instead of being "sold" on a complete makeover including an eyebrow lift.

The price difference? An estimated $17,000–$18,000 to have extensive work done by doctors who advertise themselves as "surgeons to the stars." A more modest $7,200 by a top plastic and reconstructive surgeon for routine rhytidectomy (facelift) and blepharoplasty (eyelift).

You're Going to Do What?

My Midwestern roots tugged at my Southern California attitude. To be honest, I could never spend my own money on a facelift— money I had earned, that is. But an inheritance? That's a gift. Money without strings.

I have worked for 35 years, created a home, raised three kids, paid for their private high school and most of their college education. My husband and I have bailed sons out of debt and shelled out our share for three weddings.

"It's okay to spend some money on yourself," Bob said. Then he added, "But I married you with that neck, and I love you the way you are." He paused. "Still, you do what you want to do." A wise comment, since he knows I usually do anyway.

"Go for it, Mom," my daughter said.

I scheduled the surgery. I began talking about it hesitantly, convinced most people would hoot, "What's a big old woman like you doing trying to be a movie star?" Instead, when I mentioned it in a speech to a retiree group, the women applauded. Female cousins e-mailed their enthusiasm. "You go, girl!" Mary wrote from Florida.

I got bolder. I told men.

Men, I found out, don't know what to say. If they're encouraging, they imply you need help. If they're not enthusiastic, they make you feel foolish. The typical male comment? "Aw," said Dave Threshie, former *Register* publisher, when he heard my plans. "Why are you doing that? I think age is beautiful."

Depends on who is beholding the beauty, I told him.

Even card-carrying feminists concede appearance has value. Gloria Steinem had her eyes lifted.

What Type of Women Commonly Have Lifts?

Dr. Bruce Achauer, the surgeon I chose for my procedure, says he once checked for a common profession among his patients and came up with schoolteachers.

None of us expects to go under the knife and emerge looking like Princess Grace. "I can make you look very natural," Achauer said as he tested the elasticity of my skin with his fingertips.

Natural is good enough! A silly line from a Gilbert and Sullivan ditty popped into my head: "She may very well pass for 43 in the dusk, with a light behind her." Why Achauer? I like his style. His office in the St. Joseph Medical Pavilion suits me: simple, highlighted by paintings and artwork that reveal his intense interest in shapes and balance. He keeps toys in the waiting room to entertain the many children brought to him for reconstructive work. I know women who have been "lifted" by him, and they don't look like they are standing in a stiff wind. Achauer is listed in the compendium of *The Best Doctors in America.* He gave me a good price and didn't think I needed a brow lift.

Are We Having Fun Yet?

The surgery date was set for November 12th. Two weeks before, Achauer's office sent printed information outlining what I could expect in surgery and recovery.

We had discussed where the incisions were going—behind the ears, under the chin, in the crease of the eyelid, inside the lower lids (don't think about it).

In Achauer's view, if you have someone at home to help care for you, why go to a private nursing center? I stocked the refrigerator and cupboards with liquid-type foods and taught Bob how to make my breakfast smoothie of soymilk, protein powder and banana.

After two lumpectomies for breast cancer and lymph node surgery, I couldn't muster stress for this cosmetic procedure. Then I got positively giddy. "If I'm spending this money on my face, I must believe the cancer's really gone and I'm going to live!" I told Bob. Logically, I knew that, but this was the first time I could own that triumph emotionally.

In the pre-op room, nurses shouldered aside *Register* photographer Bruce C. Strong ("I'm her real insurance policy," he told people) and worked around my husband. The Reverend Virginia Erwin of Trinity Episcopal Church in Orange came by to say some prayers because, she said, "surgery is surgery." Achauer drew blue lines around my chin and eyes "to know where to cut." Dr. Brian Donahue, the anesthesiologist, assured me I was "in good Irish hands." He plays the old patriot songs on the bagpipes.

"I'm going to make you very happy," he said, fiddling around the IV tube in my left arm. And that's all I remember.

They tell me the surgery lasted seven hours. They say Achauer, a Parrot Head, played Jimmy Buffet CDs. There are actual photographs of needles going into my lower eyelids.

I was sleeping, beautifully.

MIRROR, MIRROR, COSMETIC SURGERY

A New Look Brings a New Attitude

Monday, January 11, 1999

Ten days after facelift surgery, I was trying on an outfit in a department store dressing room when I caught the first sight of my new face in a three-way mirror.

"I don't believe me!" I said out loud. I posed. I postured. I stood there giggling and pointing to my profile.

I was still swollen from ear to ear. My right eyelid was two sizes bigger than my left. The cheek under my left eye boasted a black-and-blue lump as big as a quail egg. But I had a chin. I didn't look like a walrus anymore.

Let me embellish that: I didn't look like an old, tired, wattle-weary walrus anymore. "I may very well pass for 43 in the dusk, with a light behind me," I sang. And I did a little shuffle-step kick.

WHEN THE RECOVERY STARTS

I woke from surgery wearing a helmet of gauze and tape. There were two drains, one on each side of the back of my head, sluicing bloody fluids out of my body. Something—they turned out to be staples—felt hard and achy along the base of my skull.

It was November 12th. I never looked worse in my life.

"I can't see," I mumbled. "I can't see anything but light." My husband, Bob Eaton, leaned over the bed in the recovery room. "You have a clear mask on your eyes." Oh. Well, when the cooling plastic mask was removed, I still couldn't see well. Eight days passed before I could read a book.

My face- and eyelifts were not routine, I later learned.

Fortunately, I had picked a surgeon sophisticated and knowledgeable enough to make a silk purse out of loose lower eyelid skin, a droopy upper-right eyelid and a thick neck.

"Essentially, you had no neck before, in plastic-surgery terms," Dr. Bruce Achauer said later. "The neck had to be sculpted." My complications lengthened the surgery from an estimated five and a half hours to seven.

Two hours after I left the operating room, a nurse was smacking my wrist and shouting at me to wake up. She and Bob helped me dress, get into a wheelchair and then the car, but I don't remember any of that. I do remember walking up the stairs at home, my hands on Bob's shoulders and my daughter, Joanne, holding my waist from behind. And I remember Joanne spooning some instant oatmeal into my mouth.

"Good practice for you to know how to feed babies," she says I told her. Even in my stupor, still nagging her for grandchildren.

What else do I remember? Pressing bags of frozen peas—they're better than ice packs—around my chin and neck, downing Vicodin painkillers and lolling off to sleep.

I was uncomfortable. I'm not used to sleeping half-sitting instead of on my side. From ear to ear, my face was tight under the bandages. I couldn't turn my head. A purple stripe ran from one corner of my mouth, a bruise from the anesthesiologist's intubation tube.

Four days after surgery, Achauer's nurse, Marilyn Carlson, cut away the helmet. As the gauze fell away, Bob and *Register* photographer Bruce C. Strong stared, slack-jawed. "Wow!" Strong said. "Wow. You've got a chin!" I wanted to see my chin, but more than that I wanted to wash my hair, which was matted and icky, bloody in places. Carlson quickly tugged out the drains and told me to wash my head and gently bathe the stitches.

Nurses and assistants in Achauer's office came to look at the doctor's handiwork. "You look terrific," a staff member said. I thought I looked like the Bride of Frankenstein.

They gave me a soft white hat to partly hide my face. As I walked through the medical-building lobby to our car, I wondered what people thought. An accident, maybe? Assault and battery?

Three days later, Carlson snipped the stitches out of my eyes. That hurt enough to bring tears.

By now, an irritated nerve that runs up the back of my head near my right ear was creating sharp pain. I got some relief by massaging my neck. The stinging nerve lasted four days, but it was the only painful part of recovery.

GET ME OUT OF HERE

"Cabin fever," I said to Bob. "I have cabin fever. Let's go out to lunch." Nurses had warned me I could bruise horribly from breast-bone to earlobes, but only my eyes looked injured. I was swollen—my ears seemed huge!—so I pulled the white hat lower as we walked into Rockwell's Cafe in Villa Park.

I could feel the eyes. Women who had "been there" stared know-ingly. The waitress was blase. She had seen face-factory battering before in this upscale community. No guilt eating here, I thought. These women regard facelifts as investments.

Two weeks after the surgery, Carlson picked out the staples. Achauer seemed pleased with my progress, but I was starting to worry.

My right eye was not healing as well as my left one. The "droopy" right eyelid remained swollen. The bottom corner of the eye drooped, and it teared constantly. When I looked at distant objects, I sometimes would see double images.

"Not to worry," Achauer said. "It's going to be fine. Give it time."

ON THE JOB

I returned to the office two-and-a-half weeks after the operation.

Talk about laying your ego on the line! Walking into the building and seeing a knot of coworkers, forcing myself to say, "Good morning." Everyone said nice things, but I wondered, *What are they* really *thinking*?

Here's what I figured out: I'll never really know what people younger than 40 think. And what do they know about aging anyway? People older than 50, though—that's a different set of trigger words.

THINGS TO THINK ABOUT

If you're looking in the mirror and seeing your grandmother—or grandfather—you are ready to think about cosmetic surgery. Ask yourself: are you uncomfortable about aging or about your appearance or both? Cosmetic surgery can make you look younger, but it can't fix the arthritis in your knees.

Can you afford the procedure? Is it wise for you to put the cost on a credit card as some surgeons allow? Looking terrific won't make you happy if you can't pay for necessities.

Are you willing to take the chance? All surgeries have medical risks, and cosmetic surgery doesn't always produce the results you wanted.

WANT MORE INFORMATION?

If you have ever contemplated a facelift, you should read *Lift—Wanting, Fearing and Having a Face-Lift* by Joan Kron, Viking, 1998. For information on surgeons and procedures, check the Web site of the American Society of Plastic and Reconstructive Surgeons: www.plasticsurgery.org.

SOME BASICS IF YOU ARE CONSIDERING SURGERY

The best candidates for cosmetic surgery are physically

"*Old* makes me twitch," said an acquaintance, Wayne Brown, 49, jerking his head. "No, no, no old." He's pretty sure boomers will do whatever is necessary to stay youthful looking, he said. "You are going to be typical."

"I don't approve of cosmetic surgery," said Gloria Davenport, 71, who saw me less than three weeks after surgery, when I went to interview her for a story. "But you have a career to think about. Besides, I have to admit you look good."

And then the best: "What fat farm have you been to?" a television viewer asked the day after I returned to hosting my show on the Orange County NewsChannel. People who don't know I have had a facelift give me the best compliments. They ask if I have changed something. New hairdo? New glasses?

"Is your sister all right?" a neighbor down the street shouts at me from her car. "My sister?" Turns out she thinks I am a younger relative come to take care of the old me.

Those who know about the facelift want to look at the stitches.

No one has told me I could have spent that money more productively—feeding the homeless, educating underprivileged children, helping find a cure for cancer. Good that they haven't. I dealt with my social conscience weeks ago. If you inherited a small pot of money, would you give one-third to some charity? Do I need to call for a show of hands?

WHY AM I SO TIRED?

What surprised me was my fatigue. I expected to have this surgery, go home, sleep for a weekend, then get up and be busy at the computer full time. I thought I would stay off work for two weeks simply to spare others the sight of my unattractive recovery. Instead, I struggled to regain energy.

"You have had seven hours of surgery," Bob reminded me. "You just *look* 45." He grounded me. He took care of me. I'm fortunate.

By early January, I felt like myself. I was back on the treadmill at the gym. I had almost stopped glancing at myself whenever I passed a mirror or a store window.

My eye looks normal and "bag-less." I have bones instead of chipmunk cheeks. I've started collecting rewards. I wear drop earrings and drape designer scarves around my new neck. As a no-neck woman, I learned to avoid anything that called attention to that unattractive area.

People ask me if I feel different. Yes, I do. And that surprises me.

healthy, without risky medical conditions such as high blood pressure, blood-clotting problems or glaucoma.

OTHER CONSIDERATIONS

Cost: $5,000 and up. Type of facility: hospital or salon-style. Surgeon: Do some research; learn the doctor's reputation. Talk about your expectations and concerns regarding results.

PREPARING FOR SURGERY

Stop smoking a week or two before surgery; this aids healing. Grow or style your hair so it's long enough to hide scars until they heal. Arrange for someone to drive you home after the surgery and help for a day or two.

AFTER SURGERY

Keep your head elevated and as still as possible for a few days. If a drainage tube was inserted, it will be removed after a couple of days. Stitches will be removed in about five days.

RECOVERY

Complications of having cosmetic surgery are usually minor and run along the lines of mild infection or reaction to anesthesia.

WHAT TO EXPECT

FACELIFT

- Temporary numbness, swelling, and bruising
- Blood collecting under skin (hematoma) that must be surgically removed
- Temporary injury to nerves that control facial muscles

EYES

- Difficulty closing eyes when sleeping
- Double or blurred vision for a few days
- Temporary swelling in corners of eyelids[1]

I feel more confident. I feel visible again. Renewed. Like having naturally curly hair, there's a part of me I don't have to fuss with anymore to feel presentable.

Uncle Mike has given me a most wonderful gift. I look as young as I feel.

[1] Sources: Bruce M. Achauer, M.D., and the American Society

Read My Lips
(and Chin, Crow's Feet, Earlobes . . .)

Monday, March 1, 1999

I have to face up to it. Measured by the traditional yardsticks of reader response, sustained interest and Web site "hits," the articles on my facelift will be my career pieces.

Not my chosen career highlights: investigative reports on sleazy state's attorneys in Illinois or deaths in the Orange County Jail or even the obscene real-estate profiteers of the 1980s. But since I exposed my "lift," I've heard from literally hundreds of readers locally and on the Internet. I've turned into the Dr. Ruth of facelifts for women—and men—who want to talk over procedures. People think nothing of stopping me and spinning me around to "look me over." Which leads me to the question, "What have I done to myself?"

One woman purports to know: Rose Rosetree, a leading U.S. face reader and author of *The Power of Face Reading* (WIW, $18.95). "The face is a spiritual alphabet," Rosetree says. Face readings—a 3,000-year-old Chinese discipline technically known as physiognomy—give clues to how a person makes decisions, spends money or works. Send Rosetree a photograph and get back a character analysis (one hour costs $85 and a "mini" read is $15). It's "more reliable than computer dating" her fans insist in testimonials on her Web site (www.rose-rosetree.com).

"Finally, California calls," she said when I phoned her in Sterling, Virginia. "Let's talk about something I've never discussed in interviews before. Let's talk about cosmetic surgery." With that psychic jump-start, Rosetree told me cosmetic surgery is a "frightening trend that is becoming wildly popular. Our mothers wore girdles. We have internalized those girdles." Facelifts can erase years of experience from your life— "Well, maybe you didn't want to have those experiences"—but they also interfere with the spiritual aspects of the face.

Pinning back ears and bobbing noses are alterations that have more impact than a simple age-erasing lift, Rosetree asserts. "Send me your picture and I'll tell you what you have done by having this facelift."

Of course, she added, I should have sent my picture to her before I had surgery, just to make sure I didn't tinker with my spiritual characteristics.

A day later, with my photos in hand, Rosetree was relieved. "From a face-reading point of view, you have had very minor cosmetic surgery. In face-reading terms, you didn't change your cheeks, for example, and they relate to power. And rhinoplasty—well, watch out. That nose is an important part of your expression in life, how you work, deal with money. Thoughtful people will not tamper with their noses.

"Women are wondering if cosmetic surgery is spiritually the right thing to do. In most cases I tell them it's a mistake." Except in mine, she added. Because I'm on television, a little cosmetic surgery is necessary.

Here's my reading:

- My nose is straight, and "I can tell from your nose you work in a systematically ordered way."
- I got rid of the bags under my eyes, and "What those are about is pushing yourself to look more deeply inside, introspection. You have healed from breast cancer, so it is appropriate to let go of that."
- My right eye is angled up more than the left, which means "in work situations your outlook is optimistic and idealistic (the right eye), but in your personal life you are aware, not in denial, hugely compassionate (left eye)."
- I still have lines from my nose to my mouth, and "that's terrific. These are your suffering lines, and suffering people develop compassion."
- The "extra chin material" I got rid of damaged my ability to be down to earth. Fortunately, the third area of my face, from the bottom of my nose to my chin, remains larger than the rest of my face, which gives me credibility with other people.

- My mouth shows a great sense of humor, although it was saltier when I was earthier. The "crow's feet" at my eyes mean I reach out to others and understand things more. And my lower earlobe position is a real giveaway to my personality. "Lower earlobes indicate conscious patterns about making decisions. When you have an important decision to make, you gather information from many sources and evaluate it carefully," Rosetree said.

I can face a future with the same lower-third features as a Jane Fonda or a Mae West. As for that Earth Mother stuff: I gave that up when I opted for the lift. Wasn't it Sophie Tucker who sang, "I'm gonna change my way of living and if that ain't enough, I'm gonna change the way I strut my stuff . . . "?

Obviously, I'm doing that—face first.

MIRROR, MIRROR, COSMETIC SURGERY:

One Year after a Facelift, Register Reporter Has No Regrets—All She Wanted Was to Look as Young as She Feels

Monday, February 21, 2000

Eat your heart out, Cher. Take a second look, Phyllis Diller.

This is the face that launched a thousand facelifts.

A year after my surgery to rid myself of wattles, droopy eyelids and that sagging sensation that comes with age, I still look in the mirror and say "Wow!" A year after my "before and after" facelift stories appeared in the *Orange County Register,* I still get e-mails and calls from women wanting to talk about having this or that procedure with this or that doctor, asking for recommendations, insisting I have inspired them to raise eyebrows, lift chins and erase those tiny lines of character that make a face look old. Upward of 600 separate e-mails and calls so far, by my last count.

"You gave all us little people permission," said an e-mail from Barbara M. "Facelifts are not just for the rich or celebrities."

Even men agree. Sam C. messaged, "I find you to be more attractive now than your picture at 40 years of age."

And then there was the shared insight of Debra F., who wrote about her facelift/eye job, now three years old. "When I first saw my surgeon, we talked about why I wanted the surgery. I told him it was because I had become 'invisible.' People don't see you when you look old." Four weeks after her surgery, Debra said, everything changed.

A sad commentary on our society? Yes. But as Sam and Debra both said, this is reality: society rates you on how you look.

I'll admit it. I'm thrilled to look the way I feel—full of pep and energy. Not bad for a woman approaching 63. People still stop me in the market and spin me around to look me over. I was working at the *Register's* mobile newsroom at the Orange County Fair last summer when a woman spotted me and started stroking my cheeks. "So smooth," she said.

Others who knew me before say, "You've lost a ton of weight!" No, just a fat face, which proves people really do judge you by the face you put forward. Heftier minds than mine have pondered that problem. I'll admit it; I gave up and went with the flow.

So what if my son in Hawaii got off the airplane in May, stared and said, "You don't look like my mom!" His kids knew who I was, which is why Grandma treated them to an extra day at Disneyland.

My surgeon, Dr. Bruce Achauer, seems pleased with the results of his handiwork. What do other doctors think? A few weeks ago, a dermatologist taped a television program with me. Talking before the show, she chastised California women for using too little sunscreen and having too many cosmetic surgeries. Which prompted me to tell her I was "lifted" a year ago.

"You don't have the typical California wind-tunnel facelift," said Dr. Amy E. Newburger, a New York dermatologist. "You have more of an eastern facelift. It looks very natural. So many California women look too tight." The author of *Looking Good at Any Age* (Doubleday), she is generally cautious about facelifts.

"Age is not a disease," Newburger said. "It's a normal process. A woman should look as well as she can but decide what risks to undergo to look more youthful. People don't understand aging is an ongoing process and often have procedures done too soon." She cautions women to understand their true motivation before they go "under the knife." A facelift can't patch up a broken marriage or land you a new job.

"Why did you have a facelift?" she asked.

Because I had aged dramatically after having a breast cancer removed five years earlier. Cancer is a stressful disease. I had radiation. I could no longer take estrogen. Put all together, I suddenly wore my trauma on my face.

"That wasn't who I was," I told Newburger, "because I am confident that cancer is in my past. I feel so full of energy and such a zest for living; I want to have that show on my face."

I had another reason, too: my bachelor uncle Mike had refused to spend money on himself in his declining years. He'd wanted to leave a legacy to his nieces and nephew. "Enjoy the money," he told a cousin. I used one-third of my legacy for my facelift, saved one-third, and gave the last third to a son as part of the down payment on his house.

"I decided to do this for myself," I said. "I decided to treat myself." Newburger and I discussed how I took a year to make my final decision about whether I would have cosmetic surgery, what I would have done and who would do it. In her book, which primarily discusses ways to improve skin and facial appearance without surgery, she cautions readers to take time to probe and understand why they want to have elective surgery.

I took the time to check the credentials of three doctors I consulted. Each wanted to do different work, and the price ranged from about $10,000 (with hospital and anesthesia fees) to $18,000. I had the least amount of work done, essentially just removing the thick neck that is a legacy from my Irish ancestors and the baggy eyes my German relatives passed on to me.

One aspect Newburger found important: I had my surgery at age 61. Most aging around the eyes is finished, she says. Brows have dropped, skin is thinned and fat has seeped out from behind the eyeball. "If you have such a procedure in your 40s, watch out! You can expect to need to do it again at least once. And that's not good."

All her comments confirm what Achauer had told me before surgery. He promised to make me look natural, and he said I would not need to repeat the procedure. I've been to see him twice for regular checkups since my surgery. "I could tinker," he said.

"Don't do it," I replied. A tug here, a pull there isn't necessary.

"Good," he said. "I don't want you to have that tight look."

One question I am often asked is, "Was it painful?"

Well, duh, as the kids say. It was seven hours of surgery. It was a drag getting over the anesthesia.

Painful? Not really. Not compared to abdominal surgery or any surgery that cuts muscle. But sleeping on metal staples stuck in the back of my head was uncomfortable. Heck, sleeping on my back was different and unnatural but certainly survivable.

My bruising was minimal. That varies from person to person. The major aftereffect I noticed was numbness. I couldn't feel the hole where my pierced earring went in my earlobe. The numbness, which basically stretched from ear to ear, disappeared gradually in about six or eight months.

I still have my bitty crow's feet, some lines that stretch from nose to mouth, some fine lines above my lip. I'm still me.

Energetic. With a zest for life. And looking like it.

Monday, January 10, 2000

I thought I was ready for the millennium. As the century ended, I lifted my face and lowered my cholesterol. I launched my own Web page and figured out my VCR. I stopped eating red meat and pretended to love tofu.

But I forgot my feet. Ignored, disenchanted, my feet decided to get old.

Some night, about 10 months ago, they decided to grow. Like alien beings, they took on a life of their own. Now they're a whole size larger. They want a size 11 shoe, a difficult fit for a woman.

"I can go water skiing without using the skis," I complained to Dr. Laura Mosqueda, director of geriatrics at the University of California, Irvine. Not true, she said. "But you probably can go snowshoeing without the snowshoes." Very funny. A doctor with a sense of humor.

"Actually, your feet don't grow in the sense of lengthened bone," she said, getting serious. "What changes is the shape of your foot—when you get corns and bunions and so on."

Yeah. Old feet. Old, big, "bunioned" feet. I have a sudden vision of Fats Waller, the derby-hatted jazz pianist, hunched over his upright pounding out his 1939 version of "Oh, your feet's too big; don't want you 'cause your feet's too big . . . your pedal extremities are colossal." Those hikers in the Northwest don't see tracks of Big Foot, a prehistoric creature. They see the slogging footsteps of old women with big feet. Cold big feet.

"The foot doesn't grow, but the ligaments can stretch out and the foot elongates," says Los Angeles podiatrist Don Feigelson. "Yes, it is part of the aging process for some people." His prescription: wear good supportive shoes all your life. If you've already failed that test, hope you don't have genes for flat feet. If you have flat feet, wear orthotics for support. See a podiatrist before your feet hurt. If you are like most people and don't see a podiatrist early, see one at the first signs of foot pain and problems.

Podiatrists are fascinated by feet. So are a lot of men. My widowed mother once was propositioned by the husband of a good friend who wanted her to take the train from New York City, where she lived, to Poughkeepsie, where he worked during the week. "I long to rub your feet," he told her, suggesting a rendezvous.

She didn't go. She told me she couldn't imagine having a rendezvous with this guy anywhere, let alone Poughkeepsie, and besides, she had ticklish feet.

Having big feet makes me feel as if my age shows despite all my best efforts and attitude. Of course, my feet have been around, and they have a right to spread in comfort. The American Podiatric Medical Association says most Americans log 75,000 miles on their feet by the time they reach 50. Those who engage in rigorous sports and fitness activities accelerate the wear-and-tear on their feet and ankles. A 150-pound person walking one mile exerts the equivalent of 63 tons—or 127,000 pounds—on each foot. No wonder I feel their pain.

So I'm shushing my "barking dogs" with the attention they deserve: a pedicure, comfy low-heel shoes, even a podiatric checkup.

But no foot massage. Like Mom, my tootsies are ticklish, too.

Part 2—The Big "C" Hits Me

SOONER OR LATER, THE DEFINING MOMENT COMES FOR US ALL.
LIFE THROWS A PUNCH. WE ARE FLAWED. WE ARE AGING.
HOPEFULLY, WE ARE ALSO SURVIVORS.

LIFE THROWS A PUNCH

Exercise, Improved Diet and Lower Weight Have Become Ideal Preparation for Battling Cancer

Wednesday, September 14, 1994

More than 1,700 Orange County women will find out they have breast cancer this year. One in seven will hear the diagnosis in her lifetime.

I heard it August 29. Two lumps were removed that day from my right breast. One was benign. The other was a seven-millimeter infiltrating ductile cancer.

"Garden-variety cancer," my doctor called it. Common. Ordinary. The type that afflicts 70 percent of U.S. women who get breast cancer.

My cancer.

My greatest fear.

A time bomb the size of a pea.

Too small to kill me. Maybe too small, too young to have sent many cells traveling. Just big enough, just close enough to the surface to push up some tissue and create a lump.

Like most women, I've heard that routine self-examinations are important. I've made that exam a monthly habit for several years. Over the years, I've figured out what lumps are harmless fixtures. This lump seemed to have appeared overnight.

A lucky lump for me. Because I found the lump, I went for my annual checkup early. As a result, my cancer is out and doctors say I fall into the "early detection" category. Cancers detected early have a 92 percent average rate of cure. I like those odds.

That's the upside. On the downside, I've "got" something that I have to worry about for the rest of my life.

For a few days, I felt old and vulnerable. Now healthy denial has kicked in. If 92 percent make it, why not me? And don't tell me denial isn't healthy. As a friend reminded me, healthy denial is what we do every time we nose onto the freeway with a certainty we'll get to our destination without incident. Still, this is not what I expected to report eight months into my health-full year.

For the past eight months, I've junked the fat in my diet, wrestled mightily to reduce my sugar intake, tried to exercise at least four times a week. My goal was to motivate myself—and some of you—to reduce your risk of heart disease. I'm 57 and expect to work for many more years. I want my retirement years to be healthy ones. Heart disease— not cancer—has been the main worry in my family.

I took charge of my physical life. I triumphed over my creaky knees and accomplished a backpacking trip. I've shined a glow on my cheeks, added bounce to my Nikes and lost about 20 pounds.

Good thing I got started on those healthful activities. By losing weight and paying attention to changes in my body, I felt a small lump in the upper inside part of my right breast in late July.

I didn't pay too much attention to it. First, the lump hurt and we've all heard the myth that cancer lumps never hurt. Second, there's no breast cancer in my family. And I've had cysts in my breasts before. I decided to wait a month to see if the lump changed, as cysts often will.

Then I invited Dr. Dava Gerard to appear August 26 on the "Our Time On Line" show on the Orange County NewsChannel. Gerard, a local surgeon, is national medical director for the Susan G. Komen Breast Cancer Foundation, which gives women access to free mammo- grams and sponsors educational and support groups in Orange County.

Researching for Gerard's interview put breast cancer on my mind. I made an appointment for a checkup. I finished the show with Gerard at 2 P.M. and was in the Breast Care Center at St. Joseph Hospital to see Dr. John West at 2:45 P.M. By 5 P.M., he had done an ultrasound on the lump, shown me the results of a fast mammogram and scheduled me for a lumpectomy the following Monday morning. It was too late in the day Friday to do the usual needle biopsy that precedes a lumpectomy. West suggested we move directly to outpatient surgery.

He was pretty sure that what he saw on the mammogram was malignant. The clue: uneven edges that made the tumor look like a dented balloon.

West called it "subtle" and hard to read. It might have been missed in my routine mammogram this year. It could have "cooked" for two or three years before it was large enough to be easily visible.

Saturday, I started my research, calling friends who write about medicine, checking other sources I know who have survived breast cancer. Saturday afternoon, West called. The radiologist saw something else on the mammogram.

A possible second malignancy. That would automatically mean a mastectomy and would change my odds in the cancer crapshoot.

Surgery was postponed from Monday morning to Monday afternoon, while the radiologist examined more mammograms. But by the time my husband, my daughter and a close friend had walked with me to the surgical center, my knees were weakening.

One small cancer was something the doctor said I could beat. He wasn't saying too much about two cancers, even though the second mass was only the size of a millet seed.

When everyone left me for a few moments in the pre-operating room, I prayed. I don't want a bookend on my life. There is so much more ahead. My daughter is getting married next June. One son is starting his teaching career. Another son is about to present my first grandchild. My husband and I have plans. Besides, this is no way to treat a woman who has done her best to take care of herself—including having annual mammograms for the past eight years.

Then West came in, looking absolutely silly in a sort of shower-cap thing that surgical people wear. "We're going to take good care of you," he promised. He hugged me. He reminded me that the lumps were very, very small. That most cancers are the size of a golf ball before he sees them. "Most women wait too long," he said.

I came out of the anesthetic singing Irish patriot songs to an anesthesiologist who told me his name was Donahue. I had good reason to sing—although I didn't know it at the time.

West, I later learned, had bounded into the waiting room, ebullient and eager to tell my family good news. Yes, he thought one tumor—the

ABOUT BREAST CANCER[2]

If detected early, 92 percent of breast cancers are curable. To detect breast cancer, women 40–49 should have mammograms every two years; women older than 50 every year. The yearly screening should include a clinical examination.

Most mammograms are covered by health insurance; Medicare pays for a mammogram every other year for women older than 65. Low- or no-cost mammograms are available through the Susan G. Komen Breast Cancer Foundation in Orange County, California, and similar organizations across the country.

Estimated new cases of breast cancer in 1994 for the United States:

Age	# of cases	% of new cases
39 and under	10,900	6 %
40–49	30,000	16 %
50–64	51,000	28 %
65 and older	90,100	50 %

Nationally, about one in nine women will contract breast cancer in her lifetime. In Orange County, it's one in seven. Doctors estimate that 40 percent of women under 60 and 30 percent of women over 60 have mammograms and are screened annually. Why do

original lump—was malignant. But it was much smaller than he thought. Only seven millimeters. He couldn't "read" the second tumor, he said.

Two days later, West called me at home. "How'd you like some more good news?" he said. "The second lump is nothing." Tears started to roll. I hadn't known how dreadfully frightened I really was.

The little cancer that I had is gone. I have a battle to fight, but I've got good odds, lots of ammunition and support troops to fall back on. My family, my friends, my coworkers have lifted my spirits. My priest and my church have shored up my soul.

I've started walking three miles a day—for myself, and to get in shape for the Susan G. Komen Foundation Race for the Cure in Newport Beach on September 25. I'm back to redecorating my bedroom, a project I had set aside. Three days after the lumpectomy, I was checking out fabric samples. I'm reading guidebooks, getting ready for a November trip to Austria. My daughter, who is studying at the University of Vienna, and I will travel to Budapest and Prague. And I already have my tickets to hear Placido Domingo sing *Otello* next May.

Sure, I'm also reading *Dr. Susan Love's Breast Book* (Addison-Wesley, 1991). I'm checking out the oncology information boards on America Online and Delphi computer networks, as well as references and boards on the Internet.

If my luck holds—and I think it will—the lymph nodes removed September 8 all will be negative. Next, I will meet with oncologists to decide a course of treatment. Radiation, for sure. Chemotherapy, perhaps.

The Sunday after my lumpectomy, the communion hymn at Trinity Episcopal Church was "Amazing Grace." It always makes my eyes smart. Ten years ago, that was the hymn I selected for my mother's funeral. She died at 72 of malignant lymphoma. The music stirred my kettle of fear. And I wondered if this simple, powerful hymn on this particular day was a sign. Except the beat was not a dirge. It was triumphant, hopeful, healing:

"Through many dangers, toils and snares, I have already come: 'tis grace that brought me safe thus far, and grace will lead me home." Amen.

women choose not to have mammograms? Doctors don't always recommend them, and many women believe they are unnecessary unless there are problems.

[2] Source: Susan G. Komen Breast Cancer Foundation.

Monday, September 15, 1997

The radiologist is squeezing my left breast into a pancake. She's the same radiologist who did the pancake number on my right breast three years ago. That time, I had a lump on the right that turned out to be a seven-millimeter cancer. I found it in a self-exam. This time, there's a star-shaped spot on my left-breast mammogram that has the specialists worried. With my history, they say, it could be a second cancer.

I have opted to have a lumpectomy to remove the spot and "clean" surrounding tissue. If it is cancer, we can move on to treatment. A biopsy procedure, which just takes a sample, could leave me without a clear answer.

I'm hanging onto the mammogram machine at St. Joseph Hospital, thankful for the nurse massaging my shoulders. When there is no surface lump, when the spot is buried deep in the breast, the radiologist has to mark the territory for the surgeon. "Needle localizations"—marking the spot with dye and a thin wire—take about 30 minutes. During that time, the patient stays squeezed.

"A man must have invented this machine," I mumble.

There are worse moments to endure. I don't want to repeat the moment when Dr. John West of the Breast Care Center told me there was a 50-50 chance I had a second cancer. A second cancer is better than a spreading cancer, he said. Small cancers are curable, meaning about 96 percent of the women survive 10 years or longer.

"Finding cancers this early means the system (of self-exams and mammograms) is working. It won't kill you, Jane," he said.

Terrific. I went home and cried.

It's not fair. I've tried so hard. No red meat. Soy milk on my cereal. Moderate exercise almost every day. Supplements and antioxidants to boost my immune system. For an hour, I wallowed in a private pity party. Then I called in my support team—my husband and children, my friends who have had breast cancer, everyone I know who prays with gusto.

"Take it one step at a time," Bob said. "Don't think about the worst-case scenario." Bob is a terrific husband for a woman of Irish heritage whose DNA carries both the "worry" and "worry more" genes.

Think about the good things breast cancer brings, my walking buddy, Lynne, reminded me. After going through chemotherapy and radiation last year, she says she is grateful for the experience. She's found friends she didn't know she had; she's deepened her relationships with family; she's reached into her soul and discovered she has the "right stuff."

My daughter put it in cosmetic perspective. Removing a lump from the left will give me a match with my "lumpectomied" right, she said, adding, "At least I made you laugh."

On the day of surgery, I am surrounded by prayer chains from people who love me and people who care. My rector has anointed me.

Worst case would be another "trivial" cancer, as my oncologist calls the one cut out three years ago. Been there. Done that. Can do it again. Having a trivial cancer is not the same as being a little bit pregnant. Trivial cancers at one centimeter or less usually have not spread to lymph nodes. Three years ago, my lymph nodes were negative. I needed only radiation. But that treatment is physically draining. A year passed before I felt like myself again.

Crab apples, as my mother would say. Until I learned about this damned spot, I was among the briskly walking energetic. Well, I can make it through the fatigue of radiation and be the walking-well again, I tell myself.

I give Bob a thumbs-up as they roll me into the operating room. West and I talk through much of the procedure. I am drugged but feel alert and vital. "Did I dream it or did I hear you say you didn't find a lump?" I ask him.

No lump, he says. This is good. One hurdle. Cancer—at a certain stage—makes a hard lump.

West sends a piece of me as big as a baby's fist—with a big, blue-dye bull's eye in the middle—to the pathologist. Two hours later, I'm healing at home with a bowl of matzo-ball chicken soup. The next day, the nurse calls. "Open the champagne," she shouts. "It was negative."

I start to cry again. She cries. Bob cries when I call him at work.

What was it? A buildup of cells in a milk duct, the surgeon says. Not normal. But not cancer. The system is working.

I can live with that.

EMOTIONS RUN HIGH SUNDAY IN NEWPORT BEACH

Hopes Take Flight at Race for the Cure:
Register Writer and Cancer Survivor Takes One Step
at a Time in the Benefit for Breast-Cancer Research

Monday, September 29, 1997

It was the doves. I was fine until they released 50 white doves that streaked west toward the Pacific Ocean, then gathered themselves into a team and arced and angled over the heads of breast-cancer survivors at the Orange County Race for the Cure on Sunday in Newport Beach.

It was my third race, my third year as a cancer survivor, and I knew I would cry at some point in the survivor ceremony. This time it was the doves and the song: "Did you ever know that you're my hero? . . . You are the wind beneath my wings."

Up came memories of women no longer among us, celebrating. For nine months, I watched Sally die of breast cancer. "I think anyone who finds out she has breast cancer should go out in the garage and shoot herself," she said once, in a dark moment. But she didn't mean it. She fought to live until the end.

I salute her; I make myself focus on those of us here now. Almost 1,000 of us are wearing the pink visors that mark survivors, hugging and holding hands, wiping away one another's tears.

These are my heroes. Women who have had breasts cut off or chunks cut out. Women who have endured incredible months of chemotherapy, toxic cocktails coursing through their bodies. Women who have exposed themselves to deadly radiation machines.

And they have returned to their kitchen sinks, their jobs, their husbands and children. Tentatively, they allow themselves dreams for the future.

And standing there, looking up at these women, are the other heroes: the husbands and fathers, brothers and sisters, friends and lovers joining in the joy and tears.

You think you know a lot about people until you walk a Race for the Cure.

Pete, the tattooed punker, is there with uncountable earrings in lobes and eyebrows. He holds the hand of his mother, Alice, who wobbles the one-mile walk wearing her newly won pink visor, her surgery only two months old.

Behind her, Brilee, 16 months, rolls along in a stroller beside her grandmother, Shirley.

Cathy and I are walking the 5K portion of the event that raises funds for the Susan G. Komen Foundation.

A team of yellow-slickered firefighters jogs by, sounding off in cadence with a flag-carrying team leader. A few Marines run around us. Show-offs!

We take the time to read the signs pinned to the backs of T-shirts of hundreds of walkers. Pink signs that say the walker is there in celebration of a survivor or in memory of someone who died.

Some walkers have several signs pinned together cascading down their backs.

So many lives touched! So many ordinary people forced to be heroes:

"Did you have curly hair before chemo?" Diane asks as I join the survivors after the walk.

I never had chemo, I tell her. I just had radiation. How about you?

"That's where the curls came from," she says with a smile. She has survived one year since her cancer diagnosis. The "chemo curls" are her bonus—a prize for being a brave mom and enduring chemo while raising a five-year-old and a six-year-old.

Tami waves a wand, her brow circled with a crown of glitter. "I am a princess," says the Covina woman, a four-year survivor. "When I make 12 years, I'll be a queen."

"I see hair! I see hair!" one woman shouts to a not-so-bald friend a few steps away. Hair returning. The signal that chemo is over.

"How long have you survived?" That's the question we ask one another.

Six years ago, Robyn Wagner-Holtz came to her first Race for the Cure. "The day I came there, I knew I was dying," she says. "Didn't everyone die of breast cancer?

"Then I saw all those women who survived! That was the day I started to live."

Sunday, she was chairwoman of the survivor ceremony.

Who needs doves? Just keep singing: "You're everything I wish I could be. . . . You are the wind beneath my wings!"

FOUR YEARS OF FREEDOM FROM BREAST CANCER?
GIVE A CHEER!

Monday, August 31, 1998

Give me a "High Four!" Four years since my breast-cancer operation! Four years cancer-free!

Celebrate good times! Come on! Four years ago, I found a small lump in my right breast one morning when I was doing a self-examination.

Three days later, Dr. John West of the St. Joseph Hospital Breast Care Center removed a seven-millimeter cancer. Later, he removed 31 lymph nodes from under my right arm—all negative.

My treatment: radiation but no chemotherapy.

The heroes of this story remain the same: researchers whose names I don't even know; the skillful doctors and empathetic nurses; and the many, many other women with whom I share this disease.

All I did was live long enough to end up with the most common cancer among women.

In some ways, it has been a gift. I have learned to celebrate—the good times, the little things, the overlooked moments:

- When my grandson in Maui answers the phone and says, "Is this Grandma Calipornia?"
- The wedding photos from my children's marriages—all AC (after cancer) events.
- The grin on my husband's face when he retired and shook hands with his boss for the last time.

Since I've had cancer, I've ridden a camel around the pyramid of Cheops, watched Sir Simon Rattle conduct Mahler's Sixth Symphony in the Musikverein in Vienna, seen the sun set in Hawaii and enjoyed the sunrise in Orange, waking the birds that flock to our backyard feeders.

My face is turned toward the future. Days go by when I don't think about cancer. My expectation is to live many more years.

Except for this time of the year, the anniversary of my operation.

The anxiety starts to build. Heartburn turns into stomach cancer in my mind. I prod different parts of my body, looking for lumps and lesions.

Once a year, I feel a need to share these fears and triumphs. My hope is to encourage just one woman to get a mammogram, to learn breast self-examination.

Those of us who have had breast cancer are part of a sisterhood that knows no age or economic or ethnic boundaries.

I sat in the *Orange County Register* fair booth this year as part of the newspaper's effort to connect us with readers. Two women walked across the vast fairgrounds just to talk to me about breast cancer.

In Orange County, one of seven women will develop breast cancer during her lifetime—1,650 women this year. And every day here, a woman dies from this disease.

But most of us live! That's the greater message.

Take care of yourself. And next year, give me a "High Five!"

EVEN DOCTORS COME TO BELIEVE:
FAITH CAN HEAL BODY AND SOUL

Monday, October 26, 1998

I know the power of prayer. About a year ago, when I had surgery for a potential second breast cancer, I knew I had been included on several prayer lists. Prayers, I believe, get answered. Even if the answer isn't what we want—or think we want. Knowing that helped me feel calm and confident as I was rolled into surgery. Did it change the outcome and guarantee a benign tumor? I don't know, and I don't care. More important to me was my attitude—a certainty that I could deal psychologically with whatever outcome resulted. Members of the clergy who regularly visit the sick validate that positive attitude. "A lot of doctors might not like to hear it, but I know that people get well faster if they have some religious belief," says the Reverend Virginia Erwin, rector of Trinity Episcopal Church in Orange. "People have more peace about their hospital experiences."

"Faith impacts the patient's well-being, and patients with a better attitude simply do better," says Marla Rickman, an emergency-room nurse at St. Joseph Hospital.

Older patients with some religious belief sliced hospital stays by more than half, according to a new study conducted at Duke University Medical Center. Patients 60 and older with no religious affiliation spent an average of 25 days in the hospital, compared with 11 days for patients with some religious denomination, researchers found. And there's data indicating that people who attend church services at least once a week are half as likely to be hospitalized. A review of studies in the *Archives of Family Medicine* says people who practice religion have lower depression and suicide rates and can deal better—mentally and physically—with illness. The result is faster recovery.

Lois Fiscus, who heads the daily prayer team at Mariner's South Coast Church in Newport Beach, knows faith comes from the inside.

Twenty years ago, she was diagnosed with a serious and rare lung problem. She felt she was going to spend the rest of her life as a semi-invalid, relying on a breathing machine. "One night I was watching a television evangelist—I didn't even believe in such things then—and he suddenly faced the camera, described my illness and said God was going to heal me. Two days later, a strange feeling came over me.

"I've never used that breathing machine. I am cured."

The experience changed Fiscus's attitude toward the healing power of prayer. Few of us can point to such a dramatic, direct link between healing and religion. But we want to believe such healings occur. We want to believe in miracles. Now, "Johns Hopkins Medical Letter" says that chemistry may explain how religion influences health, by minimizing stress and its effects. Still, the medical school is among those offering courses on spirituality and healing. "We can't ignore the research and the patients' desire for healing to include both body and soul," says Dr. Pat Fosarelli, an assistant professor at the Johns Hopkins School of Medicine.

WRITER'S EXPERIENCE WITH BREAST CANCER CHANGED HER LIFE

Thursday, September 23, 1999

Five years ago, I thought I would be dead today. Five years ago, a seven-millimeter lump cut from my right breast turned out to be cancer.

I immediately did the Irish thing: I planned my funeral. Play "Amazing Grace." Have me cremated but don't scatter the ashes. I have this phobia about being tossed around.

Five years later, I'm still here, thanks to excellent medical care and treatments available today. I am here—but I remember well the day I was diagnosed because nothing prepares you for that moment when a doctor says your life is at risk. Thoughts, questions speed down the hallways of your mind, bumping into walls of fear, bouncing into wells of terror.

Here is the good news about breast cancer—more than 95 percent of the women diagnosed at an early stage, before the disease has spread from the breast, are alive and well five years later.

That's me. Alive and well.

Not that the five years have passed without event. I've had two other lumpectomies, both benign, and one stereotactic biopsy, a new procedure that bores into the breast like an oil drill to carry out bits of tissue for analysis. Each time, I've waited for the results and done the Irish thing. The funeral, by the way, gets more elaborate. Lots of good music.

Five years with an occasional day of fear is an easy price to pay for the blessings I have enjoyed during these 60 months. I have learned what marriage is really about. Without my husband's support and love, I would have lost my serenity. He stops my Irish from taking over. I've watched two children marry and seen my three children flourish into exceptional young adults. I've welcomed my first two grandchildren. I have traveled to exotic places. I've kept a full schedule of work. I've bought a new computer, got a new dog, picked out carpeting, and planted trees that are producing peaches and apples. Three of my good friends have found out they have breast cancer in the intervening time. Each has endured more involved and lengthy treatments than I faced. Each also is still alive and well.

Every year I tell you about my breast cancer because maybe one woman will read my story and decide to have a mammogram and a clinical examination by a physician. Maybe others will learn the techniques of breast self-examination. That's how I found my tumor.

I said that three of my friends are still alive after their diagnoses. But another friend is not. I watched this woman die of breast cancer. Morphine did not always dull her pain. Her faith in God and her certainty of an afterlife did not keep her from crying out in frustration. I don't want that to happen to me. Or you. Certainly not to my daughter or your daughters. Take the time to have your breast checkups every year after age 40. Encourage your husbands to have prostate checkups to catch any cancer at an early stage.

Sooner or later, my family will be putting the final touches on my Irish funeral. They'll be looking for a Dixieland band to play "When the Saints Go Marching In." They tell me they're not in a hurry to start auditioning groups. I'm not in a hurry to shuffle-step out of here, either.

Stick around with me. Who knows what the next five years will bring?

Part 3—We Say They're Seniors— They Say, "I'm Old"

THE GOOD NEWS IS, TWO-THIRDS OF ALL THE HUMAN BEINGS IN THE ENTIRE HISTORY OF THE WORLD WHO EVER LIVED TO BE 65 ARE ALIVE TODAY. THE BAD NEWS IS, NOT ALL OF THEM ARE FINDING GOLD IN THEIR GOLDEN YEARS.

Help Expose a Tragic Secret: Elder Abuse

Monday, March 31, 1997

I want you to read this and be outraged. I want you to be so angry you promise to do something about elder abuse before it becomes the scandal of the 21st century.

Experts estimate 10 percent of people 60 and older are being abused today. That would be 4.1 million elderly. In a decade, the nation could have 7.2 million. Elder-abuse victims, like child-abuse victims, are frail and vulnerable. Their abusers are usually family members. The abuse ranges from physical violence to financial exploitation, from neglect to sexual abuse.

The National Center on Elder Abuse says only 1 in 14 cases are reported. It took Catherine, 91, a dozen years to make her report. When her daughter lost her job 12 years ago, Catherine offered her a home. The verbal abuse began almost immediately. Over time, Catherine became isolated in a bedroom in her own Orange County house. Malnourished. Fearful of the rats and roaches scurrying through rooms piled high with trash.

"She would not leave the house," her son said. "She would not leave my sister."

Last fall, Catherine broke her hip. Before she was released from the hospital, a social worker came to the house to make sure conditions were right for Catherine's return. The social worker was appalled. She called Adult Protective Services.

"I was in a walker, and I couldn't get through from one room to another," Catherine said. "My daughter just kept hauling trash and junk down on me. She told me, 'You should go to a rest home. I have my own thing to do and I don't have time for you.'"

Broken in spirit, Catherine finally agreed to move in with her son and force her daughter's eviction. Before the daughter left, she cleaned out her mother's checking account and stole her monthly retirement check. Catherine can hardly talk about her daughter's abuse. "Oh, lady, you don't know how it hurts."

That is a typical response, says Jack Light, head of Orange County's Adult Protective Services. "There is a reluctance to turn in your own children. It's the same dynamic as domestic violence. The scenario may be that the older person feels some responsibility or thinks he/she can change the child over time. Most of the time, these people stay in the relationship because they feel depressed and over-whelmed by it all. How can they cope? It's easier to give in."

Old women who were never assertive in younger years are partic-ularly easy abuse targets. But old men also are victims. Jim, 89, lived with a stepdaughter and her two sons in the home he owned in Los Angeles County. When his daughter called to check on him, he always told her he was fine. She didn't know that each night, before he went to sleep, Jim propped a chair under the door handle to his bedroom. He had good reason to lock himself in his room. His stepgrandsons had knocked him down on numerous occasions, one time breaking his hip. His stepdaughter fed him small bits of food and candy bars. She let him sleep in a urine-soaked bed.

"By the time I found out what was going on, by the time I got con-servatorship to rescue my father, he was acting demented," Jim's daughter said. Now that he's living in a board-and-care home, the old man is regaining some of his lost faculties. He no longer props any-thing under the doorknob of his room.

Most abusers have drug and alcohol problems and often resent the older person for being dependent or even for past mistreatment. Some are caregivers who snap under the stress. An overwhelming number depend on the old person for housing or money.

"The biggest ally of abusers is secrecy," Light said. "These people are isolated. They end up totally dependent on the abuser."

Only public awareness can help prevent this crime. Here's what you can do: befriend the old people living in your neighborhood or apartment building. Stay in touch. Don't let them get isolated. Know the resources of your community. Calls to Adult Protective Services are confidential. Eldercare nurses at your local senior center often can help identify and intervene in cases of abuse. Call the local bar association. The Orange County Bar Association has a free legal referral, Lawyers for Elder Abuse Prevention; there is probably one in your area, too.

Don't let this crime wave continue. Don't become a victim.

GRANNY IN STIR: SENIOR EQUALITY CUTS BOTH WAYS

Monday, July 7, 1997

Here's a clue that our civil-rights movement is mainstreaming: an Indiana prosecutor put a grandmother, 60, in shackles for a court appearance. Her crime: she can't pay $40,000 in estate taxes and fees.

Hortencia Bohen had already spent six weeks in jail. She got the jail time for contempt of court. She told the judge she gave away a $250,000 inheritance and has no receipts. She says she spread cash among Hammond, Indiana's, homeless. One of the lawyers for the bank involved in the civil case thought six weeks in the slammer would crack the old girl. "I figured we'd hear from her in an hour; certainly the next day at the latest," lawyer Joseph Costanza told a reporter. "But you just can't talk to her. She is, to put it mildly, a very determined woman."

Now here's the pop quiz question: What civil-rights movement does Hortencia represent? You think "women's rights"? Bzzzzzt. That's '80s politics.

Hortencia is a '90s woman. She's old. She's bold. If she does the crime, she'll do the time.

For her, age is no excuse.

Her case made headlines because Grandma was put in shackles, as if she were 25. Are you outraged? Maybe you should be grateful.

Our aging population can't demand a level playing field in the work force and the marketplace until we're willing to take our lumps along with everyone else. We can't demand equality to succeed and ask for special treatment when we err.

Not that crime has ever been age-restricted. Former Orange County Treasurer Robert Citron, 71, pleaded guilty to six felonies in connection with the county's bankruptcy. His punishment, of course, was a year of community service work. That sentence led to several public comments that Citron was playing the "age card."

Alfred Pohlmeier, 92, tried to play on jury sympathy, claiming he was being merciful when he strangled his wife because her chronic cough annoyed him. A Ventura jury said age was no excuse for his crime and found him guilty of second-degree murder.

Gray hair should not be an automatic ticket to respect. Maria de Jesus Chavez learned that the hard way. The Santa Ana woman was scammed out of $8,000 by an old man who rambled on in a pitiful fashion about tragedy in his life and asked her help in selling some gold bars. The gold bars—which Chavez bought—turned out to be brass.

These older criminals are proving to be grist for film and book writers.

Sure, sure, there were those dotty sisters in *Arsenic and Old Lace,* but they only offed lonely old men. Now, in *Absolute Power,* aging world-class jewel thief Clint Eastwood rappels down a building and outruns the Secret Service. He's puffing, but he's fast.

Aging criminals are proving as popular as those aging fictional sleuths Miss Marple and Jessica Fletcher. An example are the villains of Mission Viejo mystery writer Maxine O'Callahan, especially in her short stories featuring a 70-ish female assassin.

"She's a grandmotherly old lady who cultivates the look because it affords her the advantages you would expect," O'Callahan says. "Who's going to suspect a little old lady? Actually, her husband was a hit man and she takes over his business when he dies."

O'Callahan, author of a dozen mysteries including the Delila West, Private Eye series set in Orange County, says she's always had older villains. "When I see stories in the paper about older people committing crimes, well, it does lead a mind down certain avenues."

Reality is that the justice system traditionally has been more lenient on the old, says Gilbert Geis, 71, professor emeritus of criminology, law and society at the University of California, Irvine.

"Juries sympathize," he says. "They say, 'What's the point?' in punishment."

Of course, jurors themselves are getting older. "Retired people are the only ones with the time to serve," Geis says. These older jurors may look at gray-haired defendants with a more jaundiced eye.

As an Indiana judge told a *Hammond Times* reporter, "I'm 63 and I am capable of committing a crime, so why shouldn't she (Hortencia) serve her time, too?"

Age should never be an excuse.

POWERFUL ROLE FOR SENIORS: GUARDIAN ANGEL

Monday, February 23, 1998

I met my spirit guide once.

In the 1970s, when the trendsetters were into focusing energy through pyramid power, guided handwriting and psychic experiences, I did a series of newspaper articles on reflexology, palmistry and seances. That's where you meet spirit guides. In seances. A psychic worked with a young woman who dropped easily into a hypnotic trance and channeled spirits from the other world.

"Howard is here," she said. She was sitting on a green vinyl bean-bag chair in the living room of a small apartment in Elgin, Illinois. "Howard is your spirit guide. He was a scribe in Greece. He'll be with you until he works out his karma. Say 'hello' to Howard."

I demurred.

"Say 'hello' to Howard or you will hurt his feelings!" she said.

Discretion is the better part of valor. I said "hello" to an empty room.

I never felt really close to Howard. Greek scribes named Howard trying to work out their karma guiding me through the intricacies of investigative reporting stretched my credulity.

Guardian angels—those tall, striding creatures with long hair and big wings—long ago went the way of Santa Claus in my mind. But guardian spirits are a different bag of ether altogether. They've even talked to me.

Once, running down a street in Stockholm from one interview to another, I heard my mother, clear and strong, tell me, "Stop." Mom had been dead for a good decade when I heard her voice. Something—Mom again?—made me check my belongings. An important notebook was missing. I retraced my steps and found it lying at the top of a staircase in a Swedish office building.

Bet you've had experiences like that, too.

In fact, I believe most of you believe in guardian spirits—or desperately want to. Why else would 10 million viewers watch *It's a Wonderful Life* every holiday season? The film is about the human spirit, God and the meaning we bring to each other's lives.

One of my favorite characters is Clarence, the film's wing-seeking angel, who lets George Bailey see what life would be like if he had never been born.

"In talking about the film, many people have spoken about 'angels,' meaning someone in their lives who has been a vehicle for opening their eyes," says Connie Goldman. She's an independent producer of public-radio programs on aging.

Goldman has produced "It's a Wonderful Life: Our Lives Re-Viewed" as a one-hour radio special. It focuses on the meaning the movie holds for people of all walks of life. One of her purposes: to give meaning to the lives of the elderly.

An important point Goldman makes is that older people often have been "angels" who touched another's life in a positive way.

Think of yourself as an angel? That's a powerful message. It seems a shame to confine that thought to the holiday season.

Guardian angels. Spirit guides. Whatever you want to call them, there's some comfort in believing they exist.

But I still have trouble fitting Howard, the Greek scribe, into that mold. Maybe if his name was Zorba.

Just Being There Is What Is Needed during Personal Crisis

Monday, March 2, 1998

When someone is diagnosed with cancer or congestive heart failure or is zapped by a stroke, don't tell me it's God's will. I don't believe in that kind of God. When a loved one tumbles into the confusion of Alzheimer's, don't pat my hand and murmur, "At least they don't know what's going on." That's an insult. Just stand by me.

"Ninety percent of helping is just showing up," says the Reverend James R. Kok, director of care ministries at the Crystal Cathedral.

Now, I believe that. In my own experiences with serious illness, I remember the comfort from people who "just showed up." I also remain bewildered by good friends who never called and later told me they "just couldn't deal with it." Excuse me—I had to deal with it big time.

"People just don't know what to say, so they turn away," Kok says. "No one tells us what to say." Kok believes caring for others crosses church boundaries and generational differences. His mission is to get people out of their pews and into their neighborhoods—not to evangelize but to fraternize. His concern is that as our population ages—and our losses mount—we aren't learning little ways to help each other get through day by day. "Unfortunately, the way most people learn what help is needed is when they get slammed by life themselves," he says.

Shirley Zenk says "amen" to that. Ten years ago, her son took his own life. She called the 24-hour help line at the Crystal Cathedral, and no one answered. A few weeks later, Zenk showed up at the cathedral to train as a telephone counselor. "I thought, maybe that's what I should do to bring some good from this," she says. Now she talks about ways to reach out and help one another in schools, at community meetings and to groups outside the church. "Sometimes, we say or do stupid or inappropriate things," Zenk says. "Just learning not to run away, not to give pat answers, can really make a difference to people."

Just say "hi." "That is what most people want to hear," Kok says. Just "be what people need. Don't judge. Just listen."

Here are some ways people of all faiths can reach out to each other: give the help you would need to take care of yourself. Visit the sick and dying. Learn to listen. Remember that part of caring for others is letting others remember the past.

Treat other people the way you would like to be treated yourself.

Monday, November 9, 1998

Satisfied.

That's the only way to sum up the attitude of more than 80 percent of America's 65-plusers, who tell pollsters they feel pretty darned good about themselves, about their contributions to society, even about their finances. More of them are working—15 percent, compared with 12 percent last year—not because they need the dollars but because they like feeling productive, enjoy the challenge and would otherwise be bored.

What kind of work are they doing? About 14 percent are laborers, helpers and secretaries; 13 percent remain in management. An additional 10 percent identified themselves as skilled laborers. The array of jobs trickles down to 2 percent in farming, forestry or fishing. An astonishing number—81 percent—say they have never experienced age discrimination.

Good times for today's golden agers! But don't expect the party to last when the boomers arrive.

Today's satisfied seniors lived through the depression and world wars, the threat of nuclear holocaust and massive job-churning markets, says Arthur B. Shostak, professor of sociology at Drexel University Center for Employment Futures. He recently completed a national telephone survey of 889 adults that came up with these results.

"Today's seniors are hard-boiled and thick-skinned," he says. "They are survivors. They were smart enough or lucky enough to buy homes on the GI Bill, go to school on the GI Bill and become skilled workers. They have a history of not feeling sorry for themselves." As an example, the professor talks about his own mother, now 88, who worked 50 years as a nurse. "When I asked her how she spent all those years taking guff from male doctors, she was bewildered. 'That's just the way it was,' she said. Well, it won't be that way in the future. And good riddance," he adds.

The next wave of seniors-to-be wants to avoid that age label. "They came through a different America," Shostak says. They have had their consciousness raised by the civil-rights movement, the feminist movement and, thanks to AARP [American Association of Retired Persons] and similar groups, the age movement. Boomers will not equate aging with a time of self-contentment. The Rolling Stones' "(I Can't Get No) Satisfaction" was written with them in mind.

Instead of retiring at age 62 or 65, these "new-agers" are planning to combine part-time work and leisure to keep themselves active and busy. Shostak expects that a larger percentage of older Americans will work in some capacity in the 21st century. That's no surprise. Not many will have enough income from pensions and Social Security to retire in style. What took Shostak aback was the number of people who said they work for something besides money.

Shostak discovered that, for many older Americans, work translates into a caring community. "What they are experiencing at work is family. The importance of that environment is a good thing for employers to keep in mind." Increasingly, "family values" begin in the workplace for older Americans.

Domestic Violence Is Problem of Old As Well As Young Women

Monday, May 17, 1999

Just thinking about domestic violence drives me nuts. The concept that any human being of any age physically or verbally abuses another person is evil. And don't get me started on sexual abuse!

But why do we think all victims of this abuse are young?

"Domestic violence is the leading cause of injury to women 17 to 45," the National Domestic Violence Hotline reports. What happens when the women reach 45? Do they wise up and move out? Die? Or just suffer the batterings as forgotten victims?

An Orange County woman who lives in a large retirement community just filed for divorce from her husband of 32 years. She also charged him with personal injury. She is the first elderly domestic-violence client her attorney, Kent F. Tibbitts, has represented.

Older ladies simply are taking it on the chin, says Shirley Gellatly, program director at Human Options, a Newport Beach–based service for abused women and their children. "We had a support group at a senior center and found that many older women are in long-term marriages where they have endured violence," Gellatly says. The Human Options shelter housed four women older than 65 in the past three years. All were fleeing long-term relationships and violence that escalated as their spouses aged.

The Older Women's League reports that in 1994, 1.4 million women 45–65 were abused by their spouses. And that abuse never stops, Gellatly says. She recalls a woman in her 80s who described the way her husband, in his 90s, smashed his hand into her face and banged her head against a wall. Why do they stay?

"They stay for the same reasons younger women stay," Gellatly says. "They are afraid; they feel threatened. They've gotten used to it. They don't know where to go. It's mostly economic. These women are very tied to their husbands economically. And they usually have lost the support of their family. The kids grew up with it and are tired of hearing about it. They've given up. Many of them are mad at their mothers for staying and being treated like that."

Gellatly believes there is no age barrier to the statistic that 25 percent of the population is involved in relationships with ongoing violence. As proof, she cites a survey in Boston that found calls to elder-abuse hot lines cited spouse abuse (58 percent) more often than adult-child abuse (24 percent). "This is not solely a young woman's problem, and it's about time we got that word out," Gellatly says.

Older women who reach out can find help through the National Domestic Violence Hotline, (800) 799-7233. A call there will connect you to the closest shelter and counselors for abused women.

The time has come for you to be mad as hell and declare that you aren't going to take it anymore.

Withholding Visitation? Just Stop It!

Monday, October 4, 1999

Trends of an aging society: "My ex-husband's second wife is refusing to let our children visit him in the nursing home," the caller said. Why? Bitterness over the way assets were divided, she assumes.

Well, that might or might not be true. I've heard only one side of this family feud. But a check with elder advocates regrettably confirms an increase in end-of-life fussing between family members, particularly in families where there has been divorce and remarriage.

"I'm starting to hear a fair amount about these controversies," says Laguna Hills elder-law specialist Fay Blix. "Usually the arguments happen in hospitals over whether or not to keep people alive using various artificial means." In the case of life-or-death decisions, doctors and lawyers look for paperwork that assigns someone—usually the spouse—as the agent to make those decisions.

In the case of visitation, the answers are less certain. "Technically, the agent comes first and can make most decisions," Blix says. "But barring visitation is not usually included. The adult children could protest that." Her suggestion to save time and legal expense is to turn to the nursing-home team for mediation. Accredited nursing homes are required to have some type of ethics counselor, "who could make sure that everyone has a chance to be heard."

"Obviously, there are some underlying concerns we don't know. Are the children going to try to get Dad to change his will, for example? Maybe Dad doesn't want to see his children. But if the second spouse is just acting as a gatekeeper, that's pretty arrogant."

Arrogant, indeed, says Rosalie Kane, director of the Long Term Care Center at the University of Minnesota. "You can imagine scenarios where children could be a problem visiting, but it's difficult on the whole," Kane said. "Usually the person in a nursing home could use and enjoy all the attention he can get."

These are situations that never should occur in the first place, says Kane, who assesses quality of life in nursing homes. "We keep trying to get more and more of our human problems and issues settled by some legal formula," she says. "Why can't more people try to work things out between themselves?"

Why not? Because of the Almighty Dollar, says Rochelle Woolery of the Council on Aging of Orange County and director of its ombudsman service. Ombudsmen routinely visit nursing-home patients. "Yes, these fights among family members are increasing," Woolery says. "And when we get down to it, money is usually the cause. Sometimes the arguments are not totally unreasonable, but most of the time, I want to tell people to get a grip. Think of the person who is lying there in the bed."

In Woolery's opinion, unless the person attempting to bar visitation is the court-appointed conservator, there is no legal right to bar family members from seeing a patient. "The nursing home isn't in the business of limiting visitors," she says. "And if family members can't stand each other—well, work out a visitation schedule."

As she said, get a grip!

There Are Times for a Happy Face, Times for Realistic Outlook

Monday, April 5, 1999

"You do harm," the voice on telephone said. She was angry because a recent column said aging well depends on a positive attitude as well as healthy living.

Her point: some people cannot overcome disease or disability. Telling them to "buck up" and be positive is cruel. The caller, who didn't leave her name or number, obviously is in some anguish over a personal or family crisis. Nevertheless, her message disturbed me. I saw myself cast as some geriatric Shirley Temple tap dancing on the sunset cruise of the Good Ship *Geezerville*.

All things in moderation, please.

There are times for a happy face and times for a realistic outlook. The concept of "healthy attitude" covers both. The question is how to encourage the correct "face." An oncologist once shared his confusion about what to tell families who react positively to a diagnosis of terminal cancer. "When they say, 'We're going to fight it!' I often don't know how to respond," he said.

Elisabeth Kübler-Ross, who virtually invented the field 20 years ago with her classic book, *On Death and Dying*, says people should be told the truth, but no one needs to volunteer information.

Dr. Daniel Redwood of Virginia Beach, Virginia, says, "We all are born the same way. We all die the same way, basically." Certainly, that makes death the ultimate attitude adjuster.

But Kübler-Ross added that the way we approach death, to some extent, depends on how we have lived. "If you have lived fully, then you have no regrets because you have done the best you can do. If you made a lot of goofs—much better to have made lots of goofs than not to have lived at all."

Sounds like a Frank Sinatra theme: "Regrets? I've had a few, but then again, too few to mention." I hope I remember those words when I make the ultimate attitude adjustment. I've only skirted the edges, but I know it is not possible to always be positive. In fact, sometimes a positive attitude would seem ludicrous.

A little more than a week ago, my husband was hastily admitted to the hospital because of a heart flutter. Six days later, he left with prescriptions and admonitions to change his lifestyle, exercise more, all the usual orders. The day after he went into the hospital, I had a scheduled biopsy because of concerns my breast cancer had returned.

Did I spend the weekend upbeat and chipper? Of course not. In the dark, cold hours of the night, I would wake up in fear. I asked friends for prayers because I was too stressed to pray myself. Luckily, my biopsy was negative and Bob will be fine. I'll keep on eating my tofu; he'll start walking and stop smoking.

Having something we can do to maintain or improve the status quo makes me positive. To dwell on the limitations life inevitably deals us is what does harm.

That's my attitude.

Monday April 3, 2000

Forget this preoccupation with nursing homes. True, 30 percent of elders have said they would rather die than go to into institutional care. Fact: nursing-home care sometimes fails to meet quality standards. But constantly fingering the worry beads of nursing-home care can obscure the view of reality.

Here's reality: most people who are ill or disabled are cared for at home, usually by a spouse or an adult daughter. Family members provide 80 percent of all long-term care. Most of them are unpaid.

It's estimated that one in four Americans—52 million people—provide some care for an ailing family member. Imagine if 52 million Americans were expected to work at jobs that paid nothing: no wages, no benefits, no future.

Don't tell me that it is a family member's responsibility, caring for loved ones. Tell me how we're going to keep them at this physically demanding and emotionally wrenching task when we live in a society where money matters.

Supporting families involved in at-home care is critical, Ken Dychtwald told the American Society on Aging convention in San Diego last week. Dychtwald, author of *Age Power*, said that even with so many families providing unpaid care, the cost of caregiving looms as a budget-breaking expense for American social-service programs.

Why? One reason is the longevity of elders. Improved health care is extending lives, said Marilyn Ditty, director of South Orange County Senior Services. While caregiving once was a 3- to 4-year obligation, it now stretches for 8 to 10 years.

But there's hidden danger in that long stretch of service: about 25 percent of all female caregivers leave employment to respond to caregiving demands. They quit the work force, losing health and

Social Security benefits, to care for a mother or a husband. When their caregiving chores end, they find themselves behind the eight ball in terms of workplace skills, said Kathleen Kelly, executive director of San Francisco–based Family Caregiver Alliance.

"We need to take a serious look at this problem if we are going to encourage family members to be caregivers," she said.

President Clinton's budget includes a $3,000 tax credit for full-time caregiving. Not enough, acknowledged Jeanette Takamura, U.S. assistant secretary of aging. "But it's a start," she told me.

Technology can solve some caregiving problems, predicted Dr. William H. Thomas, founder of the Eden Alternative nursing homes. His philosophy is to keep patients interacting with life by having resident pets, such as dogs and cats, and offering gardening projects, among other activities. Thomas contends that only 700 of the nation's 17,000 nursing homes need to remain open. Most people can stay independent—and in their own homes—if technology helps out.

"Stoves that turn themselves off when a pot goes dry, refrigerators that e-mail daughters—and sons—when the door hasn't been opened for 12 hours; these are the future products that will give elders independence longer," he said. Aging boomers will demand a shift away from institutions, Thomas predicted.

Besides, Dychtwald says, "home care is cheaper than institutions."

True. But society cannot have it both ways. If aging America wants to shift away from warehousing the old in nursing homes, there must be some way to adequately reimburse family members who provide care.

No other profession is so debilitating to older people. A study reported in a recent *Journal of the American Medical Association* shows that older spousal caregivers have a mortality risk 63 percent higher than noncaregiving spouses.

Caregiver burnout is widely recognized. In fact, the National Alliance for Caregiving has some recommendations for those who might be at risk for burnout, particularly those who feel listless and frequently wish they were somewhere else:

- Join a caregiver support group. Check the newspaper or local library to find others to share your experiences with regularly.
- Talk to a professional, such as clergy, social worker or psychologist.
- Take advantage of respite-care services offered by organizations such as the Alzheimer's Association of Orange County or the Orange Caregiver Resource Center.
- Carve out time for yourself, even if it is just an hour or two.

Part 4—Don't Ever Call ME a "Senior Citizen"

GIVE ME LONGEVITY ON MY OWN TERMS. DON'T TELL ME WHAT I CAN'T DO—CHALLENGE ME TO DO MORE. I WANT TO BE TOO BUSY LEARNING NEW TRICKS TO PONDER WHEN THE BELL WILL TOLL FOR ME.

THE "GIRL" AT 71

*Helen Gurley Brown Admits Pills, Potions and
Plastic Surgery Can't Stop the March of Time*

Wednesday, April 14, 1993

You must develop style. Every girl has one.
— HELEN GURLEY BROWN,
Sex and the Single Girl (1962)

Helen Gurley Brown, 71, opened the door to her Beverly Wilshire Hotel suite wearing nothing but a man's shirt. Her hair looked like a tumbleweed—one that had bounced on Route 66 between Albuquerque and Tucumcari. Grease slathered her face—taut as a tom-tom thanks to plastic surgeries.

The editor of *Cosmopolitan* magazine, a woman totally preoccupied with eternal youth, has lost the battle.

From her knobby knees to her skimpy hair, Brown proves you can be too thin. And, no, not even dermabrasion (skin), rhinoplasty (nose), blepharoplasty (eyes), a complete facelift, 90 minutes of exercise a day, 30 vitamin and mineral supplements every morning, massive doses of estrogen daily and a lifetime of smelling food instead of eating it keeps you forever young.

Instead, it's time for *The Late Show: A Semiwild but Practical Survival Plan for Women over 50* (Morrow, 1993), Brown's newest guidebook, this one for the *Cosmo* girl who discovers she is aging.

"I can't see many laughs in the situation," she said, sitting on the French Provincial couch with one foot tucked under her, all girlish and gushy. "I worked like a dog to keep it from happening."

She's still riding the wave of sexual liberation. Still pitching daring exploits such as "borrowing" a friend's husband if yours is worn out

SEMIWILD WISDOM

Is Helen Gurley Brown talking to you? Here are some comments from her book *The Late Show: A Semiwild but Practical Survival Plan for Women over 50:*

- On weight: "If we weighed what the insurance charts say we could at our age, we could be a baby blimp." Her solution is to keep the calorie count down. "I am totally preoccupied with food."
- On exercise: "Enough exercise to make a difference (in your looks) takes a one-hour session at least four times a week for six months to a year . . . . With exercise, good posture, copious creaming, you'll look good enough from all easily visible angles."
- On health: "I have taken megadoses of vitamins for 20 years. . . . Never mind that some doctors who prescribe them sell vitamins and your bill can be bigger than the rent."
- On coping: "After you're older, two things are possibly more important than any others: health and money. Sex, work, friend-

with age. Still talking the way she writes, in surges of gamy italics. Still trumpeting her philosophy: a *Cosmo* girl "loves men and children, is traditional in many ways but wants her own identity."

She says her *Cosmopolitan* attitude flourishes in 27 international editions because she gives voice to the philosophy Germaine Greer and other feminists decry as one befitting "perpetual brides."

"There are millions of women who fit that description," Brown said. "I consider myself a devout feminist, but the feminist movement sometimes denigrates men and, well, after all . . . I knew early in my dating years that men have problems, too. I've seen my husband and other men go through stuff I wouldn't wish on Saddam Hussein."

So that's it: a generous dollop of understanding men mixed with a healthy dose of romancing men sugared with pedicures and perms plus real knowledge of intimate pleasures for men. As Brown said, "I'm sure most women think like me but they don't talk about it. I don't mind. I believe in being frank. I want to uplift and inspire."

Inspire to what? Men—how to catch, keep and, if you're inclined, get married to one of them? That message hasn't changed.

Brown, originator of *Cosmo*'s bosomy cover girl, chatters with aplomb about how the message translates as women age. On aging lovers: "I mean, we have to remember that it takes work for them." On the price of perpetual youth: "I suppose it is elitist to talk about facelifts when they cost $10,000."

Let Gail Sheehy write her *Silent Passage* about menopause. Brown will tell you she never experienced "the change." She says her doctor okayed massive amounts of estrogen to keep her libido and her body at its youthful peak.

She also admits women "have it easy in the sex department."

"I don't blame anything on menopause because I never experienced it. But I wouldn't want to be a man growing older. We can always perform like little minxes. They, poor dears, have those performance problems and it's all tied up with their egos."

As she has aged, Brown may have accepted the fact that there is more to life than catching a man. "Love is

ship, love have to be fitted in."

- On aging: "We need to accept ourselves at the age we are. . . . We didn't 'appreciate' older people when we were younger either. . . . Older is what we get. And it's okay."

no more important than work," she said. "And while I am oriented toward men, there are lots of ways to love, including friends, family and children."

Childless, Brown has devoted her attention to husband David Brown, multimillionaire Hollywood producer of *A Few Good Men.* But she and David fight, she confided. Why, just that morning they argued about which credit card she would use to pay for a hired car to drive her around Beverly Hills. Which brings her to another point:

"I never trust people who say they are fabulously, happily married," she said. "If they are lucky, they have a decent, good person as a mate. Try to marry someone who is not a creep, of course. But they are all flawed. So when we combine our flaws, it's not always a plus. People who stay married are no happier than those who are not married. They have just decided there is no point risking it all to find out if someone else is better."

So much for fidelity. Age is a different can of cream.

"To grow old is disgraceful. You must fight back," Brown said. "People think it's okay to let go, but they must not." Age, if it gets you, turns you into a boring, whiny, unhealthy person. Not someone a *Cosmo* boy wants to hang with, she said. "But it is true, maintenance takes time, care and money."

Reading about the hours and hours and hours that Brown spends on maintenance can be daunting. Who has the time? The money? The inclination?

"Well, I made the time. And it never occurred to me I wouldn't stave off age forever. It crashed in on me. I didn't like it. Getting older is the pits. But if you can't keep yourself from aging, you can keep yourself from getting older."

Attitude, Enthusiasm, Energy Separate Aging from the Old

Monday, October 7, 1996

I had the most wonderful summer vacation. Twice, I had to prove I was old enough for a 55-plus senior discount.

I hear you asking who's really fooled by this face, still natural and without benefit of cosmetic surgery? It has wrinkles—tiny lines of character, I call them—and age spots and incipient jowls. Well, I'd like to think it looks younger because I have energy, enthusiasm, excitement about living. Frankly, that's what separates the aging from the old.

Traveling through Oregon, Washington and British Columbia, I saw an incredible array of aging people and old people. Everyone had lived about the same number of years. But, wow, you can tell the difference on sight!

The aging people had bikes tied to the backs of their RVs. They were hiking the lava buttes around Bend, Oregon, and picking apples in Washington's Yakima Valley. The old people stayed inside the boat cruising Seattle's harbor, edgily watching life through salt-specked windows. They sat with crossed ankles, bobbed in recliner chairs and allowed as how they hadn't left Midway, British Columbia, for 20- or 30-odd years.

"We're talking about attitude," says Dr. Kaaren Douglas, head of the geriatrics program at the University of California, Irvine. "Attitude—as much as health—is what makes you old." Douglas contends that Californians have a cheeky attitude toward life. "Californians tend to always see another horizon. California has an attitude and environment that allows each one of us to pursue our passions and know we have supporters. We know life has got some promise. That there is joy in getting out of bed every day."

But really, you don't have to be from California to "zippity-doo-dah" after 55.

Bill Putaansuu, a retired chemical engineer, is buoyant leading tourists on a Mount St. Helens nature walk, showing off the blackberry vines and lupine and deciduous trees reclaiming the volcanic park. Putaansuu, who labored on federal reclamation projects after the 1980 eruption, divides his time between being a volunteer forest ranger and working as a ski instructor. "Life is wonderful!" he says. "I look forward to every day."

Not so the women shoving their trays ahead of me in the cafeteria line of the roasted chicken restaurant in Bend. They complained about everything from the mashed potatoes to the size of their chicken serving. These women—all gray-heads—acted as if they hadn't had a good day in years.

Said one, "Young people just don't care about niceties like we did."

The cashier automatically gave her a senior discount, so I asked, "How old do you have to be for that discount?"

The cashier looked at me hard. "You have to be 55," she said. And when I said I'd take it, she glared, "I swear, some people want to be old."

Ah, ain't it the truth? Ain't it the truth?

Men Taking a "Firmative" Action on Skin Care

Monday, November 25, 1996

You guys are carrying this equality stuff too far. First you demanded the right to be sensitive. Then you started wearing support hose. Now you want my facial appointment. Enough gender-blender!

Last week I showed up at my local spa to make a quick appointment, only to find Paul shoving in the door ahead of me, eager to book the same time. Paul insisted he had "needs." He needed to be exfoliated. He needed his blemishes expunged. He needed the peaceful tranquility of foot reflexology.

At 52, Paul said he suddenly realized taking care of his body was not enough. The years are showing on his face. Actually, he finally admitted he had a job interview and his competition was a woman. And so he turned to Toni Bush of Clinical Skin Care in Orange. Like a disciple, he listened to her intone, "Pay attention to the way you look today if you want to cut it in the marketplace. Dry skin makes a statement about the value you place on yourself." In the past year, men who value themselves have become almost 40 percent of Bush's business.

These midlifers are running scared. They know that smelling like an old sailor doesn't send your flag up the rigging of corporate America anymore. According to the Bureau of Labor Statistics, men 45–54 run the greatest risk of losing their jobs in corporate downsizing. Because older men are competing against younger colleagues—and against women—they need to take pains to look younger to get a promotion or keep a job.

That's the conclusion of Aramis, the New York–based producer of male grooming and cosmetic lines. Aramis introduced its first male cosmetic and grooming products in 1964, but they languished until the '90s recession. In the past five years, sales of men's skincare products have zoomed upward an average of 20 percent annually, reaching $1.65 billion a year.

"First it was the younger guys," said Adrian Stonehouse, who sells skincare products at Macy's men's store in South Coast Plaza, Costa Mesa. "Then it was the middle-aged guys trying to look younger. We still don't sell many of these products to older guys. Older guys still think it's sissy."

That's geezer-myopia. Twenty years ago, only 10 percent of cosmetic surgery was done on men. Today it's 25 percent, and they're having hair restoration, liposuction, nose jobs, eyelid lifts and skin abrasion. Middle-age men are ladling on the alpha-hydroxyls, the anti-oxidants and the self-tanning products. They want tone and clarity and moisture. They don't want those tiny lines of character that age a face.

"Every 15 seconds, a male baby boomer turns 50," said Timothy Rush, spokesman for Aramis. "They are looking for solutions."

In January, Aramis expects to offer fresh solutions, including an "eye time rescue gel" to reduce puffiness and circles. The eye gel joins a line that includes Sharp Shooter, a moisturizer that uses anti-oxidant vitamins.

A generation's addiction to the Marlboro Man is reduced to this: an oil-free facial cream that won't clog an urban cowboy's pores.

DOES MATURITY MAKE YOU RIGID?
ONLY IN THE CONDENSED EDITION

Monday, December 22, 1997

Here's the topic: "Do you think you're young or old?" And here's
1 of 10 questions that supposedly gives you the answer:
Every Friday night,

My spouse and I play bridge with our two closest and oldest friends.

We go to dinner with an alternating group of pals.

We try to do something different from what we did the
previous week, even if it turns out to be a disappointment.

The quiz is one of many tucked inside yet another new book on
reaching the Big 5-0, *Are You Old Enough to Read This Book?
Reflections on Midlife.* Published by *Reader's Digest,* the book con-
denses the toils and rewards of aging in typical *Reader's Digest* short
takes. Among the other questions: Do you think the good old days are
gone? How do you feel about hip-hop language? How would you
react if someone called you a "prig"?

The "correct" answer—the one that shows you're not old—is the
answer that stresses flexibility, or "c" in the sample question. But the
quiz—like so much pop psychology—is bogus because it equates old
age with rigidity.

Folks, it ain't necessarily so. As proof, let me introduce you to
Deena, a family friend.

She doesn't read newspapers because she can't stand the feel of the
paper and ink. She doesn't watch television news because it interrupts
her train of thought while she cooks dinner. She doesn't listen to radio
news because she doesn't want to be distracted while she drives. And
there's more: she doesn't fly because there was a plane crash in her
city 25 years ago. She won't drive through major cities because there
is too much traffic. She doesn't need to know who's running for office

because she always votes a straight party ticket. She won't go to new movies because she won't stand in line for popular shows. She doesn't like to shop, so she makes a list and does all her Christmas buying in a single evening.

Deena is a very content, very controlling woman. But old? No. She's 45.

Besides, when did enthusiasm for hip-hop language emerge as the litmus test that separates old and young thinking?

With age comes entitlement to do some things your own way. You do not have to associate with bores unless you really want to. You do not have to kowtow to phony social doyens unless you really choose to. You do not have to bungee jump off the Golden Gate Bridge just to prove you've got a zest for life.

There's a vast difference between being rigid and being mature. Deena could find that out if she'd just buy some gloves and pick up a newspaper.

But there's no hope for *Reader's Digest.*

IMAGES AND STEREOTYPES OF GROWING OLDER

We were strolling the beach in Maui when Travis lagged behind to pick up a dead crab. "Come along, my little buckaroo," I said.

"I not a buckroo!" my grandson shouted. "I a boy!" Being a "boy" is important to Travis because two months ago another guy, Ian, joined his family. Ian, says Travis, 3, is a "baby."

Images and stereotypes.

"I prefer to call the years after 65 the time of longevity, not aging," said Jeanette C. Takamura, assistant secretary for aging in the Clinton administration. She was speaking at the American Society on Aging meeting in San Francisco, where I went after a family visit. Boomers don't want the label of their parents' generation. They will not "age." They will "live long." "Aging brings up negative images and stereotypes. Longevity is more appealing to younger people," she said.

A rose by any other name?

From San Francisco I went to Cleveland for my Uncle Mike's funeral. "This is my niece," said my Aunt Catherine, introducing me to her pinochle club. "She writes about senior citizens."

The gray heads nodded and welcomed me with smiles. I wanted to scream "I am not a senior citizen! I am a late-middle-ager." Do I protest too much?

Kari Berit Gustafson thinks I do. "I don't agree with the programs that change words, or people who say they are going to stay young forever," she said last week. Gustafson, 34, is activity director at Marriott Brighton Gardens, an assisted-living facility in Denver, and heads a consulting company, Age in Motion. At the American Society on Aging meeting, she drew a crowd to her workshop, "Enticing Boomers to Face Their Aging Selves." Gustafson encouraged her audience to visualize what they will look like in 20 years.

"I can't believe it, but I look like my mother," one boomer shouted.

Gustafson challenged the group: Who are your role models? How has your view of aging been formed? She maintained that boomers should quit looking at aging as something to avoid. Instead, they should think about what they will look like, who they will be around, what they will be doing, what they are going to be. "If you don't like the person you expect to be, make changes now," she said.

Her theory: boomers don't talk enough about aging because they don't see enough of it. Too many elders are tucked away in assisted-living facilities, creating generational separateness.

I closed that generational gap with my trip to Cleveland, where I saw almost all my aunts and uncles, all in their 80s. They all live alone and keep their own houses. They drive—even Aunt Irene, who admits she has "a little macular degeneration."

Are they aging or just living longer? Don't pester Aunt Virginia with such a nonsense question. When she finishes painting the wood-work in her house she has the garden to ready and the acre of lawn to mow.

Whatever they're doing, I expect I'm already among them, because Aunt Julienne exclaimed, "Look at her! She looks just like her mother!"

Images and stereotypes.

KEEPING FIT IN OLD AGE IS OUR RESPONSIBILITY

Monday, December 28, 1998

Whether or not we age well depends, for most of us, on how we live from day to day.

Only about 30 percent of the characteristics of aging are genetically based, says Dr. John W. Rowe, director of the MacArthur Foundation Consortium on Successful Aging. His research concludes that if you end up sick and demented, dragging your backside around town and popping blue pills to have a sex life, you can't blame your mom and dad.

"People are largely responsible for their own old age," Rowe says.

By old age, he means 70s and 80s.

Which is why I am leaning against a treadmill in the Laguna Hills Leisure World Fitness Center talking to Gene Usow as he strides 1 1/2 miles at a rate of 3.2 mph.

Usow, a retired medical doctor, had heart surgery at 60. "I weighed more than 200 pounds. I never exercised," he says. "I just told other people to do it." Fifteen years ago, he retired and left his Milwaukee, Wisconsin, practice to move to Southern California.

And he became a convert.

At least four times a week, he works out 20 minutes on the stationary bicycle, 30 minutes on the treadmill and finishes the workout lifting weights. He weighs 167 pounds, and when he goes back to Wisconsin to visit, they don't believe he's 83.

"Not only am I 83," he says, "I'm able to do this exercising!" Usow is my kind of athlete: he came to the game late. And he admits to occasional backsliding.

Who among us can claim that we never eat chocolate-chip cookies?

Okay, some of you can, but in my heart, I know you're not really having fun.

Yet, the new year nears. Once again, I vow to rise early, exercise often, eat no fat or sugar.

To inspire myself, I went looking for mentors. But who wants a mentor like my work colleague who exercises for two hours every day and keeps his diet in "The Zone"?

Give me a guy like Usow who learned his lesson the hard way and plods sensibly toward a moderate, active lifestyle.

After all, common sense says most of us don't like to exercise or we would do that instead of lounging, loitering and lingering "at ease." So hurrah for women like Jay Marks, who admits she is less than thrilled about hitting that Leisure World treadmill! But she does it faithfully four times a week, setting the machine on a computer program that raises and lowers the walking platform to simulate climbing hills.

"You have to start easy," says Marks, who began exercising eight years ago. "Then after you do it for a while, you like yourself better.

"I'm doing the right thing, I think." Marks has survived bypass surgery and still suffers an occasional angina attack. She's 80.

Cree Groen is the new kid on the Leisure World fitness circuit.

She's 68 and moved into the retirement community after a depressing divorce.

"I know this is helping me," she says. "I feel less depressed, have more energy." Then Groen says she has nothing to complain about. "You should see the people who come in here in walkers and wheelchairs and do better than I can!"

The moral of this tale is self-evident: if you don't use it, you lose it.

Seniors Today Get Younger As They Age

Monday, April 26, 1999

A decade ago, shortly after I started writing about people 50 or older, a colleague stopped me in the newsroom. "What did you do to get demoted?" he asked. "How awful you have to write about senior citizens."

A few days ago, that same colleague celebrated his 50th birthday. "Welcome to seniorhood," I messaged him.

"I'm not a senior," he flashed back. "I'm middle-aged."

Hello? What does that make me at 62? Chopped liver?

"No," he said. "You're late-middle-aged."

And when I'm 72?

"Oh, you'll never be anything but late-middle-aged," he said, mouthing the wisdom of the wise man who covers his bases.

Behind the banter, under the fear, lurks a reality, however. We are a cohort (as the sociologists call us) without a label.

People are getting "younger" as they age in this respect: yesterday's chronological senior citizen of 65 went to the senior center. Today's senior, 65, is more likely to be trekking in the Himalayas on an ElderHostel trip to Nepal.

Chalk it up to healthy living coupled with medications that let us conquer or soften the impact of arthritis pain, osteoporosis, erectile dysfunction, cancer, heart disease and other ailments.

Our—dare I call it late-midlife?—exuberance leaves many asking questions and only a few providing answers.

For example, last week I got a telephone call from a consultant doing a survey for AARP. The purpose of the selective poll was to find out what perceptions people have of the nation's largest senior organization. AARP is enrolling 25 percent of the boomers who turn 50 and become eligible. But the Washington, D.C.–based advocacy association is concerned those "new seniors" won't want to hang around with the "older" senior citizens of the past.

To combat its image, AARP has a jazzy Web site (www.aarp.org) and different versions of its magazine, *Modern Maturity*—one for retirees and one for still-working early agers. Only time will tell if these encourage boomers to join the club founded by their parents.

Boomers view aging differently. One proof is a new nationwide survey that says getting older no longer means having to say goodbye to good sex.

About 70 percent of those 50 and older responding to the survey by the Association of Reproductive Health Professionals said they are sexually active and satisfied with their sex lives.

It's the first such survey of this age group since Masters and Johnson wrote their report postulating that sex lives basically end at 50.

The results are good news, says Dr. Louise Tyrell, medical director for the sponsoring association. She credits healthy lifestyles with promoting a longer sex life. A happy sex life benefits both men and women.

Older women, Tyrell points out, become more desirable. "Mature men will not look for . . . trophy women . . . if mature women have an interest in life," she says. "That's part of what has changed. Older women are becoming better partners."

Tyrell should know. She's 78. She has a male friend, also 78. They met skiing. "It was wonderful because we both were delighted to find someone our own age who skied," she says.

And what age are they? They sound like late-midlifers to me.

Keep On Growing If You Want to
Slow the Demise of Midlife

Monday, July 26, 1999

Tick. Tick. Tick. My biological clock is ticking and so is yours. No, not the reproductive one. That clock already tolled for me, if not for you. But what about the clock that tells our heads what time it is in our life? Demographers say my midlife clock is running down. They define midlife as the chronological years 35–50.

Let me say they *used to* define it by those years. With a boomer turning 50 every 7 1/2 seconds, I expect the midlife to stretch on and on and on in the future. After all, what comes after midlife? Let me whisper the words: senior, senior citizen, elderly, geezer.

Tick. Tick. Tick. Are we only as old as we feel? Try this definition: We are only as old as we think.

Mentally, midlife lasts as long as you keep growing, says Kathleen A. Brehony, a Virginia clinical psychologist and specialist in midlife issues. "People can grow until their last breath." All that's required is being open to change and new experiences, she says. There is more to life than sitting in front of the TV watching *Wheel of Fortune* every night.

How long we will reside in "midlife" is determined by the way we cope with life experiences. "We can't control all the events in our life," Brehony, the author of *Awakening at Midlife* (Riverhead Books, 1997), says. "We can choose how we will respond to those events." Events trigger the onset of midlife. "At some point, we react to the realization of our own mortality. We are hit with the reality that we are going to die, and that should change everything for us."

She likes to quote Dr. Bernie Seigel, author of several books on getting on with life after illness. "He said, 'People who live best are people who know they are dying.' And we are all dying."

Facing a death or a life-threatening illness triggers change for many people and a retreat into addiction for others, she says. Those addictions can be television, food, even religious dogma. Addictions cocoon us from the pain of change. "By midlife, we have left so much of ourselves as a sacrifice on the altar of conformity that most of us are encased in a deep coating of defensiveness and grief," Brehony says. "Neither old nor young, we have no control over our ultimate destiny and yet we have the power to transform within it."

In simple terms, we grow old the way we live—with gusto or with slowed gait. You can teach an old dog new tricks if the dog wants to learn. You can't force people to keep on growing, learning and enjoying life.

Meanwhile: Tick. Tick. Tick.

And you know the rest of the stuff about *For Whom the Bell Tolls*.

AGING NATURALLY

Character Reaches Its Finest Expression When We Accept the Years

Thursday, September 9, 1999

Age is starting to hang out in public on the East Coast as mover-shaker boomers nudge the 50-years notch. For instance, fashion designer Eileen Fisher, 49, wears her age Dutch-bobbed in a full-page *New York Times* magazine ad. Indeed, her gray hairdo is the only ornamentation for her black outfit and black-rimmed eyeglasses.

Well, isn't that just like those New Yorkers to celebrate the patina of years? But get real! We live in Southern California, capital of an entertainment industry that worships eternal youth. Age—old age—has no value here. And deep inside, everyone else wishes they were dewy-fresh kids, just like us, right?

Maybe.

Most of us count ourselves among the millions who rely on hair rinses and dyes, facelifts, pills and potions to stave off the obvious results of an extended life span. A few—a depressing few, according to author James Hillman—recognize that aging has a purpose and a value. "Aging can free you from conventional constriction and transform you into a force of nature, releasing your deepest beliefs, your passionate intensity," he says in *The Force of Character: And the Lasting Life* (Random House, 1999). Age confirms and fulfills character.

Hillman's ideas have changed the way we look at ourselves before. He's the author of *The Soul's Code*, which proposes that each of us is born with an innate character that calls us to pursue our lives a certain way. Now he extends that theory by examining aging. "Why do we live so long if there isn't some kind of value in it?" he said in an interview. "If it takes a long time to grow up and out into the world, maybe it takes even longer to grow inward and downward in age." Hillman says there is no recipe for how you should age, but he does believe you should just do it, without resorting to cosmetic surgery or excessive fitness regimes to artificially maintain youth.

"You should be you. You don't need self-help books to be yourself." In being yourself, Hillman maintains, you become more in character for yourself.

And so we looked in Orange County for some people willing to expose their character through natural aging. And we asked the questions "Why?" and "Does this make you feel better about yourself?" What Price Youth?

Women who felt empowered through the women's movement surely reject false symbols of hair dye, eyelifts and cellulite treatments, don't they? Wrong. Aging naturally is not synonymous with the women's movement. Even Gloria Steinem had her eyes "done." Barbara McDowell, 53, director of the Women's Center at California State University, Fullerton, has dyed her hair since high school, but she wears no makeup and runs 50–60 miles a week to keep fit. McDowell considers herself aging naturally, but that does not mean sitting back, crossing her ankles and letting the years take their toll without a fight.

Women's attitudes toward aging remain ambivalent, in her opinion, a conclusion expressed by many we interviewed. "I am for holding onto youth at any cost, as long as possible," she says. "The question is, what is an individual's limit?" She hears women talk about rejecting the trappings of youth, "but I'm wondering if women don't talk a better story than their values. We talk about aging naturally, but if we have a long enough discussion about this, it becomes defensive. We resent society's messages, but we feel we fail if we don't live up to society's images.

"It's a paradox."

No Way to Judge

Women focused on business certainly don't muddle their heads with hair dye, do they? Puhleeze!

Of course, Lynne Lawrence, president of U.S. Net, a national computer-service company based in Santa Ana, stopped dying her hair after chemotherapy for breast cancer. "It looks silly to have dark hair and an aging face, I think," says Lawrence, 55. "Besides, in my business, I'm a matriarch and can afford to let the gray show." But if she won the lottery? "I'd have my eyes done instantly," she says and laughs. And if she was looking for work, "I'd make myself look as young as possible."

Judy Rosener would like to think women don't have to bow to false idols of youth. Now 69, she won a national reputation with her article "Ways Women Lead," and she champions the special talents of women as a professor at the University of California, Irvine, Graduate School of Management. Rosener has let her hair gray, and she's never had cosmetic surgery. But she hasn't washed her own hair—unless on vacation—since she married 48 years ago.

"Hair and nails. Those two things are important to me," she says, "and lately I've been thinking about lightening my teeth." Good grooming and a bright smile do not define her; they are essentials for everyone, she says. Trashing Southern California's "absorption" with outer appearance, she insists the result is a society that pays attention to images, not words.

Maintaining a youthful appearance has never been Rosener's personal style. She earned her doctorate at 50 after raising her family. Her husband, she says, "loves me like I am." She speaks all over the world but has never held a job in corporate America. "I know, on one hand, that appearance shouldn't matter in the business world. On the other hand, it does because we have become such a visual society. I would not work for a company that I felt judged me based on what I look like rather than what I contribute.

"But that's me. I have pretty high self-esteem."

THE MALE MODEL

If we judged men and women equally, gray hair would signal the age of distinction and wisdom, right? In your dreams. Men increasingly are shrugging off signs of aging. Kevin Costner, for example, had his hair digitally enhanced in the film *Waterworld*, spending millions to thicken his locks, according to published reports.

Robert Frazier, 73, of Cypress, had his first facelift 15 years ago and is ready for round two. "It made me feel better about myself," Frazier said. "It was well worth the time and effort." Atop his lifted brow he plops a gray hairpiece. "If you can afford it, go for it," he trumpets.

Johnny Vigil, hairstylist at Belcourte Salon in Newport Beach, tells men they shouldn't color their hair, that gray makes them more distinguished.

"But now for women, there's more prejudice," he says. "I tell women, 'I hate to tell you this, but in the business world, if you want to look put together and polished, hair color is the start of it.'" The entertainment industry sets the standards, he says.

RESPECT FOR AGE

Okay, this obsession with youth is an American phenomenon—something that goes along with our history as a young country built by brash youth.

"Bull," says author Hillman. "We are the oldest constitutional democracy. We are a graying nation walking around with a youthful fantasy."

Other cultures usually put aging in a place of respect. "Asian customers particularly respect me," says Minh Le Vu, 49, branch manager of the Wells Fargo Bank in Westminster. "They see me as the mature person, and they trust me more." Yet Vu, with a client base primarily from Asian cultures, colors her hair. "Actually, I dye my hair not because I look old but because it looks weird. It's white on the top," she says. Vu is not denying her age because it works to her advantage in a culture that respects wisdom conferred by years of life.

"I think more of us are realizing that we have too much to do to try to deny age," says Mary Leigh Blek, 53, of Mission Viejo. Blek and her husband, Charles, founded Citizens for the Prevention of Gun Violence after their son, Matthew, 21, was shot to death in a New York robbery by teenagers toting cheap handguns. Among their victories: a recent California law requiring safety tests for handguns, which effectively bans the manufacture and sale of Saturday-night specials. Blek also is founder and regional director of the Bell Campaign, a new national effort to tighten firearm regulations and registration rules. She hopes to have chapters in 50 states pressuring federal and state legislators for reasonable gun control.

Blek believes many in her generation are changing their attitude, finding value in being natural and healthy, valuing exercise and proper food. She decided to let her hair go gray this summer. "But I reserve the right to be a woman and change my mind if I don't like it."

NO COOKIE CUTTER

Some people have always just been themselves, rejecting the fads and trends of teen years and refusing to bow to conventions. To them, age is a natural part of life.

Laguna Hills therapist Carol Hughes, 50, has always been this way: natural, in tune with the earth, reflecting her Cherokee roots. "Because I work with eating disorders, I know one of the key issues is body image. The media constantly feeds us with images of what we should look like. As a therapist, I see what that does to create serious problems for some people."

She wears only eyeliner. Her hair is straight and combed back. If she goes to a corporate meeting to make a presentation, "Sometimes I pull it into a bun. Either they like me the way I am or not. If I can't live that way, I have no integrity with my clients." Hughes believes people will value her for what she is inside rather than what she looks like outside. But she is a realist. Very few women share her attitude, she says. "I think it's a personal decision for each one of us. Who am I to judge others?"

To change our fixation on youth, "we would have to have a very enlightened society, a lot of growth in the American culture. . . . Our attitude toward aging is what we've been sold."

Hughes looks forward to future aging, she says. "One day I will be even older. I will have more of a voice and probably be out there talking about what we are talking about today—honest, natural aging. My message will be: 'Stop looking at the outside. Start looking on the inside.'"

As author Hillman puts it, "It takes courage to go against the stream, but it's more dangerous to deny your character than to deny your aging process."

Steps That Lead to Being More Active

Monday, November 1, 1999

Jessie Jones boogied down the runway, calling out to seniors in the Crystal Cathedral sanctuary to "get up, get on your feet, shake it out." Jones, 50, is an apostle of fitness. She's also director of the Center for Successful Aging at California State University, Fullerton.

"Getting old is not always a choice," she told the elder crowd. "But the way we live our older years is our choice. Everything we do or don't do, everything we eat or don't eat, everything we think or don't think, can impact our successful aging." Her audience—seniors from Orange County attending the first countywide Senior Summit on Aging sponsored by Supervisor Charles Smith—waved their arms at her commands, swayed their hips, lifted their knees.

They already had heard the Reverend Robert Schuller tell them that positive aging is their responsibility. Living longer is nice, Schuller said, but "the price of nice" is the occasional aches and pains and the effort it takes to keep older bodies in shape.

Why bother? Because from age 30 to 80, most people lose 40 percent of their physical capabilities, Jones said. As a result, many become disabled and are forced into nursing homes and assisted living.

Now, that's scary. But being physically active adds 10 to 15 active years to a senior's age, Jones says. In other words, use it—or lose it and suffer the consequences. "We cannot go back and make a new start, but we can start now to make a new ending."

Jones has developed steps to maximizing vitality in later years. They result from research she did with Robert Rikli, also a professor of exercise science at CSUF. More than 7,000 people ages 60 to 94 participated in their two-year nationwide study on fitness and mobility in older adults. That database lets Jones speak with authority.

THE STEPS

1. *Evaluate your current fitness and activity level.* Do you sit all or most of the time? How many days a week do you participate in moderate exercise? For how long?

2. *Set your physical-activity goals.* How active and independent do you want to be? What short-term goals (such as increased strength or balance) do you need to achieve your long-term goals?

3. *Develop a plan of action.* What type of physical activity will help you achieve these goals? What are you willing to do, starting tomorrow?

4. *Develop motivational strategies.* Expect setbacks. Find someone to help motivate you.

5. *Reevaluate.* After a few weeks, review your physical status and long-term goals.

6. *Readjust your activity plan.*

Successful senior years ultimately depend on the ability to remain active—which, in turn, allows you to stay involved with life. There are three keys to successful aging, said Dr. Thomas Cesario, director of the University of California, Irvine, School of Medicine. "See your doctor regularly. Never slow down. And always have something to look forward to." Everybody, get up and move it!

AVOID FOLLY OF TRYING TO DENY AGING

Monday, November 29, 1999

We are now deeply infected with the virus Seniors-Not-Us—and it threatens to turn us into a nation of blithering gray-haired adolescents.

We reach a calendar milestone—age 50 or 60 or even 70—and we don't know who we are and refuse to be what we've become. For inexplicable reasons, we've decided everything worthwhile in life happens before 50; everything that happens after 50 has to mimic youth to be worthwhile or successful. Consider these examples:

The *Today* show has a running feature called "Forever Young," a title that is, itself, insulting. Last week, the focus was the importance of a sense of humor. The subject was an older man who tells his jokes at a Chicago senior center. Who can argue with the essential benefits of good humor? But when did having a sense of humor get attached to youth?

Television and print ads featuring so-called seniors usually show them involved in something athletic. My favorite is an ad for a bladder-protection product that lets the woman continue mountain biking, a sport she presumably could not enjoy if she had to stop for occasional relief. But when did "success" get itself equated with running a marathon? I know a lot of "successful" seniors who raise grandchildren, volunteer, even keep working.

We haven't even decided on what to call ourselves, wandering between the cutesy (prime timers) to the neutral (older persons) to the downright depressing (elderly). Ask someone in their late 50s or early 60s if they are going to use a senior center when they retire. "I'm not a senior citizen" is the usual response. But what are you then? A senior? A geezer (aw, come on!)? An elder?

Who is causing this age denial? Most of us honestly can point a finger at ourselves. We never want to grow old. Why should we? The images of "being old" are images of disease, despair and disappointment.

The only salvation, says Richard Browdie, Pennsylvania's secretary of aging, is knowing that all of us eventually will be neck deep in the waters of aging and discover that the later years aren't so bad. "No matter how we reinvent aging or the language we use, there will still be old people," he says in *Aging Today,* the newspaper of the American Society on Aging. "The rhetoric of 'ageless aging' is one of the most striking and rather sad forms of ageism that I've seen. It is ageist in that it denies aging itself, and it is sad in that it denies each of our personal realities."

In other words, there is no single way to age, folks. You do it however you feel like, hopefully with wisdom and grace. Once we all understand that, maybe we can get on with making these years meaningful.

Listen to Joanne Handy, president of the Visiting Nurses Association of Boston, also in *Aging Today:* "With the extension of life expectancy, aging takes on a whole new meaning. Sixty or 65 can be seen as the start of the third or fourth age in terms of work, creativity and personal development. It also means the world has greater access to the wisdom of experience."

Please, let's all be grownups about growing up. If you never skydived, you don't have to start in your 70s to earn the title of "successful aging."

Part 5—Women—The 21st Century Gender

"Retirement" isn't a guy thing anymore.
Significant numbers of women have earned their own
pensions *and* the right to plan their own leisure time.
Some are taking a tip from Mrs. Casey Stengell, who greeted the
Yankee manager's retirement with the observation that she had
married him for better or for worse but not for lunch.

WOMEN NEEDN'T GET WORKED UP OVER RETIREMENT

Monday, October 14, 1996

When my great and good friend Carolyn wailed to me that her marriage was as rocky as the coast of Maine, I referred her to Peter Drucker. Drucker, the guru of modern business management, once told a female colleague weighing retirement against a new position that she had a choice: you can speed up or slow down.

Nothing better defines the options for 50-plus married women. Particularly those whose husbands are talking about retiring, as is Carolyn's husband, Tom. "He started talking about it, and suddenly I felt like I was inside a room with no windows and no doors," she says. "I'm not ready to quit and play golf. I'm still on the top of my game!"

Carolyn admits that the thought of spending day after day after day with a husband she now sees only occasionally has her in a panic. "I've worked hard, too. I'm entitled to retire on my own terms."

Ah, is this yet another hurdle for the pioneer liberated woman? You betcha.

Experts are realizing that there is no retirement literature dealing with the emotional or social issues of retirement for 50-plus women, says Rosalie Gilford, professor of sociology at California State University, Fullerton. "Retirement traditionally has been on a timetable set by men. Yet there are different ways men and women approach retirement."

Men nearing retirement often have worked more years than women and feel burned out, she says. These men figure if they have money and health, why not quit? Women, on the other hand, have concerns about loss of freedom and privacy. "The big question will be what clock are we timing our lives to. Our own or our husband's?" Gilford says.

Here's where independence makes its play. More women are financially, emotionally, socially—and informationally—independent,

Gilford says. They know the answers to everything from combining casseroles to investing in stocks.

"Men need to realize there is such a thing as postmenopausal zest," says Wendy Reid Crisp, spokeswoman for the National Association of Female Executives. "Many women have just made varsity in their 50s, and now the guy wants them to turn in their letter! Would he?"

Crisp, author of *100 Things I'm Not Going to Do Now That I'm Over 50* (Perigee, 1994), says women need to be understanding about men's needs but that they don't have to give up unless they want to. "You have the right to pursue what he feels he has earned," she says. She argues that marriage will be redefined in the next decade by these 50-ish women. "It's a critical point in a relationship," she says. "If you never really liked each other or have nothing to share, you have to basically reach agreements that a significant portion of your time will be spent doing separate things."

Separate things?

"Yes," says Crisp, who advises, don't get divorced. Move into another room down the hall.

WOMEN FINALLY ARE GETTING THE TREATMENT THEY DESERVE

Monday, November 18, 1996

When I remember Momma, I see her striding across the vast marble lobby of Grand Central Station, weaving and bobbing between commuters to catch her train to Westchester County. She has a novel in the tote bag slung over her shoulder, cigarettes in her purse and determination in her heart. Momma was no pushover. She knew how to get a good table in a restaurant, fix basic plumbing problems and make a meatloaf that qualified as classic cuisine.

Momma was an accomplished woman of her generation.

And just like other women of her generation, she rarely questioned advice from her doctors. In fact, doctors could transform this executive assistant from a take-charge woman to a totally dependent female. Momma believed the doctors who said her increasing fatigue was all in her head and probably related to "womanly problems." She accepted five years of abdominal pain as "typical female stuff."

Momma died of cancer at 72. The cancer had nothing to do with her female organs. Were her symptoms ignored? I'm not sure, but I do know that Dr. Bernadine Healy is on the mark when she says, "There's more to us than those female organs and ailments."

In 1991, Healy launched the Woman's Health Initiative, a $625 million, 15-year effort to study the causes, prevention and cures of diseases that affect women. The initiative—Healy dubs it the "mother of all clinical studies"—is trying to make up for the decades of research that focused exclusively or primarily on men.

Today's midlife women, who demanded equal treatment as humans, deserve credit for creating a pro-woman political climate, which in turn fostered support for the study, she says. "Until this generation, women were never really taken seriously. Not in terms of their brains, their hearts or their bones," says Healy, dean of the College of Medicine at Ohio State University.

The national study is separated into three clinical trials involving 64,500 women. Researchers are trying to determine the effects of a low-fat diet, hormone-replacement therapy (estrogen) after menopause and supplements of calcium and vitamin D. They'll also observe 100,000 women in an attempt to uncover clues that can predict disease in women. Thousands of women have signed up at 40 research centers nationally, but there is still a need for 100,000 women 50–79 to become part of the historic study. For information, call (800) 54-WOMAN.

"Women are making this happen because we finally think we're worth it," Healy says. An extra benefit for volunteers: complete health monitoring at government expense.

"There are lots of unanswered questions about women's health," says Dr. Loretta Finnegan, director of the initiative. Admittedly, the questions might not get answered in our lifetimes. But midlife women participating in the study will help their daughters and granddaughters receive good medical care.

Of course, those women probably still will grapple with affirmative action, glass ceilings and that ever-present Barbie doll attitude. We can't solve everything.

RETIREMENT MIGHT NOT MEET EXPECTATIONS

Monday, April 20, 1998

We were driving up Oregon's Route 97 two years ago when Bob first mentioned the "R" word. "I'd like to retire at 62," he said. "I thought we could open a bed and breakfast."

Tipped slightly off psychological guard, I shrieked, "Did you say 'we'? I didn't work for 30 years to spend my old age cleaning bathrooms."

That interchange was my first realization that retirement isn't all it's cracked up to be. Many are called, but few are chosen to live a life of leisure that matches their expectations. I know. I've spent the past two years doing research. And I've concluded that deep down inside, most retirees are honestly bored.

"How was retirement?" I shouted at hearing-impaired Uncle Mike, 90, as he lay on a Tampa hospital bed.

"Boring," he shouted back. Mike, who spent 28 years not working, said, "After the first 10 years of playing golf, it was all downhill."

Three weeks ago, I was sitting on the lanai of my oceanfront vacation condo in Maui when the guy renting the condo next door stopped by. He's a retired pharmacist from Minnesota who lives in Tucson. He collects desert rocks and makes them into jewelry that he just happened to bring to Maui in case anyone wanted to buy an Arizona trinket in Hawaii. He had lots and lots of jewelry to sell and was on the verge of being a pest until his wife came by to call him to supper. Don't tell me that guy isn't bored.

Boredom knows no state boundaries. "I am not particularly enthused about retirement," said Leroy Clemens, my editor-mentor in Illinois, when I called him about the topic. "I've enjoyed it, but I'd rather be working." Clem gave up editing at 69 and stopped writing his column four years ago at 72. Now he says, "If I had it to do over again, I'd look for a position to at least stay active. I miss not being involved with the community."

Clem would approve of the way Barbara Resnick is marching toward leisure years. Resnick, of Orange, won't sit despite inching closer to the so-called retirement time. "I'm still doing all the things I did earlier, and I've just added some new ones," says Resnick, a real-estate developer who became a gerontologist when interest rates went to 19 percent. Now she's formed a nonprofit housing corporation that will build senior apartments on Catalina Island. ("It just breaks my heart to have to go over there," she jokes.) She also operates a school for administrators of assisted-living facilities.

Energy? "Sometimes I wonder how I have so much energy," Resnick says. "I go from the crack of dawn until late in the day. Maybe expending energy creates more energy."

All of this research takes on added significance in 10 days. That's when Bob is retiring—at least from his current job. Six weeks ago, his employer offered him one of those golden handshakes only a fool would turn down. After almost 30 years with one company, he heads into the future with a mixed bag of ambitions and expectations.

Some days he's ridiculous: "You'll be able to let the cleaning service go because I'll be home to take care of the house." Then he's optimistic: "Now I can do things I haven't been able to do for years." Occasionally, he's realistic: "I think I'll find new opportunities."

Many are called. Few are chosen to be among the wise people who know that we never outgrow our need to feel useful and meaningful.

WOMEN IN THE "INVISIBLE ZONE"
WON'T ACCEPT SOCIETY'S DECREE

Monday, June 28, 1999

Last week's column about pheromones—those odorless scents that keep men sniffing around younger women—inspired spirited e-mail from several over-50 women who are, frankly, fed up with worrying about what men think of their looks, their attitude or their sniff-appeal.

"And that goes for younger men, too," Tracy said. "They better wise up and start recognizing us. We've got our own Platinum Visa cards. We're not going to be invisible like our moms were." She's talking about the generation of women now entering the traditional "invisible zone." In other words, women over 60.

Tracy's still steaming about the experience of an older friend, 75, and her daughter, mid-40s. Together, they hired a lawyer to deal with some family matters. Both women are professionals. Both are experienced at handling complicated financial affairs. But in repeated meetings, the young attorney directed his questions and comments to the daughter, ignoring the older woman.

"It's ageism!" Tracy said.

Darn right. Ageism that is not confined to young men. Young women are just as guilty.

In stores, women clerks gravitate away from gray-hairs. In fast-food restaurants, they look beyond the senior to serve the teen. In medical offices, they call the gray-hairs by their first names, often patronizingly.

I know what I'm talking about.

Five years ago, doctors discovered I had a small breast cancer.

I had radiation treatments. I cannot take estrogen.

In five years, my face and body aged aggressively. My figure changed. Everything drooped.

I became "invisible" to the rest of the world.

Six months ago, I had a facelift. What a difference a nip here and a tuck there makes!

Men nodded, smiled at me at a recent cocktail party before a social gala. "So wonderful to see you again!" one gentleman exclaimed, pressing me to his ample chest. Imagine his confusion when he read my name tag and realized we had never met.

He was embracing youth without concern about his own balding, aging appearance.

Sight and smell are only two of the five senses, yet obviously they control the aging of women just as they controlled their youth.

Not!

Those of us edging into the "gray zone" today are cut from a different cloth than our mothers.

We are the pioneers who insisted the world recognize us as human beings. Don't even think we will become invisible.

"When will men care about us for our brains?" Louise wailed to me in an e-mail. "Looks aren't everything."

Ah, just remember, Louise, as Gloria Steinem once said, "Any woman who chooses to behave like a full human being should be warned that the armies of the status quo will treat her as something of a dirty joke; that's their natural and first weapon."

The question, of course, is who's going to get the last laugh?

Daughters Have Full Range of Options for Life Open to Them

Monday, August 9, 1999

We were three sages—women of zest ranging from 51 to 67—sitting on the grass in the park, drinking wine and watching the sun slip into the Pacific. I am a journalist. Rosalie is a therapist. Jesse is a professor who teaches exercise science. We talked about our present: aloneness. Marriage. Divorce. Toe fungus. Fibromyalgia. Yoga. Why red wine is good for you.

Once Cindy arrived, we were plunged into our pasts: limitations. Mistakes. Wasted time. Disappointments. Success at great effort. Accomplishment. Empowerment.

Cindy is 38. She couldn't understand why we shared a peculiar pride of achievement in doing what, to her, comes naturally. That is, fulfilling her potential as a person. "Why didn't you just do it?" she asked. "I mean, if that's what you wanted to do, what happened?"

We sages looked at one another in the fading daylight. So much has happened to our worlds in the past 40 years. How to put it all in perspective? "We couldn't do those things," Rosalie said. "We were girls. We didn't have many choices. When we were young women, we could be nurses or teachers, nuns or secretaries. That was about all the career opportunities we had." Rosalie joined the Civil Air Patrol in hopes of becoming a stewardess, a glamour job in the 1950s. She became a suburban mother and didn't graduate from college until she was in her 40s.

Jesse remembered when girls were not encouraged to enjoy sports. As a young teacher, she fought for equality in girls' sports programs—won the grant but lost her job in the process. "Girls were not supposed to be competitive," she said.

No, I said, we were supposed to be mothers. I had three children in four years. "The most creative mental stimulation for me was poring over cookbooks, figuring out ways to stretch the food budget and still cook exotic meals," I said.

Cindy—and all our daughters—have a full range of life options today, including motherhood. Not that I would change my choice to have children. "What do you consider your primary identity at this time?" I read in a survey. "Are you a mother or a career woman?"

Well, that's easy. I am a mother. Always. But I am also a career woman. The achievement is that the two roles are compatible today. Not every door is open to young women, however. Beating the last ones down will be the task of the emerging generation of women. I'm enthusiastic that they have some goals left to achieve.

Knowing we have succeeded in becoming the people we wanted to be gives all us sages a quiet sense of satisfaction. Our daughters need to earn the same life stage. We went beyond the status quo of our mothers and our grandmothers. Now our daughters must surpass us. At least, for starters, they are accepted for themselves.

At a luncheon last week, Ruth, in her 50s, put it all in perspective. "Today, I am introduced as Ruth," she said. "I used to be introduced as Jimmy's wife or Steven's mother. Today, I am myself—and that is a wonderful feeling."

Monday, March 6, 2000

Is your life different from your mother's? How?

Ask those questions of women 50 to 70—as I do on my Web site www.womansage.com—and tally an overwhelming chorus shouting, "You bet! I have an education!"

A college degree. A high-school degree. An education is the common separation between women born before and after the depression. An education opens the door to meaningful jobs and careers. Sure, you can argue that women still make less than men at similar jobs. The important consideration right now is that women have made and are making money. A large proportion of women reaching 65 have pensions in their own names. They increasingly are covered by retirement plans and Social Security. They have 401(k)s.

They have a sense of independence that money can buy, an important point to ponder in March, officially National Women's History Month. That independence sets us apart as mentors for our daughters and granddaughters. We are pioneers. We blazed the road map for their future sense of self-achievement.

Or did we?

Before we start a hearty round of self-congratulation, maybe we should check out the territory. Look at the media—television and the movies, says Kimberly Salter, a NOW activist and cochairman of a recent Orange County conference for girls 12–16. The overwhelming message is that girls shouldn't compete with boys, says Salter. But, I argue, surely times have changed. Although my mother told me, "Never let a boy know how smart you are," I didn't say that to my daughter.

Times have not changed, Salter says. "The education system does not tell girls to take math and science classes. Those are for boys." If girls listen, she argues, they will lose out on job opportunities. Hence the efforts by the American Association of University Women, the

League of Women Voters and NOW to emphasize a different message. The effort worked for some girls at the conference:

- "I found out I can get a good job if I want to," Indira Mazon, 13, a Santa Ana high-school student, told me.
- "I learned I can be a doctor if I really want to," said Sasha Mercer, 13, of Costa Mesa.

Lofty ambitions—and why not go for the gusto? Adult women should be encouraged to reach for achievement, too. "Well, that doesn't always work out," Joanne VanDerHyden told me. She's 52, a community college student in a certification program for a health-field job. Many older women are among the students in her biology class, she told me. The teacher has "flat out" told them they will fail because they are women, because they can't "get it" like the guys can.

Society better "get it"—fast. Women are in the work force to stay. Three out of every five women are working today. By 2005, the Bureau of Labor Statistics projects 72 million women will be in the labor force. That's 63 percent of the women 16 and older, an increase of 24 percent since 1992.

Women are in the work force longer than ever before. And they are likely to stay. AARP pollsters and others report baby boomers plan to work well into the so-called retirement years of 65-plus.

Many of us are doing "man's work," although getting a "man's job" isn't easy. Forty years ago, when I graduated from journalism school, I sat across a desk and heard a managing editor offer me a "man's job" covering city hall instead of society but at a "woman's salary." He said he would pay me $10 a week less "because some man will take you out to dinner."

Put that in perspective. First, that 10 bucks was a big chunk of dough when I was being offered only $55 a week. But how demeaning to be "auctioned off" as a weekly dinner date with some creepy guy. I had a choice: take a man's job and live on tomato soup or take a woman's job and shove my career into a box of tea-and-sympathy stories. I took the job, without the weekly date. My dad sent me $10 a week instead.

Within six weeks, the city editor wrangled me a raise and within a year, I had won some major awards for the newspaper doing "man's work." That definition of "man's work," by the way, required a certain amount of logic, determination and guts—qualities I have never considered gender-specific.

The women of my generation, I've decided, have been like salmon—swimming upstream all our lives. We've climbed that darn ladder, dodged the predators, reached the calm pool of achievement. And what do we get for it?

The challenge to make sure our trip hasn't been in vain.

Part 6—Ah, the People I've Known

I LIKE PEOPLE WITH GUTS. THE TYPE WHO MOUNTAIN BIKE
UP A HILL JUST BECAUSE IT'S THERE. THE ONES WHO LIVE
EVERY DAY THE BEST WAY THEY CAN—AND THEREBY INSPIRE OTHERS.
MEET A FEW OF THE PEOPLE WHO HAVE INSPIRED ME.

A Good Attitude Helps to Make a Good Sport

Gordon Kelly is one lanky, tall drink-of-water guy lucky enough to have lived with the wind on his back for 87 years. He has spent a lifetime going to baseball games—and getting paid for it. Nice work if you can get it, "and I've got it and I'm not quitting," he says. "About all that's wrong with me is I needed an artificial knee."

Gordon lives in Chico, where he scouts full time for the Cincinnati Reds. His territory ranges north into Oregon and east to Nevada. When he finds a hot prospect, he calls his boss, who flies out, eyeballs the kid and decides about negotiations. He works a 12-month "season." But this week he's taking time off, making his annual trip to Southern California to visit a son, Kevin, in Newport Beach and to go to the annual Alhambra High School Reunion. "It was my 64th reunion," he says. "My football coach was there, too." The coach is 91.

Gordon played football for the University of Southern California back in the days when players wore leather helmets and didn't get scholarships. He ushered at Tunnel 14 in the Coliseum during the 1932 Olympics. He went on to spend 26 years as a football and baseball scout for USC, then began scouting for major-league teams. Among those he lured to the Trojan banner: O. J. Simpson.

A guy can't spend all that time in dugouts and locker rooms without developing a philosophy on life. This is Gordon's: talent and desire are important, "but 50 percent of success depends on attitude." In his view, "if a boy listens to you, he's going to understand how to develop his talent." Sadly, over the years, Gordon has met and signed players who thought all they needed was talent. Most of them, he says, fail before they make the big time.

Jerks, he says, have flourished in every generation. "Kids are no different today. Not really. There have always been great ones and know-it-alls." The know-it-alls are the kids Gordon labels as talented but with "parent problems." In his book, parents have the attitude that "bends their twig" the wrong way.

Not only parents but also grandparents, says Jill, my morning walking partner who has two daughters in Travel Ball, a softball circuit for girls. The players in Travel Ball are a big cut above average. College scouts just like Gordon sit in the bleachers, eyeing the talent. Parents and grandparents, anxious for their girls to win college scholarships, are in the same bleachers, she says. "Some of them have turned their daughters into prima donnas, always praising them and arguing with coaches and other players. These kids expect to get a free ride to college. They think more about themselves than the score. There are more and more kids playing team sports, but that doesn't mean everyone understands what team playing is all about." A big dose of desire and a lot of listening to the coach often mean more than talent, Jill says.

Each generation has kids who don't respect authority, says Gordon, who has lived through four generations. I find that predictability comforting. We're not going to hell in a handbag right now. Gordon assures us we've been hellbent for decades and—despite those meddling adults and arrogant kids—we're still surviving. We can count on consistency. So I ask Gordon where he's going on his vacation.

"To Anaheim Stadium," he says. "Thought I'd catch an Angels game."

CREATURE COMFORTS UNNEEDED
BY SOME ADVENTURESOME SOULS

Monday, July 14, 1997

I've reached a point in life where I can go only so many days without a flush toilet and a hot shower. Like three days, at the most.

But hurrah for the undeterred adventurers among us: the late-lifers who rappel down mountains, kayak in the Bering Strait and bike around Europe. People such as Martha Marino, 69, who rents out her ocean-view home in Laguna Beach each summer to pay for her escapades. Marino has boxed up her bike for a three-month tour of Denmark, Scotland and England. This will be her eighth summer on the road, with clothes stored in saddlebags and a tent and sleeping bag strapped on the back.

"Life without adventures would be awful!" says this former teacher, who still substitutes during the school year. She's chanted that mantra since graduating from Berkeley in 1949. Her goal was to circle the globe, a trip that took 15 years because she paused to teach in different countries. "I have always wanted to learn about different cultures," she says. "Europe, Japan, India, Africa—studying them makes you feel that there are a lot of ways to live this life."

She was engaged to a Muslim in India in her 20s. "I loved the spiritual aspect of that country," she says. The relationship didn't work out. Instead, she married an Italian in Africa and settled in Laguna Beach to raise two sons. Marino spent 15 years teaching French, German and Spanish in Anaheim schools. Divorced and no longer responsible for her sons, who were in college, she joined the Peace Corps. The Corps sent her to Thailand and China, to small villages where she coped with unusual customs, unwelcome critters and understanding natives. She recounts her escapades in a self-published book, *Asian Adventure* ($14.95 through Marino Press, P.O. Box 4818, Laguna Beach, CA 92672).

Marino has no intention of letting age get in her way. But she admits to slowing a little. "I can't do as much as I used to," she says. "I've got to get the right amount of sleep. As we get older, we have to listen more to our bodies." She does her listening biking alone through "pretty places." She's already been through the Loire Valley, the Chianti area of Italy, the Danube Valley, the Cotswolds in England, parts of Ireland. She pedals about 25 miles a day, stopping to talk to people who interest her.

"I'm not afraid," she says. "I think sometimes I should be afraid, but I feel I'm in tune with what I want to do. I was born this way. I love adventure and taking risks." Marino says she'll do her traveling on about $40 a day. "I'm on a budget," she says. "All of life is a budget."

She proves that a rich attitude contributes more to successful aging than money in the bank. And as far as those flush toilets and showers are concerned, Marino acknowledges she doesn't always camp out. Some nights, she sleeps in hostels.

"I don't expect everyone wants to do what I do," she says. "But it works for me."

*Jennie Faires, Whose Birthday Is Today, Celebrates with Her Family
and Shares Her Secrets for Longevity*

Monday, August 18, 1997

She never drank, she never smoked, she walked every day and she baked the best coconut meringue pie in Santa Ana. Jennie Faires says those are some of the reasons she's 108 today. And then she adds, to live a long life, "you need to trust the Lord" and "take each day as it comes." Seems like pretty standard centenarian advice.

"Well, it works!" Faires said Sunday, winking behind thick lenses. As she gathered with family to officially celebrate her birthday at Town and Country Manor, where she has lived since 1975, Faires skipped over the past, turning 108 years into a sound bite. She was here, now, in the present, yearning to see the future.

"I spend my days sitting in a chair and rocking, thinking over my life and sometimes making up stories about the future," she says. "I won't be here but I like to think about what the great-grandkids will grow up and do." Finally she grabbed the hand of the person beside her and whispered the secret of longevity: "Live in the future, dear. That's what works."

In fact, it worked well enough for Faires to make her one of Orange County's oldest residents—perhaps even the oldest. Social Security records are sketchy, making such achievements difficult to verify, said Bob Hartnet of the Santa Ana Social Security office. "I do know that so many people are reaching 100 we can't count them fast enough," he joked. In the county, 170 people hit the century mark this year. By 2000, the Census Bureau expects to tally 75,000 nationally, compared with the paltry 14,500 counted in 1980.

Many are old; few, like Faires, are old in great style. Faires is one of the unique American women that British author Rudyard Kipling wrote about after a trip to Philadelphia the year she was born. "The girls of America are clever—yea it is said that they can think," he wrote.

Faires proved him right. She went to business college as a young woman. When her husband died in 1935 after 23 years of marriage, she went to work in a doctor's office. She married again and was widowed after eight years. With her parents, she homesteaded in Nebraska, traveled to Washington state on a train, rode a covered wagon to Oregon and returned to Nebraska before she was seven. Her father decided to take a job in a New Haven, Connecticut, wire factory, so the family set off again. It moved back west, this time to California, after she left school. She and her first husband moved to Santa Ana in 1919.

"Oh, I've seen plenty," she said. "Plenty of things change." Among the changes were tragedies that buffeted her life. "My mother never let anything stop her," says Dorothy Pack, 72, of Mission Viejo. Not even death.

"My daughter is adopted," Faires said. "My greatest sadness was when my little boy died when he was seven. Both my children died. But Dorothy came into our lives and she has given me a wonderful, wonderful family."

In return, Faires has done her part not to be a burden. She says she hasn't an ache or a pain. She wears two hearing aids and needs help moving around, but she tucked a green linen napkin into the neck of her blue print dress and dug into a plate full of party food: baked ham, macaroni salad, fruit, rolls and butter. A white cake with custard filling waited on the side table, surrounded by several boxes of chocolate candy.

Faires had a squeeze for great-grandson Travis Gutierrez, five months, and a hug for his brother, Tyler, nine. She took a minute to check with her sister, Gertrude Smith, 96, to see that her plate was full. "Jennie raised me," said Smith, who also lives at Town and Country Manor.

Nephews Henry Holland and Ted Humphrey, visiting from Maine, talked about the eastern branch that is planning to come for her 110th birthday. Her grandson Robert Pack of Cota de Caza reminded her they used to watch Lawrence Welk on television on Saturday nights. "I remember! I remember!" Faires said.

So many people are living so long, longevity by itself is not noteworthy. But only a few can remember running down the hills of Oregon beside a covered wagon and playing with American Indian children. Who's left who was born in a sod hut in Nebraska? And how many women cherish the right to vote today?

"I voted, oh yes, I voted," Faires says. "I voted for Harding. I voted every time I could vote until I gave it up before Clinton. You know, I've lived through amazing times. So many amazing things. I was amazed to talk on the telephone, amazed to ride in an auto, and it was wonderful to fly in an airplane."

On the table in front of her, an arrangement of lavender and pink flowers matched the colors of her wrist corsage. "Pink is my favorite color," Faires said. "You know, I have had an ordinary life. But I have had a good life."

It sounds like a cliché. But clichés exist because they are real.

LET CREDIT ROLL FOR ENTERTAINMENT FIGURES WHO CARE FOR THEIR ELDERS

Monday, October 13, 1997

Tom Selleck is a boomer role model. He's 52. He oozes star-quality sex appeal. He has his values straight: "Who you are is more important than what you are," he says. "Fame is a vapor; popularity an accident; money takes wings. All that endures is character."

And there's more. He loves his mother.

Selleck talked about family values to a room full of women who cast longing looks in his direction and flicked envious eyes over his mother, Martha Selleck, also in the audience.

Selleck should be every mother's son. He's tall, handsome, rich, glamorous and doesn't mind spending time with older women. His recent appearance at the Screen Smart Set Auxiliary luncheon and fashion show at the Regent Beverly Wilshire Hotel in Beverly Hills netted him the Heart of Hollywood Award. But more important was the spotlight focused on a little-lauded role of actors and actresses: volunteering, supporting charities and taking care of their own aging community.

This auxiliary, which runs a vintage and designer clothes shop featuring gently worn items, has raised more than $3 million for the Motion Picture & Television Fund. Among its programs are assisted-living centers, hospitals, health and medical centers and retirement care for those in the entertainment family.

Does it seem out of step to hear Hollywood types talking family values? Maybe we haven't been listening. "If your family loves you, that's the whole ball of wax," says June Haver, accepting the Mary Pickford Achievement Award. Haver gave up the screen for family. She was Mrs. Fred MacMurray for 37 years. Her charities include the Mary and Joseph League, ChildHelp USA and the Motion Picture Mothers.

The luncheon ended with a parade of klieg-light volunteers modeling donated clothes. There was Anne Jeffreys and Beverly Garland,

Constance Towers and Janet Leigh, Tippi Hedren and Betty White, Frances Bergen and Janice Williams, strutting and pirouetting, encouraging friends to bid on the outfits as part of a charity auction.

A highlight of the event was the publicity—or lack of it. Media coverage was discouraged. This was a private, industry moment and that was refreshing. Entertainment types don't often show their "ordinary" faces in public. Diapering babies, helping old ladies across the street, serving ladles of soup-kitchen food are no longer "boffo" at the box office.

Too bad. The industry's influence is deep and wide.

"The entertainment community is the third-largest employer in California," says Dr. Kaaren Douglas, director of geriatric programs for the Motion Picture & Television Fund. "We're dedicated to enriching the quality of life for our community and we have a special interest in seniors, retirement and family issues."

Does this signal a shift from youth, sex and violence on the screen? With boomers like Selleck passing the half-century mark, there's hope even the entertainment industry will age gracefully.

Monday, January 12, 1998

Somewhere during the second or third year researching her book on control, Judith Viorst lost it. "I was thinking about the book all the time," she says. "It had taken control of me." The realization proves her point: sometimes negative, often positive, control is an issue for all of us. We vie for, hang onto, rebel against, abuse, lose and sometimes willingly let go of control. But we are ever drawn to master it. And we never quite succeed. The ways we gain and give up control—with our parents, our spouses, our children, in the office, in bed, even in dying—define us and our relationships for life, Viorst writes.

And writes very well, by the way. The author of the hugely successful *Necessary Losses*, which examined issues of letting go, writes with ease and élan in her new book, *Imperfect Control: Our Lifelong Struggles with Power and Surrender*. She explores our lives, forces us to admit some events are simply not controllable, helps us recognize our imperfections. With humor. Always with a touch of humor. Viorst, after all, is the poet who wrote "Forever Fifty and Other Negotiations," among other works. She is the mother of three sons, inspirations for several children's books, including *Alexander and the Terrible, Horrible, No Good, Very Bad Day*.

In fact, it is those children, now grown, who inspired her new book.

"I had been hearing a lot about control issues," Viorst says. "It comes up in very different ways. Certainly, the heart and passion and most emotional issue for me was—what do you get to say to your adult children?" Sometimes, not much. But most of us keep trying, she says. And when those children don't measure up to our expectations, we blame ourselves. That's part of what Viorst calls "the fantasy of control: If we do everything right, if we follow the recipe correctly, we will produce a happy, healthy, creative, well-adjusted child. If the child does not wind up that way, well, it's got to be our fault. We didn't read the recipe right. We did something wrong."

The solution? Don't look to Viorst to give you seven easy steps to losing control. No advice, she says. "I'm really interested in getting people to be aware of the way control issues pervade their lives; being able to ask themselves, 'How much do I want? How much do I really need? How much do I have to give?'"

Viorst says parents sometimes come to realize that they are not God, that they cannot be completely responsible for how their children turn out. And, sometimes, there is no resolution to yearning for control. About control in marriage, Viorst writes:

> Even if I had a Ph.D. in psychology,
> Even if I were a diplomatic whiz,
> Even if I were Queen of the Charmers and more irresistibly sexual
> Than whoever the current reigning sex-pot is,
> And even if I had a fortune to squander on payoffs,
> And even if I had Mafia connections,
> It still would be impossible to persuade my husband, when lost,
> To stop—please stop—the car, and ask for directions.

From baby's breath to last breath, we continue to seek—and rarely find—control. Viorst holds a mirror to our imperfections and reminds us nature, nurture and our life events control our urges to control.

Seeking balance between power and surrender is our lifelong quest.

CELEBRATING A CENTURY OF LIVING— HE AND HIS BREATH STILL STRONG

*Former Boxer Peter Whitman, 100, Credits
Garlic for His Longevity and Fighting Spirit*

Wednesday, May 6, 1998

He has a grip of steel, legs of iron and breath that would make a dragon weep.

Hey, what Altoid is strong enough to mask years of eating four cloves of raw garlic every day? "Garlic keeps your whole body alive, inside and out," says Peter B. Whitman.

Garlic made him a better boxer, he says. It made him a stronger wrestler. And, he says, it's the reason that come today, he will have lived to be 100.

Whitman's standing on his head on his weight bench, scissoring the air with his legs, and not even wheezing while he talks. Before he started flailing the air with his feet, he was hoisting 50-pound weights over his head. And before that, he was pedaling his stationary bike.

Sound like a hearty workout? Whitman isn't even breathing hard.

"So, what's (turning 100) mean? I'm tough." He lifts his arms, feigning a boxer's stance.

Tough. Spunky. Junkyard-dog mean. At New Horizons Lodge, the Stanton board-and-care home where he lives, Whitman cackles with delight when he shakes hands with a guy and squeezes, and squeezes, and squeezes, pulling the fellow toward the floor. Women get their hands kissed.

He was eight when his home collapsed in the 1906 San Francisco earthquake. He crawled out. His parents were dead, pinned under tons of debris.

"I was out on the street and I saw the cops coming, and I thought, 'I don't want nothin' to do with them guys.' So I joined a gang. We didn't kill nobody. But we fought hard. We scratched and kicked and bit."

He lived on the streets for several months, eventually running his own gang. He was in the middle of a fight when a man came along and offered him a home. He got a bath.

"I thought I'd died and gone to heaven," he recalls. His eyes mist at the memories. "I loved my momma and my poppa. Mean. My life as a kid made me mean," he says.

Whitman's foster father ran a gym, a hangout for boxers. It wasn't long before Whitman was hanging out around the ring. He started working out.

On the wall of his room are photographs of the young Whitman at his peak. Charles Atlas with a mustache. Bulging biceps and rippling chest. Thunder thighs and massive fists.

"I coulda gone to college," he says. "But I wanted to play rough. I wanted to be a boxer."

Regrets? Well, boxing "wasn't much of a life," he says.

Weary of fighting, he turned to wrestling. That, he says, was worse. He ended up in Chicago, living in a hotel where Al Capone had his headquarters.

"We used to think he was making all that up," says his son, Gilbert Whitman, 63, of Yorba Linda. "But we found out it was all true. He knew Capone. He says Capone was kind to poor people."

Whitman settled down. He went to work for Chicago's transit system, driving a streetcar and a bus. He kept working out, reading books and magazines about healthy living.

"I eat very little meat and nothing that's greasy. I eat lots of vegetables, raw and cooked. And fruit. And garlic. Don't forget the garlic."

A widower, he came West a few years ago to join his adult children, who had settled in Orange County. He likes living alone. "I'm one of those guys who's got to do it my way."

His son agrees: "He can be—independent."

Independent and opinionated. One evening, in the New Horizons dining room, Whitman pounded the table with his fist to make his point. The glass tabletop shattered.

"Sure, I'm strong. Strong and healthy," he says.

He talks about his fights, the guys who tried to take him down over the years, the muggers who moved in on him while he was jogging in the park, maybe 20 or 25 years ago.

"I could tell they was stalkin' me," he says. "I pretended to fix my shoe, you know? And then I turned around and grabbed the first guy sneaking up behind me.

"I pinned him here and here," he says, mimicking wrestling moves, "and I mashed his head on the sidewalk. Did the same to the other guy. Never saw 'em again."

True or false? Gilbert Whitman just chuckles. "Who knows?"

Whitman's family celebrated his 100th birthday Sunday with a trip to Disneyland. His son and his daughter, Diana Dahn, now living in Las Vegas, four grandchildren and five great-grandchildren took him to the park at 10 A.M., "and we finally got him to leave at 11 P.M.," his son says.

For the day, Whitman wore a T-shirt proclaiming "Kiss Me, I'm 100!" and had a great time fighting off the women, his son says.

"He kissed them all!"

COUPLES FIND RETIRING CAN BE A TRICKY TIME

Monday, May 18, 1998

In the great Circle of Life, men and women are out of sync entering their last "Passage," author Gail Sheehy says. And while I have had difficulty with Sheehy's glib approach to life "Passages" in the past, I have to give her credit on this one. Because I'm living through the out-of-kilter one right now. And may I suggest that boomers take heed. Don't stumble into our footsteps.

In her latest book, *Understanding Men's Passages* (Random House, 1998), Sheehy writes: "It is predictable that couples will be out of sync when it comes to the point of actually planning for the last third of life. Men are generally in a greater hurry to retire for a very realistic reason: the mortality clock starts ticking for them earlier than for women." She goes on to say that "couples must share the picture in their heads of what retirement will be like."

Hello, Bob! How many times did I ask you, "What do you want to do when you retire?" And how many times did you say, "I'm thinking about it." And suddenly, you are retired and we have never talked about our expectations. Granted, retirement came up five years early, encouraged by a golden handshake. But, fact is, it's here and we weren't ready—except financially. Proving once again that money is not the answer to everything.

You want to veg. You're ready for what Sheehy calls "Gender Crossover," taking over responsibility for cooking and cleaning and stuff like that. I've got to learn to go with the flow, even if I can't find anything in the cupboards anymore because you put things in different places after it's been my kitchen for 35 years! A big issue? Absolutely not. In fact, you're welcome to spend your afternoons mucking about with the disposal. But where did you hide the yogurt and cottage cheese? All I can find is mayonnaise.

"Most women would die for this change," Sheehy says.

The truth is that Bob and I must muddle through a few months, setting new parameters, establishing new experiences to share. Even eating dinner together seems strange because his newspaper work hours forced me to eat alone for years. I got used to grabbing some melba toast and nonfat cottage cheese. Yesterday, he served me chicken pot pie.

Women adapt to change easier than men, Sheehy tells me. She's encouraging. Do not give up your independence, she says. Do not become a doormat. Then she regales me with tales of men and women who didn't make it because they had different attitudes toward retirement. Women often flourish after 50, while men start wrapping up. The result can be a fork in the road not bridged by communication.

No, that won't happen to Bob and me. He's been home only a week. Once I got over the shock of placemats on the table and dinner simmering on the stove, I started to relax. It's like dating again. That's fun because we really like each other.

What does Sheehy call it? The lusty winter? Phooey. We're just in the autumn of our years. The jug is filled with wine that pours sweet and clear. They will be very good years.

But please, Bob, read the food labels!

Monday, August 17, 1998

As the fourth movie preview starts, Lynne Lawrence shifts in her seat beside me and groans. "I'm getting nervous," she says. "I don't know if I can go through this. But I know I must go through this." What Lawrence feels compelled to do is watch Steven Spielberg's film *Saving Private Ryan.* The previews simply delay the inevitable.

Lawrence is about to witness the most graphic World War II movie made—and see a glimpse of how her father, Lt. Verne W. Robinson, was killed November 27, 1944, near Antwerp, Belgium. More than 180,000 American children lost fathers somewhere, sometime to that great war. Most of them, like Lawrence, have no memories of these men.

"A Wall of Silence was raised after that war," says Ann Mix, founder of a network for these adult children. "It was never all right for families to talk about the experience."

Lawrence tenses as the bombs explode on the screen, as bullets cut down young men on the Normandy beach, men even younger than her father, who was 26 when he died. "Even my own son is older than that now," she says. Her son, my two sons. None has experienced war. Before the film began, we told ourselves we were the lucky mothers. But soldiers have others in their lives besides mothers. They have wives, children, sisters and brothers. There is no room in this film to tell all those stories.

Stories of men like Verne Robinson. He shipped out for England the day his daughter was born. "Lynne is a beautiful baby. I can't wait to hold her in my arms," he wrote her mother. He never had that chance. Four months after her birth, he was dead.

"I have often wondered how my life would be different if he had lived," Lawrence says. Her mother remarried and bore two more children. She never talked much about Lawrence's father. "I know

now my stepfather was a fine man, but at the time, I somehow felt outside the family," she says.

Lawrence's feelings are typical, Mix says. "There is a feeling of aloneness because we never had our fathers or our losses mirrored back to us. No one talked much about it." Mix believes only in recent years did adult war-orphan children try to sort out their losses and the impact on their lives. "Instead of the hero mythology that surrounds the war, we are finally talking about the real price of the combat, what it really cost people," she says.

On the screen, the soldiers shuffle a pile of dog tags ripped from the necks of fallen Americans. The scene shocks Lawrence. "All those men—each of them reduced to nothing but this piece of metal."

Lawrence actually has many "pieces" of her father. She has the "memory book" publication of the 604th Army Engineer Camouflage Battalion, her father's unit. The travelogue-style book is dedicated to Robinson, killed by shrapnel when a V-2 struck within 50 feet of his truck. She has letters. After *Private Ryan,* she goes home and digs the letters out, sitting up until 3 A.M. to read and reread them. "He talked about people living in fields and woods. He wrote about towns where not a single building was left standing. And then he said the countryside was so beautiful, and he had trouble reconciling that—the beauty and the horror," she says.

Lawrence picks at the pieces of her father she has tucked inside her mind. There is the old woman in Belgium who was a young girl when she met Verne Robinson. He spent some time teaching her a bit of English while billeted in her home. The woman still writes every year to Robinson's family to honor his memory. Sometimes the woman goes to Robinson's grave in Belgium. Row G, Plot 56.

Four times Lawrence has bought a ticket to Belgium and four times she has failed to board the plane. "I don't know what I am afraid of," she says. "I want to know more about my father, but, at the same time, he has become the ideal father. He's a perfect person, and he loves me to death."

The morning after *Private Ryan,* Lawrence is exhausted. "Every muscle hurts like I did a long workout," she says. Scenes from the film flash by. "Mostly the blood. You know, all the war movies from our day were in black and white. I never thought about the blood. The red of it. The bright color."

For too long, war has been pictured as heroic, and wives and mothers have been encouraged to "be proud, be brave," Mix says. "I learned most of us had spent our lives feeling isolated and knew little about our fathers' service or how they died." Mix's registry, through the American World War II Orphans Network, is the only way orphaned children can reach one another. She has found more than 1,000 orphans, expanding her network through a computer Web site. Among other services, her network helps orphans uncover information about their fathers.

Mix has few pieces of her father's life. "My mother burned all his letters," she says. "I am so angry. I cannot get over that anger. I would give anything to have one letter from him, one glimpse of him as a person."

Without those glimpses, without that sense of personality, the war orphans create their own father figures. "I have just one hope after seeing that movie," Lawrence says. "That one guy who never wanted to kill anybody—I think my father would be like that.

"I hope he never had to kill anybody. He was so sensitive."

Monday, April 12, 1999

When the remarkable Jennie Faires died in her sleep last week at 109, she gave all of us a gift. Her death proved a point: there is a "centenarian personality," a stress-resisting mindset challenging the assumption that getting older means getting sick, disabled, demented, feeble. Jennie "automatically" relied on the strength of her faith and her convictions and her feelings of peace about her life, family and friends.

People who want to live long lives need to encourage similar outlooks, say two Harvard researchers in a new study of 100-year-olds.

Both of Jennie's natural children died. She mourned and went on. When she was 108, she told me her adopted daughter is "gold through and through." Three months ago she told a granddaughter she was ready to die because "I've lived so long." She was not ill or in pain. During her life, she enjoyed working and didn't retire until she was 70, but she was a homebody at heart, famous for her coconut meringue pie. And she stayed active. She was thrilled when women gained the vote and never missed an election until 1996.

"I have loved and loved and loved all my life," she said at her 109th birthday party. "I've had so many friends. And they've come and they've gone, and I've made new ones. Life is beautiful, folks." A fitting epitaph for the woman thought to be Orange County's oldest person.

Jennie could have been a poster girl for the centenarian study outlined in *Living to 100* (Basic Books, 1999) by Dr. Thomas T. Perls and neuropsychologist Margery Hutter Silver, both on the faculty of Harvard Medical School. Her life mirrors their conclusions for successful aging: sensible diet, exercise, attitude, stress resistance, genes and a curious, active mind.

"Aging isn't a curse, it's an opportunity," Perls told me. If people get that message and are willing to make the effort, more of them can be Jennies—long-lived, basically healthy until very old age. The concept of staying healthy and alert is a win-win for people and society, Perls says. He calls it "compressing morbidity," which is scientific talk for not spending years in nursing homes or being dependent on medications and hospitalizations. "I think the vast majority of us have the right mix of genes to get to our mid- to late-80s in excellent health," Perls says. "The reason we don't see that happening in this country right now—the average lifespan is 76—has to do with significant amounts of chronic illness." You know what causes the illnesses, he says: obesity, smoking, sedentary lifestyle. To that he adds attitude and stress reduction.

"It's very basic, common-sense things that people have heard about, but the message hasn't gotten through," Perls says. Why not? Too many doctors relying on prescriptions instead of preventions, for one thing. "We need more emphasis on prevention and screening," Perls says. We must realize that the route to a healthy old age lies not in curing disease but in preventing it.

What does that message mean to people who have, say, high blood pressure? "It behooves the physician to first prescribe a lifestyle and recommend ways to treat the health problem without medications," he says. "If that doesn't work, of course you turn to prescriptions to increase mortality and decrease morbidity risk." On that list of recommendations, Perls puts vitamins and minerals but not "promises of hucksters seeking to capitalize on the age explosion" with so-called anti-aging compounds such as human growth hormone. Some of these substances are not regulated by the Food and Drug Administration, and most of them are sold directly to consumers by mail, fax and Internet outlet or in health food stores.

"People are playing with fire," Perls says. "They may feel good initially, but in 10 to 15 years they will find out they have bought themselves an early and aggressive cancer." We yearn for a pill or a potion for instant results. Aging well over the years takes time, he says. Not that Perls believes most of us will live to be 100. But adding years, healthy and active years, to our life spans should be everyone's goal, he says.

Living to 100 takes its solutions from the real-life experiences of active and healthy centenarians. Through them, we can discover tools for fruitful old age that include intergenerational stimulation, spiritual growth, acceptance of individual limitations. There are tips and tools, even a "life expectancy calculator." For continuing information, Perls suggests supplementing the book with new information on the Web site www.livingto100.com.

"If people got it into their heads that living well is worthwhile, they will live longer," he says. "In a sense, we are much more fortunate than the settlers who followed the pioneers to the West. The pioneers of aging are among us; we need only to acknowledge them and welcome them into our midst. The more time one spends with older people, the less forbidding the prospect of aging becomes . . . It can be a time of work, of family, of play and of love."

FRIENDSHIP WITH AN OLDER WOMAN ALLAYS FEARS OF AGING

Monday, March 13, 2000

If we all agree life is a journey, then surely the turning point comes at the middle of midlife. That is, the turning point comes for the lucky ones who are reading the road signs.

Leah Komaiko knows all about turning points. The author of children's books—tell me your grandchildren have read *Annie Bananie!*—was 44 when she saw the signs. She felt old and empty.

Nothing made her feel young again. She thought maybe she should get remarried, so she called a dating service—and went "ugh!" Instead, she decided to volunteer to visit a person in a retirement home because what she really had to face were her own fears of aging and loneliness.

Komaiko felt she had no future. She was amazed to meet a woman, 94, who told her, "Enjoy yourself while you can." How long is that? Komaiko asked. "Until you die," the woman said.

The volunteer organization paired Komaiko with Adele, mentally sharp but frail and blind. Adele wears a diaper to bed "just in case," although most of the time she gets up and makes it to the bathroom. Adele has adult children who never visit, a watch with a voice that tells her the time and an insight on life that turned Leah's fears to fascination.

The result is a book, *Am I Old Yet?* (Doubleday). Yes, the best seller *Tuesdays with Morrie* leaps to mind, but this is a different tale, a story of an ordinary old woman and her middle-age visitor who turns into a friend. Adele could be your mother or your grandmother. Childless boomer Komaiko at first was repelled then gradually comforted by the consistency of Adele's daily life.

Adele is trapped in one room, this woman who had lived life to the fullest. "What kind of future is this, living in a holding pattern, waiting to die?" Komaiko asks. For two years, Komaiko struggled with her reactions to the old woman's demands, her dismay at nursing-home life, her great terror of ending up in such a place. Adele's plight is bad enough. Worse to end up in such a place with Alzheimer's, Komaiko says, with no memory, no past or future.

Over the months that Komaiko visited, two of Adele's roommates died. Their bodies, their belongings, disappeared without a trace. "You know, over half the people who live in nursing homes have no visitors," Komaiko tells me. "What are those of us who are childless going to be up against? We're going to have to rent children!"

Adele is angry that her children never visit, but resigned. She is their mother. She knows their limitations.

Depressing? Sometimes. Komaiko eventually saw beyond the obvious, leaping instead into the great gifts these elders offer. "Besides, old is just in time. I don't feel old in here," Adele said, pointing to her heart.

In confronting her own fears, Komaiko found friendship and a bridge across the cursed generation gap. When she told Adele the title of her book, *Am I Old Yet?,* Adele responded, "Well, if it makes you feel any better, you don't look old to me." Hearty praise from a blind woman.

As for wisdom: "Doing for others is what makes life worth it," Adele told Komaiko. "And you can't buy that. You have to earn it. Some people think they can live for themselves. But as the end begins to come clear, their minds work in the past and they really get thinking.

"But then it's too late."

Part 7—And the Books They've Written

In the 1840s, middle-class women deferred to specific instructions on laundering, housekeeping, cooking, personal hygiene and female education set down with absolute clarity by Catharine Beecher, an unmarried virgin, 41, who had no home of her own. Today, we want credentials. Here are some self-help authors who boast the best of them.

NOTABLE "LATE BLOOMERS" CAN PROVIDE INSPIRATION FOR OTHERS

Monday, July 1, 1996

Mother always said I was a "late bloomer."

"Your time will come," she said, when I shed teen tears because I was taller than all the guys and couldn't get a date. She was right, of course. Eventually, the guys grew. I even got married.

Was that when my "time" came? I'm not sure. For most of us, that blooming—that magic, sea-change moment—is difficult to pinpoint while it's happening. Events pass, and we ooze on with life. Often, only by looking back do we realize that we have been successful here—or there. Sometimes success comes in ways we don't expect.

"It takes guts to examine one's life from one stage to the next," says Brendan Gill, the famed *New Yorker* writer. "Failure is common. It comes as part of the natural course of events in life. Success is the rarity, the oddity. And it's arduous to achieve that success."

For many, success comes after much of life has been lived. Gill, 81, has chronicled 75 people who finally made it big time in *Late Bloomers* (Artisian, 1996, $14.95). The collection reminds me of my childhood book of saints' lives. On one page, a pithy, inspirational biography. On the facing page, a portrait.

Gill rightly excuses himself from the equation. He bloomed early and never went to seed. For 60 years, he has written innumerable poems, short stories, profiles and reviews for *The New Yorker*. But here's Harry S. Truman, a failed haberdasher who proved a tough-minded president at 60. And Barbara Woodhouse, the dog trainer, who says, "Life for me began at 70." There's Harland Sanders, the "Kentucky Colonel" who started selling fried chicken in his 60s, and Julia Child, who whipped up her first omelet on TV when she was in her 50s. Gill holds these achievers up and says they should give us hope. "These people are role models because they have survived.

They say to us: look, we have come through. We have endured. We have flourished."

Middle-age Americans downgraded by downsizing need this message, Gill says. "Those people, highly trained in a particular occupation, assuming they would progress step by step and retire to a graceful old age—cast adrift! I shake my fist at this injustice!" Life sometimes is like a blow in the face, and you have to accept it without loss of confidence, he says.

Gill refuses to give in to time: "I recently went to my 60th reunion at Yale, and I was dismayed to see those old crocks tottering around. I expressed my contempt for them." He went looking for late bloomers and found hundreds, he says. The task was to winnow the list. His message, of course, is that old age can be exciting.

"It's just as thrilling as youth," Gill says, "but more poignant because the punctuation point is arriving at a rapid rate."

Monday, October 28, 1996

Erma Bombeck wrote a column just for me on June 6, 1966. The day it appeared, I was five months pregnant with my first child and dreadfully lonely. We lived in an old apartment in a new city. I had swollen ankles, itchy skin and no talent—or interest—in knitting tiny garments.

The day Erma wrote for me was the day after my mother-in-law had made a surprise visit "to help you settle." In one afternoon, she rearranged the linen closet and wondered why I didn't make Jell-O salads. She moved my stainless flatware from the left to the right-hand drawer beside the sink. She refolded the towels hanging in the bathrooms. She made me feel totally inadequate. A college-educated housewife with no discernible talent.

Then Bombeck wrote to me: "The sermon today is talent."

She said she knew what talent wasn't. "I knew it wasn't setting three clean children out on the curb five days a week. It wasn't breaking out in a rash because you baked the best chocolate cupcakes on your block. And I hope there was more to it than being able to bring an African violet to full bloom."

Talent, she decided, is being able to laugh when the kids eat the bridge snacks. Talent lets you help bear your neighbor's pain and problems. She applauded those with real talent: "The talent of patience it takes to live each same, routine day and add a personal spark to it. The talent it takes to hope and put aside your personal dreams of achieving until your commitments to everyone else have been fulfilled. And the big one, the talent to recognize what you have going for you and to use it to its fullest."

Erma thought she was writing for the world that day. But I knew she was writing just for me.

The column was part of my refrigerator decoration for months. The words—but not the spirit—were lost over time. How reassuring to find them again in *Forever, Erma* (Andrews and McMeel, 1996), a new collection of 120 of her best-loved writings.

Bombeck died April 22 at 69 of complications after a kidney transplant. She was, *People* magazine said, "the queen with a sponge-mop scepter." At her death, her column was syndicated in 700 newspapers. She had written 14 books. Although she wrote her first column for her school newspaper at 13, she didn't turn professional until she was 37, when her children were out of school.

Bombeck defended the right of women to be themselves. She celebrated the housewife and fought for the Equal Rights Amendment. She was the first woman to reveal what happens to socks that disappear in the dryer. "They go to Jesus," she said.

In her last column, dated April 17, she talked realistically about growing old: "My deeds will be measured not by my youthful appearance but by the concern lines on my forehead, the laugh lines around my mouth and the chins from seeing what can be done for those smaller than me or who have fallen."

That's the definition of real talent. Forever, Erma.

Togetherness May Prove to Be Wave of Future for Generations

Monday, December 2, 1996

Whenever my adult children give me grief, I fire the mother weapon: I threaten them.

"Be good to me, or when I get old, I'm going to sit in your family room in a rocking chair and smell bad." This usually results in a chorus of hoots such as "Oh, no, we're moving to South Dakota," or "You take her; you're a girl," or other expressions that warm the cockles of a mother's heart.

Gosh, isn't family togetherness a value we all bemoan losing?

Now comes Gerald Celente, trend-spotter *extraordinaire,* to suggest we all may be forced into old-fashioned intergenerational communion in the 21st century. His new book—*Trends 2000* (Warner Books, 1996)—speaks of societal sea changes already lapping the shores. Among them is what he calls the "re-extended family"—driven into togetherness by economic necessity.

Blame it on the government, global economics, our penchant to consume and consume. In Celente's future world, there may be less for all—if you measure what's important on the basis of separate homes, lots of cars, all that "stuff."

He casts a scenario reminiscent of the so-called good old days: small houses, small bedrooms, lots of people sharing. He sees singles living together in communes. The aging who cannot care for themselves moving in with children. Healthy but widowed or divorced parents setting up house with their single or married children.

His vision includes a renewed demand for boarding houses and other forms of multifamily housing, including "granny flats" above garages.

The challenge—if Celente's vision is accurate—will be whether all of us can get along as we zoom "Forward to the Past."

In the Norman Rockwell America, everybody—except the very frail and the very young—participated in family labors from childcare to cooking, cleaning to community service. There was love and respect between generations. The "me" gave way to an emphasis on "us."

Was the past really that good?

"The good old days always have been a myth," Celente says by telephone from his Rhinebeck, New York, Trends Research Institute. "Literature is filled with tales about dysfunctional families, not functional ones."

But that doesn't mean you can't make it work in the future, he says. We can develop respect for the wisdom of elders, tolerance for the music of teens.

"Whether or not we prefer it that way, more and more people will be compelled to live together," Celente says. "Ultimately, it boils down to two choices: either it works or it doesn't work. The choice will be up to you."

He envisions people being more self-reliant, placing greater emphasis on personal responsibility for health and well-being. Flexibility of mind, body and spirit will be the real wealth to retire on in the 21st century.

Retiring Career Women Are Making It Up As They Go Along

Monday, August 11, 1997

We were eating our Caesar luncheon salads and talking about vacations and families and Elvis when Ann dropped her fork and blurted, "I don't have my own space at home."

That's when I learned that Ann—two years away from retirement—is sweating the "small stuff." As well she should. Plenty of experts are willing to give us answers to the "big stuff," such as how much money we need and what kind of health insurance we should have when we quit working. But for women in their 60s, that big stuff doesn't loom as large as little things such as space and relationships and choices.

For example, Ann's husband, already retired, has staked out the home office and a corner of the living room. "When I give up my work space, where do I hang out at home?" she's asking. "Do I go into the bathroom and close the door?"

Not a foolish question at all, says Lucy Scott, 70, a psychologist and educator who is the principal author of *Wise Choices beyond Midlife* (Papier Mache, 1997), a book for 60-plus women entering the territory of retirement without a road map. "We represent a new generation of women," Scott says. "Women have not faced aging in the same historical context as our mothers. We have no pattern. We are making it up as we go along."

Scott is testy about the people who try to set out answers. She's tired of hearing "the right way to age is to start a new business, jump out of a balloon, enter a marathon, whatever. Nothing really describes what it is like to wake up one morning and know you have 30 more years of life to invent."

She knows. When she retired a few years ago, "I entered a 'nothing' world. I wondered what I would do. I wondered who I was." Our mothers, Scott says, knew they were wives and grandmothers. But many of us who have been employed outside the home have other, independent selves. Not that men don't face an identity crisis when they retire. "They think their real life is over in many cases," Scott says. "But women have to keep on working as caregivers and nurturers. It's very different."

Scott solved her retirement crisis by starting a woman's group. She found other women 60 and older who had a hunger to stay involved and current. Forming a group doesn't give my friend Ann her own physical space at home, however. For that space, she needs to build an "altar" to herself, says Karen Kaigler-Walker, psychology professor at Woodbury University and author of *Positive Aging* (Conari Press, 1997).

Kaigler-Walker, 51, says "altar" is a loose term. "Just find some space in a corner of a room, for instance, and start to put things that are important to you there," she says. "Find out what beckons. Then, perhaps, it will become friendly and your friend will have a place to go and contemplate what she wants to do with all those retirement years."

So I start envisioning Ann nestled in her black Eames chair with Phredde, a lavender Siamese, curled in her lap, reading a good book and humming along with Puccini arias wafting from the stereo.

I'm making it up as I go along. But I like it. I like it.

Weathering Bumps of Marriage
Takes Dedication, Compromise

Monday, September 8, 1997

Bob needed to get his mother's permission to marry Nancy 50 years ago. He was 20, and New Jersey wanted to make sure the union was okay with his parent. Nancy was 19, one year beyond the state's parental-permission rule for young women.

In a half-century, they raised their five children, moved 23 times to satisfy Bob's career advancements, and finally retired to Dover, Delaware, to play bridge, visit grandchildren and take an occasional trip. Reads like a golden Valentine? Well, it wasn't. My friends have had their ups and downs, their moments when they couldn't stand one another.

"Marriage is work," Nancy told me 30 years ago when we met in Oak Park, Illinois. I was a stay-at-home mom then. Everything I know about how to turn a leather cut of beef into a gourmet pot roast I learned from Nancy. She helped me cope with mumps and chicken pox. And potty training. But she couldn't teach me to stick with a marriage that fell far short of my expectations. The gap in our ages and education meant I had goals outside the home.

I don't regret my divorce. I do wish I had not fallen out of love, however.

Nancy and Bob stuck through the speed bumps. Two-thirds of today's newlyweds probably will not, says Peter D. Kramer, author of *Should You Leave? A Psychiatrist Explores Intimacy and Autonomy—and the Nature of Advice.* "Who you are determines whom you encounter," Kramer said in a telephone interview from his Providence, Rhode Island, home. People have some sense of their own limitations and find that reflected in another person.

In his new book, the Brown University professor encourages people to try to stick it out. Second and third marriages often seem to work, he says, because people are making efforts they didn't make the first time around. In other words, they are learning to compromise. He quotes author Peter DeVries, who once wrote: "Why do people expect to be happily married when they're not individually happy?"

Kramer ties the divorce rate to social progress, to the economic emancipation of American women, which he salutes with honesty. Marriage, he says, is easier to pull off when one person is dedicated to family.

That dedication is physically and emotionally healthy, according to a report from Families Worldwide, a Washington, D.C.–based values group. Quoting various sources, the think tank says there is evidence that divorced people are more likely to have terminal cancer, commit suicide or die from heart attacks.

Nancy and Bob have learned to live with each other. Their compromises have allowed them to live long and prosper.

Kramer urges couples to look before they leap apart. Like Dorothy in the *Wizard of Oz,* he urges people to remember that old song: "You'll find that happiness lies right under your eyes, back in your own backyard."

BALANCE IS THE KEY TO SHAPING THE NEW AMERICAN RETIREMENT

Monday, February 2, 1998

Retirement. The capstone of the American Dream. A reward for hard work. Days of leisure. Years of golf.

"This is living!" say the ads for senior communities. Living? Sounds pretty boring. To me, living means staying involved, vital, purposeful and active to the full level of your physical ability.

And this, indeed, may be the retirement of the future, says filmmaker Marian Marzynski.

In *My Retirement Dreams* he explores a Miami Beach retirement condo community and the way its residents are growing old. He finds about what you'd expect: some people are bored; some are into line dancing. A few are expanding their minds; a lot are waiting for destiny. What makes the difference has little to do with age and education; it has a lot more to do with attitude.

The attitude that works best is positive and upbeat.

Retiree Howard Saltzman says that best when he proclaims retirement is "a second chance to live!" Saltzman views his elder-leisure as time to read and study and reach a type of enlightenment.

Marzynski concludes that Saltzman has the answer to successful old age. He's buoyed by Saltzman's zest. And he's intrigued by the conclusions of Professor Tim Patton, who teaches "Retirement for Baby Boomers" at Florida's International University.

Patton says boomers know they have years to live after reaching 65. How will the nation pay for their golden moments? By letting boomers keep on working.

Marzynski tells me, "We are ready for a new concept, a new American dream in a society that already has more leisure time, more mental than physical work." Boomers, he says, "want to retire without retiring." They will downsize, changing gears from full- to part-time work, gradually changing lifestyles and keeping mental involvement until the last moment.

Now, neither Marzynski nor I are boomers. We're both 60 and officially "Eisenhower generation" folk, a group sandwiched between World War II soldiers and their offspring. If we're honest, we admit that all our lives we've been touched by both the generation before and the one after. So it makes sense for us to be the transition generation.

Will our aging give us a "second chance" at life, as Saltzman says? Or will we fritter days away?

From the "geezers" in the film, we learn retirement is most difficult for those who don't take the time to think it through. These people can take years to adjust to not working. From the boomers in Marzynski's report, we hear that work should be a part of our lives well beyond 65. Those of us caught in the middle generation can swing either way—to work or to play.

Maybe our task is to teach geezers and boomers that a little balance goes a long way toward shaping a new American retirement dream.

Monday, April 13, 1998

Marilyn is retiring. Actually, she's giving up.

After 28 years of teaching elementary school, she says she can't take any more stress. No, she's not talking about the kids; she's talking about their parents. "When I call a parent in for a conference, I get an argument," she says. "They want to know what my 'hidden agenda' is. They accuse me of not liking boys or not liking girls or whatever. I'm attacked for wanting to help their children. There is no effort to work with me to make their child a better student."

A few days after hearing Marilyn's miseries, I got a letter from an old college friend, a medical doctor in Missouri. He says he is putting away his stethoscope. "It's not the patients," he says. "It's the insurance paperwork. I am constantly being criticized and forced to justify what I do for my patients. I feel harried."

The atmosphere is pervasive.

As Deborah Tannen points out in her new book, *The Argument Culture: Moving from Debate to Dialogue* (Random House, 1998), even Congress is impacted by hostility. At the close of the 104th Congress in 1996, 14 senators decided not to seek re-election. The senators, widely respected for being moderate and fair, lamented "the increasing level of vituperation and partisanship."

"The argument culture of today is not about the shouting level," Tannen tells me. "It's more about the battle metaphor." The "argument culture" urges us to approach the world—and the people in it—in an adversarial frame of mind. It assumes the best way to get anything done is to debate, to polarize, to litigate.

"We don't value compromise as we did in the past," she says. "So we can't find a solution because everything is defined by extremes." Television panders to this mindset with its Jerry Springers and

Howard Sterns and Sally Jessys, Tannen says. "Narrow adolescence," she calls it. Fights and confrontations "that have that young male audience in mind."

So what? Well, those of us with some gray hair usually have learned to blend concepts and compromise, avoiding the black-and-white approach to life. Call it the "Life is too short" philosophy. Life is a stew, a blending of ideas and concepts, positions and purposes that need to co-exist or else there is chaos.

Tannen says she is not talking about civility. Good manners are superficial, she says, spread over society like marmalade over toast. But I think good manners are a good place to begin. With that in mind, I called New York Mayor Rudolph Giuliani's office last week. Giuliani, you'll recall, launched a citywide drive for civility. Whoever answered the phone abruptly slapped me on hold, returned in five minutes, said, "Yeah, wait," and left again. After 15 minutes, I hung up.

In Tannen's spirit of dialogue instead of debate, I will not rush to judgment about the incivility of Giuliani's office staff.

Maybe someone was just having a bad-manners day.

Disappointed in Their Own Lives, "Toxic"
Relatives Can Make Life Miserable for Their Adult Children

Monday, December 21, 1998

Just one can ruin a whole family's holiday. Those whiny, crabby, you-can't-please-'em relatives who make you dread getting together.

Most of these crabs are old. Most of them are women. And most of them can stink up a whole room with their negative vapors. So concludes Gloria Davenport, 71, an educator who has spent more than a decade researching the people she classifies as "toxic elders."

"The majority of people age gracefully, but there are some elderly adults that are just plain, well, awful," Davenport says. "They make constant snide remarks about little things. They always start out by saying what's wrong. They can contaminate a whole gathering, an entire room." They are at their worst during the holidays, she says. "I remember my own daughter saying she wouldn't come home from college for Christmas if Nana (Davenport's mother—a 'toxic') was there."

Davenport coined the phrase "toxic elders" while she was writing her doctoral thesis on "the determining factors of successful aging." Many people she interviewed, she says, had this personality disorder. "They were so negative, they sucked the energy right out of me." Later, she was encouraged to develop a group-therapy workbook for adult children who are coping with toxic parents. This month, her textbook, *Working with Older Adults: A Guide to Coping with Difficult Elders*, will be released by Springer Publishing.

"Toxic elders," Davenport concludes from her research, grew up in rigid, suppressive and abusive homes full of "shoulds," "oughts" and threats. They are afraid to love, to trust, to share. The result: they spend a lifetime suppressing their emotions, "only to see them rise up in old age as untamed, disruptive behavior," she says. Most "toxics" are older than 75, Davenport says, and most are women because the men are either dead or being taken care of by some woman who doesn't object to their behavior. Usually, a spouse absorbs the toxic behavior over the early years. As a result, adult children often do not feel the brunt of a parent's toxicity until after the spouse dies.

Davenport ticks off the toxic signs: the "feel sorry for me" looks, the glares, the scowls, the tightened jaw and fist, the turned back, the walking away, the withdrawal, the shut or locked door, the nonexistent hug or touch, the sad facial expression, the downturned mouth, the piteous sighs, the incipient pauses and those dreadful silences. And she offers no hope. "Toxics can't be cured," she says.

Too often, "toxic" behavior is passed from one generation to another, she says. The only way for adult children to break free of a parent's toxicity is to recognize it and resolve not to follow in those footsteps. Adult children must not accept the guilt and anguish toxics ladle out. Instead, they need to learn to disassociate themselves. "Treat the toxics like neighbors instead of relatives."

ADULT CHILDREN CAN BE CURED

Gerry Starnes read one of Davenport's first articles about "toxic elders" in a Santa Ana College newsletter. "She described a syndrome I did not know existed," says Starnes, of Garden Grove. "But when I read it, I knew it was my mother." After her father's death, Starnes had struggled to meet her mother's needs—consistently failing. "Now I realize 'toxics' like my mother usually only latch onto one member of a family. At the time, I thought there was something wrong with me," Starnes says. "For me, it was a difficult role. I was to be her protector, supposed to take care of her. But if I didn't do that to the finest letter, she would get belligerent and angry."

Her mother would "punish" her by withdrawing and refusing to speak. She never seemed to appreciate anything Starnes did for her. She often was sarcastic. Starnes wrote to Davenport, saying she grieved about her relationship with her mother. "I am sure I have unexplored feelings within, in regard to our relationship, but those of which I am aware are frustration, sorrow, resentment and occasionally, despair. Oh, what I would give to pass a few hours of peaceful, nonvituperative conversation with her while I still have her."

Starnes helped Davenport launch a local support group—Adult Children of Toxic Agers—that met for several years. "I found out I was part of the problem, and I didn't realize it," Starnes says. "My thinking was to fix her, to straighten her out and confront her behavior. I had to learn she had tapped me early on to fill her emotional tank. As long as I carried that role, I was her enabler. She threw out the bait and I accepted it." Two years after her mother's death, Starnes still recalls the day she asked her mother about a book she was reading. "It's about a girl who trashes her father just as you trashed me," her mother retorted.

Starnes was able to say, "Mom, you really hurt me when you say I trashed you. I love you."

Her mother reached over and patted Starnes's leg. "I never meant to hurt you," she replied.

The moment was transforming, Starnes says. "From that day on, when she lashed out, I said, 'That doesn't feel good. That really hurts.'" Before her mother died at 89, she was able to tell Starnes, "I love you." Starnes credits the support group with giving her the strength to apply Davenport's antidote to toxicity: "Recognize that you have the inner choice to accept or reject toxicity in yourself or others. The real work is within each of us."

THE TEACHER TAUGHT HERSELF

Davenport has always made career decisions and picked her activities based on where she was in life. First, it was homebuilding. She and her husband, Hugh, designed and built their own house that snugs into a tree-laden lot at the end of a private driveway in Orange. "We started in 1955," Davenport says. "This house is just the way we want it. And we built it all." When her children were young, she worked with the YMCA, volunteered at Sunday school.

For 24 years, she was a professor and counselor at Santa Ana College. "That's when I started looking at my own aging, and I didn't like what I was seeing," she says. "Aging is described as such a negative. Why are people afraid of getting old?" From behind a bookcase in her paper-and-book-jammed office, she pulls a poster she made years ago for a Sunday-school class. It shows five stages of development: physical, mental, social, emotional and spiritual.

"In aging, only the physical goes down," Davenport says. "And we can slow that down by altering our lifestyles." Davenport began interviewing "agers," as she calls them. She determined that very successful agers—she calls them "stars"—had friends, family, daily telephone calls and letters. They contribute to society and are in the forefront of volunteering. "People know about them and want to be with them," she says.

"Adaptees"—her moniker for successful agers—"flow with life. Whatever life gives them, they move through it, adjust. They are not contributing to society, but they do contribute to family and friends," Davenport says. The "toxics" are usually alone. "They have no friends to speak of except one or two who are hooked in by them. They see themselves as victims and they act out their life as victims," she says.

Now that her textbook is complete, Davenport hopes to renew her support groups for adult children of toxic agers. "It is possible to change the pattern, but one has to work on it all the time," she says. "As we get older, we need to see ourselves as alive, vibrant—then we can be loving people."

RETIREMENT BRINGS NEW SET OF MARITAL CHALLENGES

Monday, November 8, 1999

This is what I know: you should never take your marriage for granted.

This is what Betty Polston knows: the empty nest and retirement can rock your relationship to its core.

The morning after her daughter Selena's fairy-tale wedding, the Tarzana woman felt empty and lost. Her husband, Bernie, didn't understand her empty-nest distress.

The day Bernie announced he planned to retire, she felt sick to her stomach. How would this major transition in his life affect their marriage, affect her life?

Being a psychotherapist, Polston did the natural thing—she researched midlife marriages, interviewed some couples who insist they are bonded tighter than ever, came to some conclusions and wrote a book. *Loving Midlife Marriage* (Wiley, 1999) might be the first how-to guidebook for the final third of your life, Polston says.

Why bother to try to breathe vitality into midlife marriages? Because with lifespans stretching into the late 70s, 80s and even 90s, you can look forward to 30 or 40 years together after the children leave. That, as Polston points out, is more time without children than with them!

Although the U.S. Census no longer asks about marriage and divorce, sociologists say there is a trend toward midlife divorce around the time of retirement. We are no longer young and in love, Polston says. We have been reliable and raised our children.

"Now we want a soul mate," Polston says. Well, find that soul mate in the guy you began with.

She speaks primarily to women because women are the "emotional managers" in a marriage. Nothing new there. But what is new is the midlife wisdom and balance women can bring to the art of salvaging relationships.

"One person can make the difference in a relationship," Polston advises in an interview. Retired husbands who seem to be adrift after leaving their jobs and work friends often need encouragement. So give him a helping hand in doling out advice, but only with his permission.

In other words, shelve that honey-do list.

Don't dismiss her "Seven Marital Themes" as a song you've heard before. Sure, we've all been told to accept each other's differences, nurture each other, reach out to family and friends, share values and responsibilities, be flexible, communicate thoughts and feelings and learn to manage conflicts. But retirement brings out different facets of a relationship.

"For starters, it brings intense closeness," Polston says. After all, what do you do with those 2,000–3,000 hours a year you once spent in work?

Traits that irritate—a husband's perfectionism or a wife's fastidiousness—can become magnified and create havoc in retirement, Polston points out. She expects women will be the ones buying her guidebook and applying its suggestions. That's normal. "Women expect more in marriage than men," she says.

The important thing to ask, after 30-odd years of marriage, is not the old "Can this marriage be saved?" question but "What can we do—together—to restoke the fires that may be burning low?"

Part 8—Everyone's a Hero to Someone

HEROES ARE THE PEOPLE WHO DO THE RIGHT THING
EVEN WHEN IT MAY NOT BE POLITICALLY POPULAR OR CORRECT.
HEROES PUSH OUR ENVELOPES TO BE BETTER, WISER,
MORE TOLERANT, INVENTIVE, CREATIVE AND CARING INDIVIDUALS.
THE BEST NEWS IS, HEROES ARE ALL AROUND US,
EVERYWHERE, EVERY DAY.

WHEN THE KEYS ARE GONE, WHO DRIVES GRANDDAD?

Monday, May 27, 1996

Every evening my Uncle Carl—he's 89—sits down at the dining room table in the house he has lived in for more than 60 years and plots a 30-minute drive around his neighborhood in University Heights, Ohio. All right turns.

Every morning at 8 A.M., Carl backs his big Chevrolet sedan out of the garage and drives the course at 20 mph. Carl does this because he thinks he is stimulating his mind and preventing Alzheimer's. Rush-hour drivers honking behind him think he's full of cow chips. I think Carl shouldn't be driving at all. Regrettably, he continues because he's alone and no one takes away his keys.

The roads are full of Carls—very old drivers who risk their lives and the lives of others. And their numbers will grow. By 2020, the population of oldest-old, people age 85 and above, will double to 7 million, then increase to nearly 19 million by 2050.

Two-thirds of these old-old drivers live in suburbs and rural areas, says Cathy Freund, 46, a public-policy expert in Portland, Maine. Getting them out from behind the wheels of their own cars is a national problem. Cars mean independence. Cars take people places. Cars access life. But at a time when Social Security and Medicare strain the national budget, public solutions for senior transportation are in short supply. What's left? Business solutions, Freund says.

"These people are used to riding around as drivers or passengers in automobiles," she says. "They are not used to riding in buses and vans. And these people are used to paying for their transportation through car insurance and automobile payments and so on. So if they want autos, and they can't drive, why not offer them a service that is about as convenient as their own car? Maybe they will pay for it."

Freund directs a pilot nonprofit program—Independent Transportation Network—that gives car rides to Portland seniors. The service combines two cars owned by the network with vehicles owned and driven by volunteers who take people to funerals, to malls, to doctor visits. Except for administrative costs, it's paying for itself.

Here's how it works: seniors can create a "ride credit account" through a local bank by selling their cars and depositing the proceeds. Adult children can give "ride credit" gift certificates. Seniors can add to the account by depositing the same dollars they spent on routine car maintenance and insurance. Young seniors can build credits for future rides by volunteering as drivers.

Freund envisions a national transportation network linked by computer that would let a son or daughter in California, for example, volunteer to drive local seniors and the credits would be applied to parents in, say, Maine. Drivers are mostly volunteers; a few are paid minimum wage. Insurance coverage follows the same guidelines as policies written for Meals on Wheels drivers.

"You know where we take most seniors? To nursing homes to visit spouses or siblings who they would never get to see without our service," Freund says.

The plan is flexible and costs $1.00 a ride plus 80 cents a mile. Best of all, it's working.

Independent Transportation Network: one solution for an aging America.

BOOKMARK FROM THE PAST IS
A BENCHMARK OF LIFE'S CHANGE

Monday, March 10, 1997

The story of our lives is punctuated by bookmarks. But we rarely take the time to review past chapters unless some event, some moment, makes us remember. But unless we remember, unless we review the past, how can we know where we are in the present?

"Who am I? What am I doing here? Where am I going?" are questions we ask ourselves now and again as we travel through life, Dennis Wholey reminds us in his new book, *The Miracle of Change* (Pocket Books). Wholey, veteran talk-show host and best-selling author, points out that making a human being takes a long time. Change, he says, is the teacher.

Usually we are taught our lessons in an abrupt way. "I was really enjoying that movie *First Wives Club* until the college graduation scene," Ellen shared last week. "Do you know those women graduated a year after I did? Suddenly, I felt old."

Years have passed. What has happened? Have we done the work we were supposed to do? I started waxing reflective a couple of weeks ago when John Glenn announced his retirement from the Senate. He said, at 75, that age is his only reason for retiring.

Age? Surely, John Glenn is not 35 years older than the day I stood on a New York City street and cheered him during his ticker-tape parade? That would make me 35 years older than I was that winter afternoon, shortly after that day, February 20, 1962, when Glenn became the first American to orbit Earth.

Just out of college, I was living in Manhattan and making a living at my first real newspaper job. A lifetime of experiences lay before me. In my dresser drawer, sharing a box with old "I Go Pogo" buttons, a Sigma Chi sweetheart pin and some real silver dollars, there's a giant button with a photo of Glenn in his astronaut gear. I bought the button from a street vendor the day of his parade.

It's a bookmark of my youth. A trinket from a past, a lifestyle I outgrew years ago. I have experienced changes I never could have envisioned 35 years ago. I'm still not sure who I am, where I'm going or even what I'm doing. But, as former Texas Governor Ann Richards says in Wholey's book: "When you say change, I think good. There is no doubt that change improves the product. I think positively about change because I think that with it, I'll be a better person, my life will be better, or my grasp of living will be stronger."

On February 21, John Glenn made me remember how I had changed. I was proud to be an American the day he circled Earth. It took 35 years for me to develop a similar pride in just being myself.

Thanks for the bookmark, Senator Glenn.

Thursday, October 9, 1997

There are days when Kathryn Hart-Darter flees the world. She goes upstairs, slips into a robe and just sits.

She lets her son, David, 6 1/2, bounce on an exercise ball in the living room as he watches afternoon television. She leaves her mother, Helen Hart, 78, to putter alone in her downstairs bedroom. "I tell them I need to chill out. I need my time," Hart-Darter says. "I tell them I can't be everything to everybody."

That candid, mentally healthy attitude helps Hart-Darter maintain her cool as she copes with the physical, emotional and 24-hour role of the "sandwich woman": wife, mother, daughter; lover, nurturer, caregiver.

She's not the only midlifer who needs "chill out" time. Someone— usually a woman—is caring for a person 50 or older in 23 percent of all U.S. households. While 12 percent of those caregivers are spouses 65 or older, most fall in the 35–65 age bracket, most are married and a whopping 41 percent have children younger than 18.

Hart-Darter fills the bill on all the "mosts." She's even 46, average caregiver age, according to a survey sponsored by the National Alliance for Caregiving and the American Association of Retired Persons.

Experts such as Robyn Stone, public policy professor at Georgetown University, argue that the Alliance survey was too broad, categorizing people who spend eight hours a month helping an elder as "caregivers." "The larger you draw the pool, the more hysterical you get about the problem," Stone says. "It simply is not that severe."

But Stone agrees that full-time caregivers such as Hart-Darter are in a sandwich. And she agrees with Gail Hunt, director of the National Alliance for Caregivers, that "The single biggest need caregivers have is time for themselves."

Hunt's concern is the number of caregivers who don't use community services to make their tasks more bearable and to provide better care. Too many caregivers either don't know services exist or are "too proud" to use them, the Alliance survey says.

Hart-Darter is an exception. By tapping into services such as adult day care and Meals on Wheels, she keeps her mother independent and entertained. By joining caregiver support groups, she learns techniques and solutions. "This is how I keep my sanity," she says. "Mom's not going to change. I have a husband and a son. I need to deal with it all and maintain my own life, too."

A FAMILY TRADITION

As more Americans live longer and need old-age care, family members are meeting the challenge, Alliance director Hunt says. "People are not dumping older relatives into nursing homes," she says. "Women are working part-time and full-time jobs, leaving work early, coming in late, making personal calls on the job, whatever it takes to cope."

Helen Hart cared for her mother. She cared for her husband during his final illness. "So it's time for me to take on this responsibility," says her daughter, Hart-Darter. But each generation carries different personal baggage.

Hart-Darter, a retired former manager with Pacific Bell, did not marry David Darter until she was 39. She had lived alone for 16 years. "Just being married was an adjustment," she says. "Then to become a mother! Talk about adjustments." Then life forced her to adjust again.

The first months after her father died in 1992, she would visit her mother in her Long Beach home and leave her there, waving on the porch. "I began to worry about her, and so did my husband," Hart-Darter says. "I felt inside myself that she needed us. Her life always revolved around family, her husband, me or my brother."

She decided to take advantage of a buyout from Pacific Bell, trading full-time responsibilities for part-time work as a food-service worker at Aliso Niguel High School. As a full-time employee, she got up at 5 A.M. daily to get her son ready for school, returning home at 6 P.M. to make dinner and handle other household chores. "Now I can give David the attention he needs as a child and Mom the time she needs from me," Hart-Darter says. She does not regret the trade-off. "I can always go back to full-time work someday." The transition, however, was not easy.

Helen Hart moved in with her daughter, son-in-law and grandson. They lived in a two-bedroom home in Santa Ana. That arrangement lasted one year. Helen Hart sold her Long Beach home, split the proceeds between her two children and helped her daughter move to a new townhouse in Aliso Viejo.

The house has a bedroom and bathroom downstairs. That was a selling factor, Hart-Darter says. "It's like Mom has her apartment and we can go upstairs and have ours. Now that she is with us, her life has meaning again. She's not isolated."

A TYPICAL SANDWICH DAY

Three days a week, Helen Hart joins friends at the Mount of Olives Adult Day Care Center in Mission Viejo. Caring for the elderly and caring for preschool children are outreach efforts of the Lutheran church.

"I have made a lot of nice friends there," Helen Hart says. "It gives me something else to do. It takes me away from home." She travels to the center on a bus provided by the Orange County Transit Authority. Her fee of $34 a day includes a hot lunch and two snacks. She also plays games, does exercises, keeps busy.

"I took Mother to the senior center first, but she's shy and it didn't work," Hart-Darter says. Then she adds, "And I think sometimes she needs to be reminded, she needs a little more attention right now."

At the day-care center, the elderly pair up—a frail person with a person with dementia, a stroke victim with someone who can help her out. On days when she doesn't go to the day-care center, Helen Hart gets home-delivered meals from Meals on Wheels. "I like the meals because everything is already put together," she says. On Saturdays, Hart-Darter drives her mother to the hairdresser. "I take care of myself," Hart says firmly. "I feed myself. I make my own bed. I take my own shower." Or she did, until she passed out one day at the adult day-care center. The director called for help. Hart was diagnosed with colon cancer, which was surgically removed. Her daughter hired a home-helper for her recuperation.

"There are some days when I walk in the door and my mind starts going in 20 directions," Hart-Darter says. "David has to be picked up at school, Mom needs to go to the doctor, my husband needs something. I have to deal with everyone one at a time. I call it my Velcro connection."

When it overwhelms, Hart-Darter takes her concerns to the caregiver support group that meets twice monthly at Mount of Olives. She's learned to cope. To tell her mother she cannot join her for a restaurant dinner "because I need time with my husband. He's the best thing that ever happened to me. He needs attention, too."

She handles her son and her mother in the car, letting each one talk and have her full attention. "I've gotten selfish with my time," Hart-Darter says. She's not afraid to tell other family members that this is her time with her mother, her time with David, her time with her husband. Sometimes, she even claims time for herself.

She has her wish list, of course. Topping it is a wish that her mother spent more time with her son, played more with him. "But I see them together, in her room, talking, and I know he will always remember his grandmother. We could have waited until she needed some sort of daily care before bringing her into our home, but I think what we are doing is more important. If we had waited, Mom's life would be shortened because she would be depressed. And I don't want that. I love my mom."

Most Heroes Aren't Celebrities but Do Their Work Unnoticed

Monday, September 28, 1998

Heroes. Bette Midler forever labeled them as "The Wind Beneath My Wings."

They are everything we want to be. Not because they are clever or brave or really good at hitting baseballs or blocking baskets. But because they are real and genuine and teach us something about the way we should live our lives.

Suzanne says Florence Griffith Joyner was her hero. She cried when the "world's fastest woman" died. "She was much younger than me, but she set goals for us all to hope and admire." Not sports goals but life goals: work hard, overcome obstacles, take chances, be bold. "I named my new BMW 'FloJo' because it's black, beautiful and goes like the wind."

Heroes are not celebrities, but sometimes we get that confused. That's because some celebrities—people like Billy Graham and Harry Truman—are heroic. But most heroes go unnoticed. That's a big part of their heroism.

Grandparents raising grandchildren. Caregivers for victims of stroke or Alzheimer's. Single mothers. Parents of children who are physically challenged. People who do their jobs well because that is the right thing to do. People who do jobs none of us want to do—from picking strawberries to changing diapers in nursing homes. People who force us to take stock of our lives.

Who are your heroes? I asked a *Register* photographer, 32. "That depends," Bruce said. "I have heroes in business and heroes in sports." He paused. "My dad," he said. "That's my real hero."

Few heroes are contemporaries. Most of us admire people who are older, people who have lived their lives so we already know their lumps and warts. "Who is your hero?" Bruce asked me.

Gloria Steinem, I said. I interviewed her once, and she was all I hoped. She was generous, intelligent, thoughtful. "Thank you for what you did for all of us," I said as she left. She made women stand taller, forced us to recognize that we can be all we want to be. We can define our femininity on our own terms today because she raised that consciousness. Steinem is a celebrity and a hero—but which came first?

Ordinary people who rise above the occasion in a crisis turn themselves into heroes. Think about Schindler and his list, the emergency workers in the Florida Keys, David Kaczynski, who had the strength to turn in his brother, Theodore, the Unabomber.

We seem to have a shortage of heroes in this country. No one who "rises to the occasion" is free of blemish. "There's a collectivized level of social self-esteem in our society," Dr. Robert Schuller told me last week.

Commenting on the conduct of President Clinton and Congress, the television evangelist said, "A city can be proud, a school can be proud, a country can be proud, or that collective level of self-esteem can come down, and we all share part of the shame."

This is a time to focus on the quiet heroes. There are those who will lift our spirits and be the wind beneath our wings.

Share your heroes with me, please.

Our Everyday Heroes Are Everywhere

Monday, November 2, 1998

Ah, this warms my heart. *Esquire* magazine surveyed boomers and found out 79 percent of those polled believe in heroes. But 69 percent believe there were more heroes in the past.

The most popular definition of a hero? "Standing up for what you believe in." Not as many heroes now as in the past? Bosh! We just don't take the time to recognize the heroes who are all around us, I said in this column September 28.

They are the wind beneath our wings. They are the people who do the right thing even when everyone around them scoffs.

One reader took exception to my definition of heroes. Sharon Gullikson, 36, of Santa Ana, says "hero" is the wrong word to use for people who simply do their best at everyday tasks. She expects heroes to do awesome, larger-than-life actions, like John Glenn blasting into space.

But others felt inspired to write about mothers, daughters, fathers, brothers, volunteers who heroically sacrifice personal time to make a difference in their lives. This is how Ricki Mandeville, 52, of Huntington Beach, described her mother: an "Everyday Hero."

> She grew up in Europe, near Frankfurt. She danced with the city ballet, learned to smoke stylish filterless cigarettes and annoyed her mother by staying out late, hanging around the cafes with the arts crowd. She lost her beloved father to a heart attack, holding him in her arms, trying to revive him by waving a bottle of Old English Lavender cologne under his nose, refusing to admit that he was already gone. She married a young German doctor, lost him tragically in the war only two weeks before delivering his only child. The well of depression and loss was deep, but her baby needed her. She clawed her way up. A few

weeks later, she risked going into the occupied zone alone to rescue her sister-in-law and her baby, saving the sick and starving infant's life by feeding it the only food she could provide: her own breast milk. Three years later, she married a handsome American soldier, moved to America, had a second child, became a U.S. citizen, a room mother, a den mother, a nurse, a ballet teacher. She held in her arms and never-too-full-for-one-more heart a succession of ailing puppies, homeless kittens, scrawny baby chicks, stray turtles, forlorn children, lovelorn teenagers, wounded souls.

In her late 60s, she and her husband gave up life as they had known it to care for her mother, who could not walk, bathe, eat or, later, even turn over unassisted. This 24-hour-a-day care continued for the next eight years, sapping her strength, its grueling routine testing her every limit. Like a hero, she came through. Today, she's still going strong. Puts on senior variety shows. Cooks for everyone. Baby-sits her friends' dogs—and kids, when she can get them. Dotes on her husband.

Two rules she has always seemed to live by are these: be kind, even when it costs you. And do the right thing, even when you're the only one who knows it. She's not the only woman whose life was structured by tough circumstances, nor the only one who rose above each challenge. She's just the only one who combined all that with being there for *me*. Yes, she's a hero. She's also my mother.

Many who wrote celebrated their mothers. From Chelsea Fernandez, 15: "She is a single mom raising four kids. She has overcome incredible odds by putting herself through law school while raising us. . . . With great joy and honor, I was able to be at her swearing-in ceremony in June."

From Dow O'Brien: "At 46, she chose sobriety. That tumultuous year, she was diagnosed with ovarian cancer and had a hysterectomy. The wealthy husband who had left her filed for bankruptcy, divorced her and married the other woman. And yet . . . she continued to live a sober life. Today, at 71, . . . she enriches the lives of everyone close to her. And I'm proud to say this woman is a great friend of mine and my role model for strength, courage and kindness."

Many readers honored family members in their letters—fathers, children, grandparents. From Peggy Craig: "Who is my hero? My daughter, Amy . . . . She knew what she wanted, what she had to do to get it, and started out one step at a time until she did it. (She graduated Boston University) in 3 1/2 years . . . . She did it by herself with loans, grants, prayer and true grit."

From Barbara Armstrong Phillips (about her father, William Armstrong): "He was the man Diogenes was looking for but never found—an honest man."

People overcoming obstacles with courage and faith are among the everyday heroes described in the letters and messages we received. Like Maureen Glick, whose emotions overflowed as she talked about her daughter, Kristy Fisher, a young mother who must care for a child with disabilities while coping with her own breast cancer.

Others found heroes in everyday life. Joanne M. Singer at Fluor Daniel in Irvine wrote about a coworker, Lillian Seen: "Those of us who rely on her in our daily lives know her strength of character, ethics and . . . her belief in all of us."

And Kristin McCoy, 14, found a hero in volunteer aquatics coach Jeff Raymond: "This person has taught me that you don't always have to get recognition for everything you do. . . . When I'm grown up, this is the kind of person I want to be. He has taught me that it's okay to care."

Amid Glenn's Age-Defying Flight, A Gender Barrier Falls

Monday, November 23, 1998

Minutes before John Glenn pushed the envelope of age discrimination, Lisa Malone made my day. As the *Discovery* exhaust bloomed at the launch pad, as Walter Cronkite massaged our minds with memories, Malone's voice came over the speakers at Kennedy Space Center. "Ten minutes and holding."

"That was a woman!" I shouted at my husband. "A woman doing the countdown."

"So?" he said. "What's the deal?"

What's the deal? Well, ditch those nattering nabobs of nostalgia and plug into reality. To understand what Malone achieved as she ticked off the minutes, return with me, briefly, to the Pleasantville of my young adulthood. We women tucked our college degrees into the linen closet, damp-ironed our husband's Oxford-cloth white shirts and swirled around our kitchens like Donna Reed look-alikes. We were encouraged to find excitement in burping everything from babies to Tupperware.

Our husbands were in charge of the big stuff: getting the cars fixed, stoking the furnace, deciding the investments and major purchases. They determined our futures and took over the important work, including counting down the astronauts before they rode into space.

It was 1962 when Glenn first rode into orbit. Somewhere in suburbia, Betty Friedan was editing *The Feminine Mystique*, the book that launched the women's movement. Both events signaled change in the way we view our limitations and reach for our dreams. Now, 36 years later, we come full circle to Glenn and Malone.

Inside the shuttle, the elder astronaut is about to prove that age is a state of mind and health. Not only can you teach an old dog new tricks, but you can also make him star of the show. Inside the control booth, Malone, 37, counts down his glory ride. She calls her job that day "launch commentary." There are three "commentators" at the Kennedy center. She's the only woman. She's also the boss, the head of public affairs, the first woman to hold that post.

Women have come so far, we are starting to take their achievements for granted, says Barbara McDowell, executive director of the Women's Center at California State University, Fullerton. "Women came into the workplace and modeled themselves as junior males," she tells me. "We were not real successful when we tried to play the game like men, with men's rules. Today, women are more successful because we understand that we have our own style and that our style has a validity and value."

In March, Malone may do the commentary for the shuttle flight commanded by Air Force Lt. Col. Eileen Collins, expected to be the first female flight commander. Will the nation stop and hold its collective breath during the countdown? Probably not. Achievements of age make news. Achievements of women are commonplace. And that, after all, is what equality is all about.

Part 9—What It Was, What It Is, What It Will Be

"MY MOTHER ALWAYS WORRIED I WOULDN'T APPRECIATE THE STUFF SHE
COLLECTED," SAYS FORMER TEXAS GOVERNOR ANN RICHARDS.
"WELL, SHE WAS RIGHT. AFTER SHE DIED, I HAD A HUGE GARAGE SALE."

DUMPING "STUFF" IS HEALTHY, ESPECIALLY
IF IT INCLUDES OLD HATES AND ANGERS.

PRIME TIME HEIRLOOMS LOSING THEIR SENTIMENTAL VALUE

Monday, October 6, 1997

It's the old treasure-to-trash story. Who values history, heritage, tradition when food comes on paper plates and is scarfed down in front of the television?

The *Chicago Tribune* reports that in the Midwest—that bastion of family values—people are dumping family heirlooms including china, silver and that nice table stuff. As baby boomers get older, familial obligations increase, living space gets smaller and the back-to-simplicity movement gathers momentum, more people are scrutinizing inherited treasures with a businesslike eye. And as goes the Midwest, so goes the nation, says Gerald Celente, director of the Trends Research Institute, a research firm in Rhinebeck, New York.

"The stuff you got when you got married—what the hell are you going to do with it?" asks Celente, 50. "Stuff that is family history might be one thing, but a lot of what we have is just middle-class junk." So much for the plated-silver trays, well-and-tree platters, covered vegetable dishes and plated pitchers from my wedding day.

"Oh, plate has crashed in value," says Mary Colby, an antique appraiser in San Clemente. "People don't entertain like they used to," she says. Women work. They don't have time to polish silver and get out the finger bowls.

Of course, some people are selling off the goodies just to stay alive. "Don't buy that stuff that the economy is better," says one Orange antique-gun dealer who asked to remain anonymous for business reasons. He says men are selling off gun collections inherited from fathers and grandfathers "because they need the cash."

Value is value. Signed pieces, sterling pieces and Mom's Tiffany tea set can be a ticket to easy retirement. Many of the middle-age heirloom dumpers are going for the gold, dealers say. And with good reason. Forty-six percent of all adults have nest eggs of less than

$10,000, according to Fidelity Investments. More than half of those working in private-sector jobs have no pensions.

"Middle-age children who inherit stuff are usually very sharp about the values," says Becky Factor, owner of Leisure World Consignments in Laguna Hills. If they aren't going to use the crystal glasses or they don't want to deal with the Chippendale armoire, they sell it off—for a price.

My mother-in-law must be spinning in her Illinois grave. Collecting "things" was her life in the '60s and '70s. She squirreled away commemorative oatmeal tins. She had my husband's old Halloween costumes packed in the attic. She had buttons and bric-a-brac, brown dishes and blue dishes (with matching glasses), red dishes and amber dishes (with matching glasses), and assorted and sundry serving pieces. Everything was laid out on seasonal tablecloths.

Even a casual meal at her house was an orchestrated event. Most of these items were gone before she died. Sold off to pay for her nursing-home care. But every year, at Thanksgiving and Christmas, I polish her brass candlesticks and set out her salters. "Not using nice things is just a trend," appraiser Mary Colby says. "Pieces are worth saving just for the thrill of the memories they evoke."

It takes time for children to appreciate what you have, according to Marcia Radelet, a Huntington Harbor resident and collector of Victorian silver. "Eight or 10 years ago, my children weren't interested in my collection," she says. "Now they are beginning to appreciate the items, and I don't think they'll end up selling everything. That's nice to know."

Monday, June 7, 1999

"If I only knew when I will die, I'd know how to live," a 70-ish friend likes to say.

Truer words, etc., etc. If she only knew when, she could make better use of her time, and her money and her things. "If I knew I only had three years, for example, I'd take one of those fabulous millennium trips that costs a fortune. But if I spend the fortune, what will I leave behind?" Ah, truer words, etc., etc. But maybe, just maybe, she should enjoy more of her money now rather than worrying about an inheritance for her grandchildren. How much money do those kids need?

Baby boomers stand to inherit at least $8 trillion, according to a Federal Reserve Board study on household wealth. The average boomer will inherit less than $50,000, but many will be gifted with homes or stock portfolios exceeding $100,000. Economist Robert Avergy says about 60 percent of that wealth is "real wealth" (real estate, for example), and 40 percent is "financial wealth" (cash, stocks and bonds). Not included are collectibles, art, jewelry and other personal goods.

You gotta ask yourself: after the real estate and the money, will your heirs really appreciate the stuff they're getting? In our family, one daughter-in-law doesn't like crystal "with cuts." So much for my Waterford collection. Another has little use for my silver. My daughter says she will enjoy the jewelry, thank you, but she's not sure about the oil painting that used to hang above my grandmother's buffet.

All very reasonable opinions. All reflecting changing tastes and values. But how long do I hang on to the stuff no one wants just because it's family stuff that has monetary as well as sentimental value? And what would I do if my heir was someone like The Jerk pictured in a Windsor Jewelers ad from New York City?

The Jerk has a two-tone gelled Mohawk. He's wearing steel-rimmed sunglasses and a metal dog collar and boasts a nose ring big enough to hold up a shower curtain. The ad copy: "The bad news is, he's the sole heir to your jewelry collection. The good news is, there's still time to cash it in for a round-the-world cruise."

Windsor ad manager Larry Aaron says, "We're basically estate-jewelry buyers, and we're telling people to sell and use the money for their own pleasure. Like most things parents value, kids today don't want the stuff, won't use it, couldn't care less. Like flatware. They don't want silver; they want stainless steel. This is the barbecue generation." Even the best-laid plans to share family valuables with appreciative heirs often go awry. My former mother-in-law tagged special items for her grandchildren. My ex-husband sold them anyway.

My suggestion: make a list of your treasures. Distribute the list among your children round-robin fashion, letting each select one item until all are spoken for. Have some valuables left over? Sell them and take a trip, establish a scholarship, do something positive.

That's a better solution than leaving it to The Jerk.

REMEMBER, IT'S WHAT YOU HAVE BECOME THAT COUNTS

February 1, 2000

My Irish grandfather was a boilermaker. In fact, when he died, he was vice president of the fledgling International Boilermakers Union. When his son, my father, graduated from high school, he decided to work his way through college. The concept outraged my grandmother: "What makes you think you should go to college?" she demanded. "You're nothing but a boilermaker's son!"

My dad never forgot that cutting remark. Her lack of pride in his ambition still hurt, even when he was named vice president of a Wall Street firm. After she died, he learned she bragged him up around the neighborhood. She just couldn't bring herself to compliment him to his face. She had too much pride to admit he was right, she was wrong.

Sometimes I think pride is our worst enemy—and the one fault that makes life miserable for many elderly people. Too much pride often goes hand-in-glove with failing independence: no, I don't need any help; no, I like to do it my own way; no, I won't take your advice. Too little pride in family often leaves elders alone in their final years: after all I've done for you, this is all I get? Remember where you came from. It was good enough for us, so it should be good enough for you.

Who wants these people? How did they get this way?

The simple answer is they spend too much time looking at the hole and not at the doughnut. Focusing on what they don't have instead of what they have leads to lonely old people sitting alone in nursing homes, says Charney Herst, Encino-based psychotherapist and author of *For Mothers of Difficult Daughters* (Villard, 1998).

Not that the prideful elders don't love their children and grandchildren. They just don't know how to tell them. "Listen to yourself," Herst says. "Listen to what you are saying. Make sure you are giving the right message." Our children and grandchildren need more "attaboys" and fewer putdowns, she says. How our children and grandchildren choose to live is their business, not ours. Yet some parents cannot forgive children for surpassing them.

"I was the first person in my family to graduate from college. I even have a doctorate," Herst says. "My mother would call me 'the big shot—a doctor, and you don't even operate.'" Yes, sometimes it takes a great deal of generosity of spirit to see children do better than we did, because it raises our own past regrets. Let those regrets go, Herst advises.

And then there are the children and grandchildren who don't live up to our expectations. Instead of telling them what they were "supposed" to do, look into your own heart. Perhaps you are disappointed because they failed to live out your fantasies, fulfill your fondest dreams. "It's not what you are doing, but what you have become that counts," Herst says. "Parents and grandparents need to remember that. A person who is satisfied with his or her lifestyle, a person who is happy and achieved his or her potential—this is enough."

As one poet wrote, "As you travel through life, buddy, let this be your goal. Keep your eye upon the doughnut and not upon the hole."

Part 10—There Are Friends, and Then There Are FRIENDS

FRIENDSHIPS TAKE ON A DIFFERENT MEANING WHEN WE GET OLDER. LIKE LONGTIME LOVERS, BEST FRIENDS MAKE YOU FEEL GOOD ABOUT WHO YOU ARE. IN FACT, AS WE AGE, WE REALIZE FRIENDS HAVE ONE ADVANTAGE LOVERS LACK: YOU CAN HAVE MORE THAN ONE AT THE SAME TIME.

Names Change, and Finding Old Friends Becomes Difficult

Monday, January 5, 1998

Where are you, Mary Agnes Conlin, Cheryl Hyatt and Geraldine Seitz, my pals from St. Rose of Lima grade school in Buffalo, New York? And Rosemary Craddock! You were my best friend when I moved from Buffalo to Hyde Park in Chicago. Are you happy somewhere? I can't find any of you on the Internet or in the nation's phone books. I expect you've all married and have different last names.

Women have real problems hanging onto their roots because they are, traditionally, pushed into giving them up, academics say. They change their names, move away from family and friends, live according to the male order of things.

"Well, we might have done that once, but we're not going to do it again," my friend Carolyn says. She is a widow who just began "keeping serious company" with a gentleman. "If we marry, I won't change my name."

A feminist? "No," Carolyn says. "A person. An individual." An individual but not a feminist? "Oh, that's an important distinction," says Carolyn Harrison, a spiritual director specializing in women's issues.

Harrison says younger women in particular are leery of the feminist label because it conjures masculine, assertive behavior or a lesbian label. "The younger women are all for equal pay and so on, but they don't see that as a feminist issue," Harrison says. They don't understand the definition of feminism—the principle that women should have political, economic and social rights equal to those of men.

I'm not trying to be a "feminist" (as defined by masculine, assertive or other orientation that has nothing to do with the cause). I am all for "feminism." How did that get twisted up with memories? Some scenes in a recent movie caused me to wonder what happened to the girls I played dolls with, learned to knit argyle socks with, even had my first discussions with about sex? It's frustrating to realize finding them will be a chore.

"Our generation never gave hanging onto our name a second thought," says Gloria Davenport, an author specializing in aging issues. "How stupid. How conditioned. How programmed we were!"

When I started in this business back in 1960, we had definite rules for the way we wrote about women. Married women never had a feminine first name (e.g., Mrs. John Doe) and divorced women did (e.g., Mrs. Jane Doe). Single women were always "Miss." Reporters spent incredible amounts of time verifying the married status of women. Better we spend our time on more substantive issues.

But I still wish I could find those old girlfriends.

Monday, February 8, 1999

Over the past weeks I've re-established one friendship and ended another. What surprised me was how easily both the connect and the disconnect happened. Each friendship was an in-depth relationship that had weathered many years. But only one, it turned out, could survive mutual lifestyle and personality changes.

What made the one old friendship work?

Tam and I met riding to high school on a Chicago city bus. We were "best friends" back then, eventually separated friends who saw each other only occasionally for more than 30 years. Yet when we got together recently, it only took moments to re-establish connections. Our lifestyles, our goals, our experiences have been different, but a basic honesty remains between us. We trust each other. Friendships take on a different meaning when we get older, Tam says. Ours helps connect her to her roots. And I like the comfort that comes with her familiarity.

"Relationships work because another person makes you feel good about who you are," says Dallas psychotherapist Bob Carver. "If that changes, relationships fail. You need to be able to say, 'I'm going to be me and you can be yourself,' and honor that."

Just like a marriage, friendship fails when there are unexpressed expectations, undelivered communication or thwarted attention.

That explains why I cut off another friend in Chicago. I no longer felt I could share. I heard from this friend only when it suited her agenda. Suddenly, I realized this person always took from me and rarely gave anything back.

"Thank you for your e-mail," I wrote her last week. "But we don't seem to be really communicating well anymore. Let's take a six-month break and see if we miss each other." So much for Carole King's song "You've Got a Friend" and her promise "winter, spring, summer or fall—all you've got to do is call—and I'll be there." In her book *Just Friends*, Lillian Rubin says friends accept each other so long as they both remain essentially the same as when they met. Or, if they change, they need to change in similar directions.

"If they change or grow in different or incompatible ways, the friendship most likely will be lost." The www.cyberparent.com Web site offers a list of suggestions on "How to Grow a Friend." Do we need to be taught how to make friends?

Younger people often don't know the basics of friendship, Bob Carver says. Those of us over 50 have let our kids down with our high divorce rates. "They don't have any role models."

I'm not sure that's entirely true. Marriage and friendship are alike only up to a point. Most of us, hopefully, have more friends than lovers—or spouses.

How do you grow a friend? Do you really need directions? You grow a friend the same way you grow any relationship. You take time. You talk—and you listen. You pay attention and you share confidences.

> People can be so cold. They'll hurt you, and desert you.
> They'll take your soul if you let them. . . .
> Ain't it good to know you've got a friend?

Monday, December 27, 1999

Bob, my husband, spent the night alone in a hotel a couple of weeks ago. The alternative was to hide upstairs in the bedroom, the door tightly closed so his testosterone didn't waft down to the house full of women below.

Once a year, I throw Bob out. There's no delicate way to put it.

The occasion is my "Chick's Celebrate" party, a potluck that this year brought more than 50 women carrying everything from casseroles to jugs of wine into our kitchen. Women do this kind of party so well. They mingle. They meet new people. They rummage in kitchen drawers for needed utensils and pop things into the oven without asking twice.

"Chicks Celebrate" started the year after Bob retired, when I realized I was spending a lot of time with him and a lot less time with women friends. And Bob wasn't seeing his men friends, either, because most of them were from work. Our solution: the women come to our house and he goes to a hotel near his former job. He has lunch and dinner with friends he rarely sees since he no longer commutes 60 miles a day to work. He maintains his network. I end up expanding mine because the women I invite tend to bring others.

Keeping old friends and making new ones takes work, psychologist Ruth Harriett Jacobs says. The effort may be essential to aging well. How do you make friends? By going more than halfway to meet people. Women tend to be better at the job than men, says Jacobs, author of eight books including *Be an Outrageous Older Woman* (Harper-Collins 1997). Most women, she says, recognize that they need "support system people." Not all our friends are intimates. Some like and affirm us; some share our values; a few build our self-esteem; the best challenge and stimulate us.

At 75, Jacobs still counsels male retirees, often at the behest of their wives. "My favorite was the guy who retired and was hanging around the house all day in his bathrobe," Jacobs says. His wife made a deal with him. He was to get up every morning and get dressed and go to the library. He was to read the newspaper and magazines there and maybe talk to some other men, if he saw any. A week later, he came to her office.

"I'm smarter than you are," he told her.

"I knew that," she replied.

Then he raved about the bulletin board he found in the library with notices of choral groups, great-book clubs, other activities he had joined. "My calendar is full," he boasted. He had discovered her second point on friendships: read your local paper and bulletin boards; go to meetings, events and gatherings that interest you. You cannot make friends sitting at home.

Jim Conway, 67, of Fullerton, finally figured that out about a year after his wife, Sally, died. "I was sitting at home wondering why people didn't call me," he says. Conway, a pastor and head of Midlife Dimensions (www.midlife.com), jokes that God said, "Well, why don't you go ask someone to join you for lunch?"

Just talk to one person, Conway advises. One conversation makes it easier to have another and another. Rebuilding friendships and nurturing new ones is one New Year's resolution that doesn't require a gym membership.

Part 11—Family, Family Everywhere

FAMILIES LIVE THE CLICHÉ: THE CIRCLE OF LIFE. WE RAISE OUR CHILDREN AND THEY LEAVE US. OUR PARENTS, AUNTS AND UNCLES GROW OLD AND DIE. WE ARE NO LONGER ANYONE'S CHILD. WE ARE ADULT ORPHANS. WE ARE THE ELDERS. WE ARE THE GRANDPARENTS. THE CIRCLE SPINS ON.

Baby Steps Take Strides to Heal a Rift

Monday, October 30, 1995

It happens in every family: angry words between parent and child, heated arguments between brother and sister, somebody walking off into the night. And the family tie is broken.

It happened in my family without an argument.

I still don't know what triggered it. I just know my oldest son married, moved to Hawaii, stopped calling or returning phone calls. It took a child to break the silence.

So proud he could burst, my son had to call and tell me about Travis Hanalei Haas, born a year ago. Gradually, hesitantly, we started talking again. Photographs arrived of a chubby, blond, blue-eyed baby with Asian eyes. What a hunk! "Come to Travis's first birthday party," my son said in a telephone call. "Please come."

Baby steps could close the family circle once again. "Go," my aunt said. "Life's too short."

Even my neighbor offered advice. "Go," he said. "I wish I were so lucky," he added, referring to a similar unfathomable rift in his own family.

"Go," said my husband, pulling the suitcase from the closet.

Tom was late meeting me at the airport in Maui. We both were nervous. After five years of silence, neither of us knew where to start. We had to find neutral ground somewhere. The baby became safe territory.

At the restaurant, Travis sat beside his mother, eyeing me from a safe distance. He slapped the table. I slapped the table. He slapped the table again and caught my eye. One, two, three times we played the game. Then he looked way, made a pout just like his dad's, turned and slapped both hands on the table, trying to catch Grandma napping.

That was the moment when I finally understood what being a grandma is all about. Travis was no longer a photograph. He was a wonderful, bright and beautiful boy.

I brought a toy piano to the birthday party two days later. Sure, it was a grandma gift. I wasn't going to be around to hear Travis pound away at two some morning. He loved it. It makes lots of noise.

Guests at the party all talked about family. Most had left relatives on the mainland. "I don't like LA," Murray said. "I hate to go there, but I sure do miss my family at birthdays and Christmas."

The next day, Tom drove me to the Haleakala Crater for sunrise and along the 53-mile Hana Highway, past waterfalls and sacred pools. He made a point of helping me down the moss-covered stairs leading to the ocean. It was comforting to have a guide who is 6 feet 5 inches tall and built like a rock.

The water is crystal clear. It's impossible to hide here. We healed somewhere among the 617 turns and 56 single-lane bridges on the Hana Highway that day. We healed without talking about the past. Instead, we talked about the future, his plans and dreams and ambitions for himself and his family.

Travis is walking now, circling the backyard in Makawao.

At the art gallery in the Grand Hotel, I got into a conversation with the saleswoman. She moved to Hawaii a few years ago from Laguna Beach. Maui is a wonderful place to raise children, she said. "They are safe here."

My son says he will never let the family tie break again. "I missed you, Mom," he said.

I wanted to ask, "Why didn't you call months ago?" I wanted to ask, but I didn't.

Life's too short.

Mom, after Vowing Better Life for Child, Sees Her Move to Simpler Life

A Daughter Rejects the Corporate Life but Finds It Anyway

Tuesday, July 9, 1996

Joanne is my baby. The youngest of my three children. The "fixer" in the family.

When the Irish gene kicks in and her brothers and I view life in thundering bathos, Joanne turns into a mother superior who admonishes us to get on with it. This woman walks the walk and talks the talk of major management material. Paneled walnut desk. Original lithos on the wall. Hotshot car parked in a private space. Proud mother joining her for lunch at some expensive restaurant with heavy linen napery, limited but esoteric menu, excellent wines. The parent payoff for all those years of working momdom.

I went to work in that "olde" era when women were nurses or teachers—or stayed home. I had the same job as the men but got paid $10 less a week because that's the way it was. I vowed my daughter would have better chances.

Joanne earned her master's degree in business administration from the University of California, Irvine. She used years of experience to land an excellent management job in banking. Her future seemed secure. I relaxed.

Then, two months ago, she chucked it all for a quieter, slower lifestyle in Bend, Oregon. She and her husband, Steve, yearn for a nice house on a big lot, children playing in a safe backyard, a small town where everybody knows their names.

I'm no better than most mothers. I pointed out the pitfalls: no live theater. No South Coast Plaza. No relatives living nearby. She focused on the advantages: cheaper living. Cleaner air. A nearby airport with shuttle service to Portland, which has shuttle service to LAX. (Book early for holidays.)

I put all my guns together: you are wasting your talent and you will get bored. She said she would find some way to expand her mind.

Six weeks ago, she was hired by a major Oregon bank to open and manage his premier supermarket branch in Bend. She's trained in Las Vegas, filled in at a bank in Salem, monitored projects in Portland and now she's in Seattle.

I asked her how she likes Bend.

Who knows, she said. I haven't lived here yet. Instead, she's talking about ways the bank can improve its training program and how older workers can be better workers because older workers have corporate loyalty. Two weeks ago, she was at a branch opening. Executives stood around in clusters. No one was networking. Joanne walked from group to group, stuck out her hand and introduced herself. She told me she thinks there are opportunities for her.

So for a while the desk is Formica, not paneled wood. So the pictures on the walls are prints. So the teeny plane flying over the Cascades from Bend to Portland is an E-ticket ride.

Joanne will thrive. She will learn she can have it all. She just can't have it all at once.

Like mother, like daughter.

Monday, November 4, 1996

Travis Hanalei Haas is dumping blocks in the middle of the living room, creating a mountain of red, yellow, blue and white plastic shapes.

"Mine," he declares, topping the heap with more flotsam from his toy chest. His energy is boundless: walk to the toy box in his bedroom, rummage for a toy, return to the heap, proclaim ownership. Travis is showing off, of course. Spreading his wealth before me. And he is indeed a very wealthy boy. He's brilliant, beautiful and my only (so far) grandchild. But his wealth comes from his parents, who work separate hours to share his care.

Grandparents know real wealth is measured in love, honesty, good humor and that stuff we call values.

Travis and I are spending our first evening alone together. We've shared a Happy Meal and an orange candy stick. We've read books and walked around the yard. And his parents have been gone for only 90 minutes.

This visit to Maui is my time to really get to know the grandson I see only once a year. When he grins, I see flashes of my father in the twinkle in his eyes. When he tells me "No, no, no," he reminds me of his own father at age two.

How did I handle that? "Grandma forgets what she did 28 years ago," I tell Travis. He giggles and climbs on my lap, dragging Winnie the Pooh with him.

Back on the mainland, on my desk, sits a survey of California seniors, ages 65–69, commissioned by Cypress-based Secure Horizons, a Medicare HMO. I remember a statistic that startled me at the time. Do you know that four of five California seniors have grandchildren? Do you know that 80 percent approve of the way their grandchildren are being raised?

Of course, we might be just patting ourselves on the back. We did such a good job with our own kids, naturally they're great parents. No one has asked them in a poll to give us a parent-approval rating. Meanwhile, we struggle to live up to the grandparent expectations. There are moments such as diaper changing that we all share. I'm struggling to find the tabs on the paper diaper. They didn't have things like this when my children were little. Travis thinks I'm silly—until he stands up.

"My diapa," he says, perplexed as he waddles across the room. Travis is clearly troubled. He doesn't really settle down until his mother comes home and laughingly explains that I put the diaper on backward.

It isn't easy being a grandparent to your first grandchild. It's a lot like being a parent for the first time. There are concerns about limitations on love, about sharing responsibilities, about being supportive to young parents.

This grandparenting business is no stroll around the park. One generation must always learn from another. The street goes both directions, and we all are wealthier from the experience.

Nothing new about that, you say. That's right. But keep that in mind as politicians and pundits intone about the coming intergenerational warfare over public spending in the 21st century. Wars happen only if people let them. I'm too busy stuffing photos in my brag book to show up for battle.

LOVE AND CONCERN HELP MIKE COME TO GRIPS WITH CHANGES

Monday, February 10, 1997

Mike qualifies as a much-loved old coot. My uncle is 88, a bachelor living in his own small Florida house and cussedly stubborn in his old age.

Two weeks ago, Mike fell out of bed. And no, he couldn't get up. A congenital hip problem has crippled him. Worse, in the fall, Mike broke his dentures and misplaced his hearing aid. Friends found him a few hours later, and he was transferred to a hospital. Doctors diagnosed pneumonia. When a hospital social worker found out Mike was living alone, she freaked. You can't be alone, she told him. Where is your family when you need them?

Whoa, lady, don't be so quick to assign blame. Mike has a nephew and a niece in Florida checking him regularly and a sister and other nieces who routinely call. We've been telling him for more than a year that he needs to live where his meals are provided, where he won't be alone.

Mike just wants to be independent, a trait that's not uncommon among the old, says Pat Messinger, head of the Garden Grove Gerontology Training Institute. "If he's competent, he has the right to make his decisions and live his lifestyle. He can refuse help," she says.

I think Mike's "independence" is rooted in fear. He's heard nursing-home horror stories—maybe even seen a few. "I'm never going to a nursing home," he told me at Christmas. "I want to die in my own bed." None of us were surprised to hear that Mike fibbed when the hospital suggested he go to a nursing home after discharge. "Aw, I've got help at home," Mike said.

Two days after he got home, a visiting nurse found him sitting in a chair, unable to move. His freezer was full of food, but he had no teeth to eat it. The nurse called the local Adult Protective Services. After a tearful call from his sister in Cleveland and pleas from my cousins in Florida, Mike finally agreed to go to a nursing home—but just "for a few days."

Mike's stubbornness is common among elderly people. "We have a lot of clients like this," says Margaret Beck, head of Orange County's Adult Protective Services. Families might find there's little they can do to force an elderly person to move to assisted care. Sometimes, it helps to get some counseling for the older person, Beck says. To find resources in your community, start with the Area Agency on Aging or Adult Protective Services or call a hospital social worker for details on mental health services for older people.

My Florida cousin is pretty sure that he has persuaded Mike to move from the nursing home to an assisted-living facility nearby. All he had to do was promise to visit Mike every day. Meanwhile, Mike's in a nursing home, where—to his surprise—"the food is terrific!" (They must be serving him milkshakes.) He sounds stronger and more confident than he did a week ago. He hasn't given up; he's just come to grips with a reality, sweetened by the love and concern of his family.

Mike's an old coot. A lucky old coot. Our favorite old coot.

A Lifetime of Grudges in a Gunnysack

Monday, August 18, 1997

Social worker Gemma Heffernan calls them "gunnysackers"—crabby old people who make you so mad you want to, well, spit.

"Gunnysackers" have spent a lifetime bagging up slights and hurts that come spilling out in their elder years. "When they get older, they lose some of the social governors that younger people have," says Heffernan, who works with elders at Leisure World Laguna Hills. "Things come out of them unfiltered."

Yup. They came out unfiltered from the mouth of a real grouch I'll call "Hal." He told me last week, "I call 'em like I see 'em and that means all the G.D. words I need to use."

Hal, 93, is alone by choice. He divorced two wives. Never supported his children and doesn't care to see them. "All those reunions with people crying after not seeing each other for 50 years are for the birds. If you dump, you dump. That's it. Forget it." We can only hope the kids Hal dumped—five of them, he says—feel the same way about the father they never knew.

What goes around, apparently, comes around. It did for the world's most married man. Only one of the 19 or so children of Glynn "Scotty" Wolfe showed up to claim his body when he died in Riverside in July. Wolfe, 89, made 29 till-death-do-us-part vows and was alone when he died.

So was my Uncle Carl, the family crab, who died two weeks ago in Cleveland. Carl, 90, was so mean all his life that he drove away his wife and his son. He lived in the same house for 50 years, and during that time he never changed the carpeting. Draperies were rotting at the windows the last time I visited him. He told my husband to make sure he had his own shelf in the medicine chest because "women take everything away from you."

Carl sat in a worn easy chair, wearing a cardigan and heavy shirt in mid-August. Anyone who has ever been in Cleveland in August knows that hell isn't a firepit, it's August by Lake Erie. He was missing some teeth. His spine was bent. He thumbed through old photo albums—the kind where pictures have those little paper corners holding them in place—and told me how terrible his parents, my grandparents, were to him.

They made him go away to summer camp, for gosh sakes. He showed me the photos. "I hated it," he said, pulling the misery out of his gunnysack. They made him be an altar boy, go to college in town instead of away because it was the middle of the depression. His mother even made him eat tapioca pudding. Carl had a pretty full gunnysack.

But he showed his parents and everyone else. He lived his life exactly as he pleased. He never went to family gatherings. He never sent a Christmas card. He made everyone attend to him on his terms. Once, when my mother, his sister, was visiting from New York, he pulled aside the curtain and saw she was in the driveway, and he wouldn't answer the door. "I don't talk to people unless they come around between one and two," he later said.

Carl carried his bitterness to the grave. He made no effort to pay for his funeral or a gravesite. He wrote a will that disinherited his only grandchild.

Aunt Virginia wanted to have him cremated, dig a hole over their mother's grave, pour him in and plant a bush. In the end, the family did "the right thing" and gave him a little funeral. But it wasn't satisfying. They harbored vague feelings that Carl had somehow won. Until Virginia told them about her last conversation with him. "Don't ever reflect about the past," he told her. "You may have regrets."

Virginia looked her brother in the eye and said, "I think about the past a lot. It comforts me because I have no regrets."

What goes around eventually comes around. Amen.

Monday, November 17, 1997

They write books about grandmothers like me. Long-distance ones, who get to see their grandkids only every year or so.

I bought some of the books before Travis came from Hawaii to spend his first weekend with me. He's three. He wears a child's size 13 shoe. He'll be on some football team just as soon as he figures out the potty thing. Meanwhile, he's a typical preschooler. He asks, "Whazzat?" and "Why?" and won't eat his vegetables. That didn't worry me.

But I wondered if I am a typical grandmother because I really have trouble identifying with this kid. I've seen him only twice before. I'm not a caring grandmother, according to the people who make a living telling faraway grandparents how to connect. Their symphony for togetherness is conducted by aging Martha Stewart types who decorate birthday cakes to match kiddy party napkins while they tape-record individual messages for each grandchild and make up storybooks about cute kitties.

"Create memories by making holiday decorations," one writer says. "Periodically bake and send the child cookies or other treats," another says. And, best of all, "knit or crochet a family heirloom."

Alas, Travis, before you hit the California coast, I knew that all I could give you was a bucket of sidewalk chalk to spark your imagination, a passport to Disneyland and a promise to spend three whole days with you figuring out exactly who you are.

We rode an elephant and a train. We gave the dog a bath, even though she didn't want one. We went to a toy store to check out the merchandise. It was in the toy store that I figured out the real Travis. You scrambled to the large play-with-me display of wooden trains and tracks. But you were a gentleman. You dragged over a chair for me. A very small chair.

"You sit there," you commanded.

"If Grandma sits there, Grandma will never get up," I countered.

"You sit there," you said, turning back to spend several industrious minutes linking railroad cars together.

It was when you left the train you were building to pick up another car that I experienced a seminal moment. Another little boy came over and choo-chooed off with the cars you had linked together. "Stop!" you shouted. "Mine!" Your lower lip came out and your fist came up.

Ah, echoes of your daddy. I wiggled and woggled to get out of that wee chair and save the life of the unsuspecting lad clickety-clacking your train down the track. It all came back: the pleasures of the playground and the sandbox, weekend trips to the zoo, picnics at the park. And the many little boys who escaped near-death experiences when your daddy and your uncle yelled, "Mine!"

That's when I realized both my boys grew up to be big, strong men who know which fork to use at the dinner table and who open car doors for women. They grew up respectable despite my bumble-fingers at creating holiday decorations and knitting family heirlooms. I'm proud of them. I'm lucky to have a Travis now and more grand-children on the way.

Parents are different. So grandparents end up being different, too. So come back soon, Travis. We probably won't make a quilt out of snippets of your old shirts, but we can go to the mall and ride the escalators.

Experts in Eldercare Can Ease Burden

Because he was a product of the depression, he ate the cheapest TV dinners. Their high sodium content intensified his congestive heart failure. His legs and abdomen filled with 35 pounds of fluid.

He never looked into home health care or equipment that his supplemental insurance or Medicare might cover. Instead, he piled eight cushions on his Barcalounger so he was propped high enough to stand up. He became incontinent, but he didn't want to change his Depends very often because they cost money. So he developed bedsores.

He is my bachelor uncle, Mike, almost 90 and, until a week ago, living alone in his two-bedroom house in Tampa, Florida. After six days in a local hospital, Mike is now in a nursing home where they hope—stressing the word hope—he will be able to move out of bed. If he can move, he will shift to assisted living, a cheaper level of care than the nursing home. He will never go home again.

"We hired people," my cousin Edy kept telling the nurses. "I don't want you to think we ignored him. We hired people, and he fired them."

For more than a year, the family has fretted about Mike, watching his decline, trying to ease his days. My cousin Kevin tried to move him to a care home he could visit. But Kevin lives almost three hours from Mike's house, and Mike refused to budge.

"I'll die here," he told me on the phone. He almost did. If we hadn't arrived for a little family reunion and found him in such a sorry state, he would be dead today. Instead of a family get-together, we spent our time cleaning out closets and drawers. When I left, nine bags of trash lined the curb. Bags stuffed with empty jewelry boxes, old letters, newspaper clippings, broken rosary beads. That's just a dent. There's an outside shed with old telephones, unworkable toasters, teakettles with holes in the bottom.

"Ya never know when someone's going to want something I have," Mike says. He's right. I found my father's high-school diploma and a fez from the Buffalo chapter of some Knights of Columbus fun group Dad once joined.

Mike loved to save. In the end, his penchant for saving could wipe out his small estate. His diet, his lifestyle did not keep him healthy. Instead of independent living in a retirement home, he may have to spend his last days in an expensive nursing home. My cousins were astonished to discover Medicare will pay for only a limited number of nursing-home days. They don't know how to explain to Mike that the cost of his care will force the sale of some assets. At least Mike had paperwork that lets a cousin act as his financial agent.

Talking elderly relatives into accepting needed care can be difficult, says Deborah Newquist of Senior Care Resources. She's a geriatric care manager, and many of her California clients are aging relatives of people who live outside the state. Care managers find solutions and implement care plans for the elderly. They also can monitor their care for relatives who live out of the area.

"There are different ways to get people to accept changes," Newquist says. "I often compare it to sailing. Sometimes, you have to tack up the channel."

With Mike, we need to find a way around his Irishness. "I'm not long for this world," he said to me as I left him in the hospital. "Tell them to play 'Danny Boy' as they wheel my coffin out of church." An hour later he was eagerly slurping down a chocolate milkshake.

What can you do to ease your burden in caring for an aging relative such as Mike? First, make sure the financial paperwork is in place. You might need the help of an elder-law attorney. For information on how to select an attorney, send a self-addressed stamped envelope to the National Academy of Elderlaw Attorneys, 1604 N. Country Club Road, Tucson, AZ 85716-3102.

Consider a geriatric care manager to help you through the decision process. For names of qualified people in your area, call the National Association of Geriatric Care Managers, (520) 881-8008.

A Different Way to Look at Race in U.S.

Monday, January 18, 1999

Ian Michael Francis Kai Nalu Haas is one year old this week. Family and friends who live on Maui will gather Saturday for a traditional one-year luau celebrating my grandson's healthy life. Next year, Ian officially joins millions of others redefining "race" in America.

In 2000, the U.S. Census will allow people to specify themselves as being of more than one race. In every other census, individuals have been forced to choose a race—and anyone not 100 percent "white" often was shoved into a minority category.

"We hope people will check the racial box that qualifies how they live daily," says Angela McDonald Thomas, a spokeswoman for the Census Bureau. I think, rather than how they live, she means how individuals perceive themselves.

Alas, the Census Bureau, so used to easy pigeonholes, still hasn't figured out how to talk about "mixed" people, and it's a long way from figuring out how to tally the "mixed" results. Meanwhile, advocates for multiethnic issues are split: should there be racial identities or simply a category multiethnic? For example, does a drop of American Indian blood qualify as part of your race? How little or how much?

Bottom line: in the 21st century, minorities will be the majority. Ian, for example, qualifies as white, Japanese and native Hawaiian—a hapa haole, or half white/foreigner. Once considered derogatory, today the term is a simple way of identifying persons of partial Asian or Pacific Islander ancestry.

"Hapa haoles are honored and treasured here. They are not treated the way mixed-race children are on the mainland," says Noel Kent, professor of ethnic studies at the University of Hawaii. "Hawaiians are the bridge to a larger culture. They have set the tone for interracial families and for acceptance of their children."

In Hawaii, more than 40 percent of the marriages are called "out-marriages"—from one ethnic group to another. Compare that to the mainland, where interracial couples account for 4 percent of U.S. marriages. But—and this is a big "but"—since 1960, the number of interracial couples has increased 10-fold, the Census Bureau reports.

Are we getting beyond the racial barrier just as we finally got beyond the ethnic barrier? When I was in high school, a friend's sister announced her engagement. She was the daughter of Irish immigrants. Her intended was Polish. Her father refused to walk her down the aisle and, indeed, counseled with priests in a futile effort to stop the marriage. Worse, he did the old "picture turned toward the wall" bit and treated his daughter, and her children, as if they were unclean.

Ian's ancestors apparently were attracted by something more than fusty ethnic roots. In addition to the native Hawaiian and Japanese cultures he can own, my grandson's heritage includes Irish, German, Portuguese, English, Welsh. And those are just the ones we know about.

As he grows up, I suspect he will follow in the footsteps of his brother, Travis, four. Travis qualifies as a local, a Hawaiian by birth and common heritage. Ian has a darker complexion and brown hair. Travis is white and blond. Both boys have Asian eyes.

My hope is they will grow up to be like champion golfer Tiger Woods. "Yes, I am the product of two great cultures," Woods said. "On my father's side, I am African-American; on my mother's side, I am Thai . . . . I feel very fortunate and equally proud. . . . Ethnic background . . . should not make a difference. . . .

"The bottom line is that I am an American."

Monday, May 24, 1999

Last week I found out what it means to be a "good" grandmother. Being a "good" grandmother means being willing to wait in line at an amusement park.

I spent eight hours being "good" to my grandchildren who were visiting from Hawaii and simply had to go to Disneyland. And I had to ask myself why those eight hours stretched longer, were more irritating, weighed heavier on my feet than they did 20 years ago when I took my own kids to the Happiest Place on Earth.

The short answer is that 20 years have passed and I have a touch of arthritis in my knee. The long answer is that people are less pleasant today, probably because they are spending a fortune to wait in line for more than an hour to experience less than five minutes of thrills.

I leave the commentary on why people are willing to wait for an hour to see mechanical pirates in the Caribbean to sociologists. Instead, let me reach out to all of you who will be entertaining grandchildren this summer with a few tips on surviving the horrors of these theme parks or amusement parks or other overcrowded, overstimulating, overpriced kiddy-oriented money holes.

For openers, remember, this day is not designed as a relaxing experience. Expect at least one hysterical kid to demand a corn dog for lunch when the corn dog stand is at the opposite end of the park. Draw up a battle plan. If a map of the park comes with your ticket, circle the loos. You will be ready to board the "Small World" boat when your grandchild announces the need to go potty.

Sneak snacks. Tuck them in your pockets or purses. Weave them into your wigs, whatever it takes to avoid paying movie prices for a small tub of popcorn. At Disneyland, that tub—a souvenir tub, of course—costs $2.75.

Carry a cell phone. I had to walk a quarter of a mile to find a phone, cleverly hidden in a building that looked like a mineshaft. There were two telephones and eight people waiting. Figure it out.

Start early in the day. Be first in line. Because we arrived at the park around 10 A.M., we caught the brunt of the crowd and it took us almost an hour to get inside. Don't count on businesses that cater to kids to cater to kids-in-waiting. For reasons known only to theme park designers, the waiting areas near thrill attractions that tiny tykes can't ride are deliberately uncomfortable. I waited for an hour outside the "Indiana Jones" experience, sitting on a sharp rock ledge that served as a seat and sympathizing with mothers who kept reining in youngsters climbing up the rock embankment. What were they thinking when they created this so-called rest spot?

Be prepared to spend. And spend some more.

Realize that when you leave, the grandchildren will tell you they did not have a good time because they did not get to ride such and such or eat this or that or buy whatever they wanted. Acknowledge those kids are tired. Admit you have reached an age where gut-wrenching roller coasters, even slow boats through Storybook Land, are a real bore.

Check out reality. The day after Disneyland, we spent eight hours at home. The grandchildren helped fill the bird feeders. They watered the plants and cleaned out the birdbath. They even pulled weeds.

"This is fun," said Travis, four. That afternoon, I taught him an old song: "The flowers that grow, the robins that sing, the sunbeams that shine, they're yours, they're mine . . . because the best things in life are free."

Recording Family Memories Helps Stem Loneliness of Aging

Monday, July 5, 1999

Aunt Virginia, my mother's younger sister, remembers my temper tantrum the day she got married.

I was five when someone snapped my picture going into the church, holding my mother's hand. My face is furious under my straw sailor hat, and I'm kicking out at the world, stabbing the step with a black patent Mary Jane shoe. "I don't remember why you were so mad," Virginia says. "But I do remember what a cute kid you were."

Virginia is the last living person who remembers my childhood. I've other aunts and uncles, but they just dropped into my life from time to time. Virginia was close—and now, at 83, she's slipping away.

She remembers Lassie, my first dog, but not where she parked her car at the supermarket or when she last bought groceries or even that she's a widow. One of her sons stopped by at dinnertime and found her cooking for her dead husband and her younger son, long married and out of the house. "Well, they tell me I'm losing it from time to time," Virginia says into the telephone. "And I tell them I'm just fine. I won't let them put me in a home. I want to stay here." Virginia is fiercely independent. She lives alone. She mows her acre lot still. Almost every day she drives to the nearby strip mall to walk around the stores and see what's going on.

"I would rather die than turn into an old woman," she tells me. Fear coats her words. I remind her she is so lucky to have sons who care for her. She should be proud of herself for raising them so well, I say. I hang up the phone and hug myself, instead of my aunt so far away. She is afraid of losing independence; I am afraid of being alone with my memories.

My friend, Gerald Larue, says he has struggled to find ways to help elders cope with the aloneness that is an inevitable part of life. "There can be loneliness in this—a powerful sense of isolation and aloneness," says Larue, professor emeritus of religion and gerontology at the University of Southern California. At 83 himself, he's putting together notebooks of memories gleaned from his brothers and sisters.

"What I did was write my memories as far back as I could and then send them to my brothers and sisters," Larue says. "They added their memories of the same events. It is fascinating to see the different angles and visions. The result is a perspective I never would have had otherwise." Being alone with a splendid book of memories helps temper loneliness, he believes.

I suppose every family should take the time to record the memories of elders. I am sure most of us don't think about doing that until it is too late. I am certain too many of us are scattered far from family and personal history today.

Virginia's decline reminds me that soon I will be the oldest on both sides of the family. This is not a passage I am anxious to mark. I was pulling the coverlet of self-pity around me when my phone rang. The call was from my son in Hawaii to tell me they are expecting another baby.

"It's the circle of life," says Valerie, a colleague in the office.

Now that's a thought I'd like to share with my mother. If only I could call her up. At least Virginia and I can still talk about babies and summers at the family country house and my grandmother's elderberry jam. "I am not going to turn into an old woman," Virginia says firmly.

Thank goodness. She keeps me young.

Her Ex Reaps What He Sows with Children

Monday, October 18, 1999

In June, the Supreme Court will rule on whether grandparents have the right to see their grandchildren—even when parents object. The case, which could affect laws in every state, hinges on the rights of grandparents to see those youngsters even after a divorce or some other family split. I'm told millions of grandparents pray this ruling will be in their favor. They long to see these children, their living link to physical immortality. Most of us who are grandparents understand that yearning to share the budding life of our children's children.

Except for a few grandparents who choose to ignore their grandchildren. And yes, they do exist. I know. My ex-husband is one of them.

We have two grandsons, one five and the other 18 months. He has never held either boy. Never walked them down the street, cut up a banana for their breakfasts, spent a nickel on a candy treat. Change a diaper? Hey, he didn't do that for his own children.

Oh, yes, he says he did his duty. He sent each child a $50 savings bond when they were born.

His excuse for being so distant? Well, the family lives in Maui, which would mean a five-hour flight for him. And our son hasn't written him often; of course, he never wrote to our son after we separated. He reasoned he should not interfere with outside parenting as I struggled through my boys' teen years. Instead, he did his duty. He sent child support, and for that I am most grateful. Considering the number of single moms who don't get any monetary support, perhaps I shouldn't carp about my ex withholding emotional support from his children.

But like most mothers, I know my kids and I know how their father's attitude affected them. He could have been their friend. He could have influenced their life decisions. He could have guided them when they were drifting. The quick retort is, "That's his loss." As, indeed, it is. Now that our children are adults, they have little emotional room for their father.

I had occasion to talk to him the other day. I mentioned we were about to become grandparents again, that another baby is due to join the family in Maui. "I wouldn't know," he said angrily. "I never hear from them. They never send pictures."

Did you mention the grandchildren in your last Christmas letter? I asked. He checked with his wife and acknowledged her grandson was mentioned but not his. "So what's the big deal?" he said.

The big deal? Your son is proud of his family, I said. He wants to know you are proud, also.

I honestly wish my ex would visit our children and tell them he loves them. I hope someday he gets to meet our exceptional grandchildren. Meanwhile, I'm content with the reality of the letter our son sent to my husband, his stepfather, last Father's Day. He wrote that he had to become a father himself to understand the love and support his stepfather gave him.

"You've been more of a father to me than my own father," Tom wrote.

The letter made Bob cry. The one who should be weeping is my ex.

A Mended Family Rift Brings Joy

Five years ago my son Tom and I had not talked for three years. I don't remember what caused the curtain to fall between us. I'm not sure I would share the reason if I did remember. The point is, my oldest child walked away.

I blamed myself. I blamed him. I blamed my husband, Bob. I blamed my daughter-in-law, Judina. I tried to bury the blame and called a couple of times. No response. Then I blamed myself again. I went through denial and anger. I wallowed in grief. This is not the "happily ever after" ending I had in mind for my "once upon a time" family fairytale. This happens to other families, I reasoned. This does not happen in my family.

I was wrong. Disagreements with adult children—some creating chasms so deep they are never crossed—are common. In quiet conversations, parents admit this to each other. In public, they put on a Norman Rockwell family face. "My daughter is doing so well in her medical job in Las Vegas," a friend said at a recent dinner party. Privately, I know she hasn't talked to her daughter in months because the daughter is gay. Her mother cannot accept her orientation or her partner.

In my own extended family, there are whispers of ruptures between parents and children. Who can forget Uncle Carl, who drove away his son, Bob, with his strict demands? Carl didn't reconcile with Bob, even when his son was dying of lung cancer. When Carl died a couple of years ago, he disowned Bob's only child because, he said, she didn't visit often enough.

"Life's too short to shut doors," my Aunt Catherine counseled me when I finally heard from Tom. She reminded me she was angry at her daughter, Eade, years ago for marrying "a guy who didn't know the meaning of the word 'work.'" Oh, they had their "words," but Catherine paid Eade's gas bill and bought food when he walked out.

Tom broke his silence when his son, Travis Hannelei, was born. He called from Maui, where he lives. We took baby steps—an occasional call, finally a visit—to trust each other again. Without discussing it, we set up rules. The first one: no finger-pointing about the past. Instead, we talked about today and tomorrow. At first, we talked once a month. Now we talk two or three times a week, visit at least once a year.

In June, Bob and I travel to Maui again.

Ten years after Tom and Judina married, they are renewing their wedding vows. They will exchange promises in front of a kapuna, a Hawaiian priest. Travis will be there. So will my other "rainbow" grandsons, Ian Michael Francis, two, and newborn Collin Patrick Kauwaiki Pao'o.

Bob and I will stand there, too. Like Tom, Bob will wear his best Hawaiian shirt and a maile lei. Like Judina, I'll be in a muumuu, with a haku lei in my hair. After 20 years of our marriage, Bob and I will renew our vows. Tom and Judina invited us to join them, to share this special moment in their lives, to promise to always stay together.

Once upon a time, I dreamed about a fairytale future. Now I know everyone crosses speed bumps in life. Life isn't fair. The rain does not fall equally on each of us. Excuse me while I enjoy this moment of sunshine.

Part 12—Modern Motherhood

MEDICAL SCIENCE IS PROVING THERE ARE NO AGE LIMITS TO
BIOLOGICAL MOTHERHOOD. EMOTIONAL MOTHERHOOD? THERE'S NO
PILL TO STOP YOUR KIDS FROM BECOMING THEMSELVES. BE GRATEFUL
IF THE ONLY BODY PART THEY PIERCE IS AN EARLOBE.

Being a Grandma Is Great,
but Being a New Mom at 50 Isn't

Monday, February 24, 1997

The older I get, the more I like babies again.

That's because I can do the grandmother thing—cuddle and coo to them—and give them back. I had three children in four years and spent almost seven straight years diapering somebody. Seven years of cloth diapers. Some women thrive and some of us wither at the thought of repeating those days and nights and days and nights. As a witherer, I have special empathy for the four million grandmothers nationally who have taken on the task of raising their grandchildren. But they do it out of necessity.

A 50-year-old Lompoc mother of seven, grandmother of six, had fertility treatments and gave birth to four babies Thursday because she and her second husband, father of three, wanted a child of their own. How selfish! These parents were thinking only of themselves, not of the children or the cost to society. Is this why scientists researched fertility treatments? I don't think so.

Raising children is hard work, says Irene Koontz, founder of Hearts United Grandparents, an organization for grandparents raising their grandchildren. Keeping up with kids gets harder as you age. There are the bottles and the diapers and then some, Koontz says. And if you plan on a vacation, if you plan on retiring, forget it.

"Plus, we're not in our 20s and 30s anymore. We have less patience," she says. The doctor who did the fertility procedure is quoted as saying that he had no qualms about the parents' ages, although both will be drawing Social Security when the kids are in high school. Women are living longer and have better health, he says.

But it takes a lot more than health and patience to raise kids. It takes money. Lots of money. Grandparents know just how much money it takes. "Beaucoup bucks," Koontz says.

Why do I suspect that taxpayers are going to provide a few buckets of those beaucoup bucks? Well, for openers, the hospital expects the cost of caring for the premature quads to exceed $400,000. Delivery—with 20 doctors and nurses attending—is extra. That's got to exceed the weekly take-home of Daddy, an electrician. It probably will strain Mom's budget, too, although she just finished law school.

NEVER TOO OLD?

Becoming a Mother at 45? Fifty? Sixty-three? Older Moms Ask, "Why Not?"

Thursday, May 1, 1997

Jacquelyn Beauregard Dillman says the trade-offs an old mom makes are small change compared with the rewards. Sometimes a stranger compliments her on her "grandchildren." Big deal. Occasionally she gets a twinge of self-pity when she looks out the kitchen window and sees women power-walking, striding down Newport Beach streets toward a coffeehouse and a steaming cup of latte. Oh, well.

"I'm making school lunches, asking my sons if they are sure they have all their homework papers or if they remembered to bring their projects, and there are my peers out walking and having a good time," says Dillman, 57. "Do I miss joining them? Not enough to give up my children. I know my time will come."

Dillman is happily choosing to spend her 50s doing what most women finish in their 40s: rearing children. Relying on a boost from technology, more women in their 40s are seeking fertility help to conceive at ages when their mothers became grandmothers.

The National Center for Health Statistics says 66,195 children were born to women ages 40–44 in 1995, a year that saw 3.9 million births in the United States. Mothers ages 45–49 had 2,660 children. The federal bureau doesn't track births after that age, but it might have to up its age limit in the future.

"Since we started this practice in 1982, the median age for women coming to us for fertility help has risen from 32 to 37," says Dr. Lawrence Werlin, head of the Werlin-Zarutskie Fertility Center in Irvine. "That means half our mothers are a lot older than they used to be."

These women are proving that there may be no age limits to motherhood, as a Highland woman, 63, demonstrated when she gave birth to a healthy girl five months ago. "I wasn't trying to make history; I just wanted a baby," Arceli Keh told the British newspaper *The Express.* "Our age doesn't matter. We feel young at heart, and we love our child. Isn't that what counts?" Keh became the world's oldest woman to give birth, but only after in-vitro fertilization procedures at the University of Southern California.

"It may be said that women have not one, but two biological clocks—the clock for the eggs and ovaries seems to run out much earlier than the one for the uterus," said Dr. Richard Paulson, chief of the infertility division at the USC School of Medicine.

Fooling an old womb into thinking it is young again may let women test the biological limits of childbearing, but should they? If a mother is 80—or dead—by the time a child graduates from college, is that fair to the child? On the other hand, not so long ago, women died younger—often in childbirth—and their children continued to thrive. And why shouldn't older women become moms when men—actor Tony Randall, 77, is a current example—become fathers late in life?

But do older mothers have the wisdom, stamina and patience to deal with the perils of child rearing, from finger-painting in the living room to sleepless nights waiting for teenagers to come home? And why do women want to do this, anyway?

FILLING THE SECOND NEST

Most older mothers resort to technology to fool Mother Nature into late-life childbirth. They go to extraordinary expense and physical effort to have these babies, usually because they delayed marriage or children or are in a second marriage and want a child to complete the union. Often, the women are married to younger men.

In these ways, Dillman is typical: She is the mother of two sons, ages 14 and 12, born when she was 43 and 45. She is the stepmother of another boy, age 16. Her second husband, Robert O. Dillman, is seven years younger than she is. She has already raised three sons, ages 32, 31 and 28, from her first marriage. She has put full-time work on hold to concentrate on her family. But in another way, Dillman is an unusual older mother: she had her late-life children without using donor eggs.

Doctors say few women 45 or older have adequate eggs to conceive healthy children. Most older mothers give birth to babies conceived in a laboratory by uniting their husband's sperm with a younger woman's egg and then transplanting the embryo into their own uterus. Couples spend a minimum of $12,000 for each attempt at pregnancy using in vitro procedures. The 63-year-old woman had been trying for three years to get pregnant.

Actress Adrienne Barbeau and her husband, Billy Van Zandt, spent four years attempting to have their family. The actress, 51, gave birth to identical twins, William Dalton and Walker Steven, on March 17. The birth was important to her husband, age 39. Van Zandt can trace his roots to the 1600s in the Netherlands. "He was not open to adoption," Barbeau says. She already has a son, Cody, 13, but "Billy really wanted to have a child of his own."

Six weeks into late-life motherhood, Barbeau is euphoric. She believes she has more experience and wisdom than she did the first time she gave birth. But Barbeau cautions against others following in her baby steps. "Ours is a very unique case," she says. "We were with various infertility specialists. It was difficult and draining, emotionally and financially."

Her pregnancy had some problems, including severe edema in her legs. "And I have the kind of career that let me spend two or three days a week in the doctor's office when I had to," she says. "This is not for the person who works nine to five."

She'll be getting close to 70 when her twins graduate from high school, but Barbeau says chronological years are not her concern. She expects to see the children of these children. "I always anticipated living into my 80s," Barbeau says. "My mother is 77 and still works. My aunt, at 82, just quit. We are strong and long-lived."

Do Older Women Make Good Mothers?

Mother-fears tend to be different at age 40 than at age 20. The first fear is simply getting pregnant. "Often I see women in their late 40s married to a man 25 to 30 years old," says Dr. David Diaz, Anaheim fertility specialist. "These are usually women who put their career first. Or they are women who have had children but want to give their new husband the joy of being a father. Having a child together really matters."

Once the child arrives, the older mother faces a different set of dynamics. "I've met very good older mothers, but, unfortunately, many older mothers are extremely overprotective and anxious because they have only one child and that one late in life," says Alice Sterling Honig, emerita professor of child development at Syracuse University.

She counsels women considering late-life pregnancies to be sure they are willing to "give up the serenity that accompanies later years. Are you willing to have other kids playing around your house? A lot of people have no idea that a baby is a 25-hour job and that you'd better really want to love a child, whatever child-assorted genetics come out. A child is not a toy."

One of her clients, a medical doctor with a Ph.D., told Honig there were times when her crying late-life baby "left me so upset I wanted to throw him out the window of the 18th floor where we lived." But these feelings can overwhelm mothers at any age, Honig notes. "If a mother knows that her child can be supported, enters into this later-adulthood phase of motherhood with her eyes open, and can accept the fact that she will probably never live long enough to see her grandchildren, I don't see what's wrong with this," she says.

Children First, Careers Second

Some older mothers say that in their younger years, they were anxious to drop babies with caregivers to free themselves for careers. Late-life children changed their priorities. Ann Koff, 48, mother of a daughter, age 20, and twins—a boy and a girl—who are 3, and her second husband, Barry, 39, share the rigors of child raising, even to the

point of both working part time so that one is always with the youngsters in their Dana Point home.

Friends tell the couple the children should start nursery school, but
they are unwilling to push them into the world. "We made a conscious
decision to do this, and it's not as hard as you think to stop working
full time," says Koff, who works part time giving technical support to
customers of an Irvine software company. "I went to work when my
older daughter was five months old. I would never do that again."
Career came first when she was younger, Koff says. "I felt very alone
with my first daughter. I was 28, and the responsibility was overwhelming. I was anxious about everything." With experience comes
wisdom and a sense of relaxation, Koff says. "Oh, of course there are
moments—there are moments with all children—but so what?"

Young Older Mothers

A late-life child gave her a second bonus: "Being married to a
younger man keeps me young," Koff says. "I feel like I'm young."
Because Barry Koff is director of education at a Jewish school, many
of their friends are younger, she says.

Late motherhood also focused Mary Shearing on a younger
lifestyle. Shearing, 57, had twins in 1993, becoming the oldest woman
in Orange County to give birth. Her husband, Don, is 36. Like Ann
Koff, she spends time with a circle of friends younger than herself. She
quit her job to raise the children. "All of our contemporaries have
small children," says Shearing, who now lives in Redding. "It's almost
as if I've turned back the clock."

She has three adult children and two grandchildren, but her perspective on child rearing has changed. "It's a lot of responsibility. This
time, I look at these children as little human beings, as opposed to little kids who are annoying me and whom I want to shut up. I don't
think I did a very good job with my three older children."

With the twins, age 4 1/2 , she's gone through chicken pox and dirt-
laden wildflowers strewn across her clean kitchen floor. She grows
impatient with some of the day-to-day realities, but her real concern

is about the future. "I know they are going to be embarrassed by me. I try to teach them that it's okay to be the same but also okay to be different. I don't make any bones about my age."

WHEN MOMMY IS OLD

Amelia Warwick, 54, was emphatic about not having children when she remarried. Her husband had other ideas. "I talked about all the negatives," says the Los Angeles nurse and psychotherapist. "I had a mother with Alzheimer's. I was concerned my children would be embarrassed by having older parents. I was afraid I wouldn't be there for a child, physically and mentally," she says.

After considerable discussion, Warwick, physically unable to bear children, agreed to adoption. They worked with an adoption attorney, supporting their daughter's mother for more than a month and paying for her hospitalization. The child is now 2 1/2, and her biological mother has made a legal effort to get custody. Warwick is haunted by fear that she could lose her daughter.

Beyond that, she does believe that older mothers approach parenting differently. "I think we're a little bit renegades because we don't follow a truly traditional path," she says. "Almost every woman in my support group has said we would have liked to have been a mother younger. You do have more energy. You do have an opportunity to spend more years with the child. On the other hand, our children are very much wanted, and most of us have the resources for support, like in-home help."

Older mothers, she says, tend to bring more balance to child rearing. "The more affluent younger people get into a frenzied preschool search so their kids can get into top colleges. The youngsters are running around in poopy pants and the parents are talking about Harvard.

"The reality is, most of us do not need to go to Harvard to have a decent life, and because we are older, we know this." Nevertheless, Warwick is fearful that her daughter will suffer because of her mom's age—whether from teasing friends or from possible age-related physical ailments.

Other older mothers understand that fear. "In the beginning, I let the children think I was younger. I was young looking and active. Now they know, and they don't care," says Jacquelyn Dillman.

These are women who thrive on the joys children bring. "I know when I nursed my last baby, I thought, 'Oh, this is the last time.' That had a real element of sadness to it," Dillman says.

*Rifts Can Run Deep, but Healing Often
Comes with the Passage of Years*

Thursday, April 2, 1998

Carole Blalock remembers the dinner almost two decades ago. Her mother sat across from her in an Orange County restaurant. She listened as her firstborn daughter buried their relationship with harsh words. "You are the reason for all my problems," Blalock told Peggy Grant. "I will no longer be in contact with you."

The webs of personal history that bind mothers and adult daughters also can strangle relationships. Most eventually rebuild the bond. But some never again achieve closeness. Mothers often blame themselves. And daughters blame them, too. When Blalock's second marriage failed, she said it was her mother's fault.

For four years, Blalock kept her vow to avoid her mother. Grant honored her daughter's distance, not calling even when she was diagnosed with melanoma and underwent surgery that left a painful open wound in her back.

"Was it easy? Of course not," Peggy Grant says. "But you raise children for society, not for yourself. I let her go off on her own."

Blalock did keep in touch with her sisters, so Grant, 70, knew where she was and how she was doing. And how was she doing? "I lived a parent-free, guilt-free life," Blalock, 50, says today. "It was easier to blame my mother than myself." Mother was her scapegoat, she says, because "all the self-help books and psychoanalysts said mothers were the underlying problems."

When she married a man who came from a large family and was anxious to meet hers, she finally called her mother. She was ready to mend the rift. Like the prodigal son, she was welcomed. No mention was made of the separation. Her mother's open attitude helped Blalock deal with her own guilt.

"When we talk now about those lost years, she tells me that she has always held me with open hands. She did not try to possess me. I love her very much—my mother and my best friend," Blalock says.

Blalock was among a dozen women who sent letters when we asked readers to share stories about the rough spots in mother-daughter relationships. Although the rifts, in many cases, were long healed, the pain, blame and guilt seemed fresh. We asked a professional for insight on these mother-daughter eruptions.

BLAME MOTHER

What did your mother give you? Too much love? Not enough love? Complexes about your weight, your height, your clothes? Great self-esteem or none? An appreciation for family? A fear of relationships?

Adult daughters tend to blame their mothers if life goes awry, says Los Angeles psychotherapist Charney Herst. She wrote *For Mothers of Difficult Daughters* (Villard, 1998).

If Herst's book title seems slanted in favor of mothers, it's because, she says, mothers often accept blame when they should not. Or they get stuck wallowing in blame and guilt, never allowing themselves—or the mother-daughter relationship—to heal and grow. For 25 years, she's listened to mothers who sag into her sofa, complaining of problems with daughters and asking, "What did I do wrong? There's a school of psychologists that says if you don't like the way your mother is, or don't like something she does, abandon her," Herst says. "This is wrong. Mothers have rights, too." Herst tells the mothers, "You did not do anything wrong.

"I do not give them permission to carry guilt. If you were there for them when there was a problem, if they were not battered, abused and neglected, and they turned out different than you expected or even hoped, it's not because of you." Maybe it was genetics. Or outside influences.

SEPARATION ANXIETY

Why do rifts occur? Herst has a laundry list of trigger points: there's the daughter who resents her well-educated, post-feminist mother whose motto is "I don't bake cookies, I buy." Herst's answer is that there is no right or wrong here. Not all mothers are "cookie mommies."

There's the mother, a highly influential professional woman, depressed because her daughters didn't turn out as she fantasized they would. "Not one is doing what I had in mind," she told Herst. Herst's advice: mourn the loss of your dreams and then accept the children as they really are.

There's the daughter who was ashamed of the way her immigrant mother dressed. And the mother upset because her daughter refused to use sterling silver.

Herst works with mothers, helping them understand how their relationships with their own moms directly affect how they deal with their daughters. She encourages mothers to catalog not only their own strengths and weaknesses but also those of their daughters. Most mothers believe in the myth of the perfect mother, the perfect daughter. Television and film portray families in which female members are almost impossibly close, she says. And in the real world, friends embellish relationships to save face. The reality is that most mothers and daughters have difficulty as their relationship matures.

Mending the rift takes time. "Every time there is a major life turning point, usually there is a movement closer to the mother," Herst says. "All of a sudden, these peak experiences occur and reality sets in. The daughter is coping with her own children, for example, and she says, 'Mom, how did you ever do this?' "

Eventually, the daughter usually accepts Mom, Herst says. One of her favorite examples: the daughter who rejected placemats at the table simply because Mom used them. The years passed. One day, the mother came to visit and saw placemats on her daughter's table. They were a symbol she was accepted, at last.

A QUESTION OF CONTROL

"Fire and ice" is the way Deanna Smith, 38, describes her relationship with her mother. Almost two decades of fire and ice. They fought.

They argued. "I got so I dreaded getting together," says Smith's mother, Ann Clark.

What changed their relationship? The birth of Zachary and Bellamy, Smith's twins. "I needed my mother's help," Smith says. But once the baby years were past, prickly heat returned to their relationship. Clark, 58, a psychologist who specializes in employee relations, suggested therapy. "I said, 'Wait a minute, I'm not going to go on being treated this way.'"

The issue was control, Smith says. "It's really always about control."

What kind of control? "Not letting my daughter grow up," says Clark, who remembers the day she reminded Smith, then in her 30s, not to leave her soup spoon in the bowl. "I didn't give her credit for being a grown woman."

By meeting with a therapist, by agreeing between themselves to repair their rift, mother and daughter worked things out. Today, Clark has a room in her daughter's home. She drives up from La Jolla every weekend to be with the family. "Maturity lends perspective," Smith says. "As long as you maintain that slight thread of contact and don't cut each other off, you have a chance to work it out."

Says Clark, "Today, we recognize that each of us has rights."

MYTH AND REALITY

Over the years, Herst says, she has learned that the women she counsels have one thing in common: The daughters and mothers all had bought into the myth of the perfect mom. Somewhere, the myth goes, a perfect family lives in a clapboard house. The mom is always available, generous, supportive, unconditionally accepting. She has no problems of her own. She never gets angry, doesn't complain. She puts her children first. She's always strong. Daughters and mothers alike subscribe to this myth, Herst says.

"What about fathers? All these kids have fathers and siblings, and sometimes war and poverty. But it's Mother that the daughters blame," Herst says. In response, she offers her "Mother's Bill of Rights," which includes the right to be treated with respect, to say no, to reminisce and be sentimental, to buy nice things and to go places and have opinions. Herst tells the mothers to insist "I have the responsibility to respect each of my children and to grant them the same rights I expect for myself."

UNHAPPY ENDING

"You can't fix your daughter's problems or make her happy," Herst writes in her book, "and you can't live your life through her. No matter what your relationship with your daughter is like, you are not just a mother, you're a person."

Ellen Cook knows this. She also knows there is not always time to heal broken relationships. Cook's daughter, Laura, had teenage ups and downs but seemed to be getting her life together until she was in an automobile accident. The crash left her in constant pain and addicted to pain medication, Cook says. "Laura became someone I did not know, getting drugs from whomever she could," her mother says. "I had never known anyone who lived on the streets and did not know how to deal with this problem. I finally tried 'tough love.'" The last time she saw Laura alive was June 12, 1992.

"We had unkind words with each other about her lifestyle, and we parted that day with bad feelings," Cook says. The next day, she was told her daughter had died. The cause was not determined, she says. "I no longer have anyone to call me 'Mama,' no longer have my daughter to laugh with. . . . I beg any mother and daughter who are estranged to read this story and reconcile as soon as possible," she wrote to the *Register.*

Despite her pain, Cook finds comfort in the one good thing that came out of her daughter's death: Laura's House, a shelter for battered and abused women and their children. It was Cook's compelling letter to a committee studying domestic violence issues that helped raise awareness—and funds—for the shelter, says Sandy Condello, director and co-founder.

Not all relationships heal, Herst says. When that is the case, she urges mothers to reach out with volunteer work—as Cook has done. Most mothers can hope rifts will heal, she says. Meanwhile,

> Instead of nursing your old grievances against your daughter, imagine that you are placing them all in a metal lock box like the ones in the bank vault. Then imagine that you are taking the box, boarding a rowboat and rowing to the middle of the nearest lake. Dump the box in the lake and visualize it sinking to the bottom. . . .

> When you finally meet with your daughter, you'll probably discuss the past. . . . The conversation will be a lot more productive if your anger over her injustices has cooled.

Monday, September 13, 1999

Sue and I were halfway through our platter of sushi and sashimi—yes, we use low-sodium soy sauce—when the topic of kids came up. One reason we get together is to dish about our kids, alternately complaining, kvetching and bragging.

"They never fulfill the vision you have for them," Sue said, plucking a piece of raw tuna. "I mean, you have this ideal in your mind and, damn it, they grow up to be themselves. And then they expect us to accept them the way they are!" Sue says all this with a wink and a nod, of course. She's an eternal mother. She'd mother a mother hen. Her only disappointment is that only one of her two children has given her a grandchild.

But she makes a point. Children do grow up to leave home and be themselves. The wise parent raises them to do just that—even if, once in a while, we moan a bit about their choices.

Which reminds me of a wedding we recently attended, arranged by the bride's mother, who admires lovely things and has chests of heirlooms to pass to her two daughters. But neither of them wants any.

One daughter married before a justice of the peace in a simple ceremony attended only by family. The second daughter—after living eight years with her "friend"—announced they were going to have children. She was persuaded to have a full-blown wedding where she wore a white gown, exchanged vows under a flower-bedecked gazebo, even registered for wedding gifts, although she and her husband live on 10 acres where they raise pigs, horses and cows. No room for china teacups in their lifestyle.

Neither daughter in this family fulfilled her mom's fantasies. The heirlooms are packed away, but there's always the potential a grandchild will want to treasure Grandma's treasures.

Who can predict what children will grow up to do? Margie Kleinerman of Buena Park has three children, one of them gay. She also has two grandsons, both of them adopted by her gay son and his partner.

"Isn't that ironic that he's the only one who made me a grandparent?" Margie muses. Admittedly, she faced personal issues with her son's homosexuality. "I wondered what other people would say, I'll admit that," she says. "Then I realized there's a lot of—there is no other word but 'garbage'—out there. Misinformation. My son grew up in a loving home, had a close relationship with his father. He is not a stereotype.

"But even we had to unlearn the misinformation because, even though we were very liberal, when it's your own child, your response is different."

Margie is an activist now in Parents, Family and Friends of Lesbians and Gays. "Let me tell you," she says, "my son and his partner live like everyone else. They get up and they go to work; they come home and watch TV. And they have saved two wonderful little boys from a life bouncing around in the system. I love them all."

Family is what counts, all these women acknowledge. Life's too short to sit around crabbing about what your children don't do. Like them or not, they are always your children. And you have to love them for that.

Part 13—Boomers in Prime Time?

BLESS THE BOOMERS. AS THEY EDGE OVER 50, THEIR VALUES ARE CHANGING. "WHEN WILL YOU BE OLD?" POLLSTERS ASK THEM. "AT 79" IS THE FAVORITE REPLY. AND BY THE TIME THEY GET THERE, "OLD AGE" WILL NO LONGER EXIST IN A CLONED, RECONSTRUCTED, REPLACED AND REPAIRED WONDERLAND OF MEDICAL ADVANCEMENTS.

BOOMERS JUST CAN'T STOP TALKING ABOUT THEIR G-G-G-GENERATION

Monday, June 17, 1996

Everyone's asking boomers what they think about as they reach 50. What they say they think about is themselves. Constantly.

Who's surprised? Del Webb Corp., builder of retirement communities, commissioned a poll that paints a "boomer profile." I'm not sure you want to look.

Pollsters found that most boomers rank financial security as their greatest priority. Not world peace. Or God. "Moral decay in society" gets mentioned in passing. But not wearing a necktie is a big boomer concern. That's the generational summation by *Life* magazine in its current issue on the 50 most influential boomers. Who wins? Steven Spielberg, the "mythmaker" who lives every boomer's secret dream: "He never has to wear a tie."

To be sure, *Life* editors take the generation to task. Gently. After heaps of nostalgia and self-congratulations on the first television generation comes a dollop of remorse: they waited too long to have children. And when they finally got around to procreating, they were, "as parents always are, found wanting. Our high divorce rate, our drug excesses, our preoccupation with material goods . . . we had all the fun, they got the hangover: the busted families, the shopping malls, the AIDS virus," writes *Life* editor Robert Friedman.

In an editor's note, Friedman writes that no one over 50 had any input in the issue that touts the boomers as the first generation that had to "duck and cover" in school atomic bomb drills; the first whose dreams were shattered by the Kennedy and King assassinations; the generation defined by Vietnam.

I don't think so.

A few of us Roosevelt babies—folks born just before boomers came along—bobbed under our desks. And we were just stepping into adult life when those assassinations changed the nation. We also had a few guys who paid the price in a place called Korea. Of course, they did it before TV.

Friedman's conclusion that boomers—at 50—are "entering the land of our parents" is absurd. Boomers will never be their parents because they will never let themselves grow old. Del Webb pollsters found that boomers who once thought 50 old have changed their minds. Now 50 themselves, they mark 79 as the start of old age. Perhaps by the time boomers get there, old age will no longer exist. The American Academy of Anti-Aging Medicine, a Chicago-based outfit headed by Dr. Ronald Klatz (age 40), plans to give people physical immortality.

"Aging is not inevitable," Klatz told me on a tour promoting his book *Stopping the Clock* (Keats, 1996). A few growth hormones, a dash of estrogen, a dollop of melatonin and your body can live forever. "We should treat today's elders carefully, for they are like vintage autos," Klatz said. "Their likes won't be seen again."

Hasten, Jason, get the basin. Oops, plop, get the mop.

LOW RATE OF CHILDBEARING HAS CONSEQUENCES FOR THE BOOMERS

Monday, November 11, 1996

Boomers are playing *Jeopardy* with their future. You know *Jeopardy*—the program that gives you the answer and you win by asking the right question.

The answer is: children.

The question is: what did boomers forget to have on the way to the bank?

Who doesn't know that more than 76 million people were born in 1946–64? And who hasn't heard that this boomer generation won't have enough money to retire in style because it isn't saving? Well, scratch that sob story.

University of Southern California economics professor Richard Easterlin has charts and graphs that show boomers will reach their mid-60s with more lucre than their parents—barring a recession, of course. He said boomers make about 57 percent more than their parents at the same age—and that's in real dollars, factoring in inflation and cost of living.

Easterlin's boomers are rich in the bank and poor in relationships. Millions will count old-age coins all alone, with no one to share their lives. A typical married boomer couple has one fewer child than their parents and may grow old with few children to depend on for concern, support or care. At least 15 percent of boomer women will never have children, Easterlin said. "The reason why boomers have improved incomes is because they sacrificed family for economic gains," he told a seminar on boomers at the Andrus Institute at USC.

That's not the only reason millions will be alone. Women are working, and this causes strains in relationships, he says. While boomer women's income is 60 percent higher than their mothers', strains in the households are leading to divorce. Some 20 percent to 30 percent will enter retirement alone, compared with fewer than 20 percent of their parents left widowed and divorced at 65.

Boomers are in denial about their coming old age, said Fernando Torres-Gil, who just retired as President Clinton's assistant secretary for aging. At the same conference, he said that without children to care for them in their late years, boomers "will need to look to someone." That "someone," he predicts, will be government. "People say they don't want to be a burden on their families, but they don't say who is going to step in," Torres-Gil says. "It has to be government."

He expects boomer concerns about old age to reshape public policy in the next administration. Torres-Gil's predictions: a bipartisan committee to study ways to keep Medicare solvent and changes in Social Security, including a strong push to privatize parts of the program. Boomers will unite to get what they want, Torres-Gil said. He expects they want a high-quality old age with Social Security and Medicare. "We must seek new sources of revenue," he said.

The answer is: taxes.

The question is: where's the money coming from?

Basics No Longer Come Naturally

This is not a column about recycling broccoli rubber bands into jar openers. (Place the band on the lid and twist, says Beverly Kendall of Seattle, Washington, in *The Tightwad Gazette III*). Instead, it's an observation about how we were frugal once—and how some are learning to be frugal today. Frugal, I know. In my Midwestern nonworking mother years, I canned tomatoes, made grape jelly, froze applesauce and thought about living in a commune in Taos, New Mexico.

I did all that stuff—shopping at thrift stores and buying in bulk and mending (*yes!*) sheets—because we had three kids, one income, and it snowed 96 inches in Chicago, raising our heating bill and ruining the car tires. Now, experts who make their living telling other people how to spend their money say the aging of the boomers and the downsizing of America have created a similar harmonic convergence.

That is, although most families have two incomes, people are still pretty broke. Common-sense frugality is back. "We should have all learned this as kids," says Mary Hunt, 48, of Garden Grove, publisher of the "Cheapskate Monthly." Hunt spent 13 years paying off $100,000 in credit card debt, and that transformed her into a savings maven. She learned the hard way how to stick with common-sense stuff like not maxing the credit cards, not buying things she didn't need.

That's just the basics, says Amy Dacyczyn, 41. In *The Tightwad Gazette III* (Villard, 1997), she maintains the truly frugal person of the future will learn how to make braided rugs out of old clothes and return to the cheapo days of cloth diapers. Who pays attention to this stuff?

"Boomers, mostly," Dacyczyn says in a phone interview from her home in Leeds, Maine. "A lot of older people are already doing this. It's the boomers who tell me, 'You changed my life.'"

Presumably, that includes Christina Stone of Ann Arbor, Michigan, who wanted directions on washing diapers and asked specifically, "Do you rinse the messes in the toilet?" (Surely you josh, Christina?) Let's return to common sense. Specifically, to the well of common sense, those remarkable Beardstown Ladies from Beardstown, Illinois, 14 members of an investment club that stunned Wall Street with its success.

Stop and consider before you buy. Look before you leap. Listen to yourself before you open your pocketbook. That's the astute advice of Betty Sinnock, 64, one of the original Beardstown bunch. She's co-author of the new *Beardstown Ladies' Guide to Smart Spending for Big Savings* (Hyperion, 1997). In the book, the ladies even reveal when they slipped up. Sinnock still regrets the day she and her husband bought a three-year warranty on a tractor from a faraway Peoria dealer who left them high and bladeless during harvest. "Hopefully young people will learn from our experiences," Sinnock says.

People who crowd the Beardstown Ladies' appearances complain they weren't taught common sense. So let's start at the beginning, Christina. A penny saved is a penny earned. Yes, canning tomatoes is a messy job. And the stuff in the cloth diaper has one place to go.

For Boomers, Retirement Soon May Become Just a Fond Dream

Monday, May 19, 1997

Mel is a retired Irvine dentist who, at 74, says he would rather be working. He spends much of his time riding his horse and doing some volunteering. "Most of my friends who are retired really don't like it," he says. Mel, I know, speaks for a select few. And he voices an opinion that future generations will envy because retirement is about to become as obsolete as a 1980s IBM PC.

By 2020, age—and the boomers' fewer children—will overtake the retirement dreams of millions. Instead of four workers per retiree, the ratio today, there will be only two workers to make Social Security and Medicare tax payments. That's not all. Unless U.S. schools keep students ahead of the pack, a globalized economy will "even out" the wages of the world. In other words, the worker in China and the worker in Detroit will do similar jobs for similar wages. For most, the daily grind will never end.

"Working throughout a life span has to be a fundamental element in the nation's thinking—particularly for boomers," says Fernando Torres-Gil, UCLA professor. Torres-Gil sounded that warning as Clinton's assistant secretary of aging three years ago. Now, the Hudson Institute in Indianapolis nails that thesis to Wall Street's wall with a study of trends expected to shape the work force through 2020.

More years working, fewer benefits, a cutback in federal entitlement programs. "That's the future," says Bill Styring, 51, senior fellow at the institute and co-author of the study. In a century, the United States will have moved from a nation of people who didn't have "retirement" in their vocabulary, through the so-called golden years and back to square one. The average retirement age started creeping up in 1995, Styring says; it's now 63. "We're just on the wrong side of the roller coaster," he says. "Boomers will face the 'graybeard ceiling.'"

The focus of the Hudson Institute's study is the way this army of graybeards will change personnel policies. Will older workers have economic value? One important conclusion: a shrinking army of young employees will not benefit by adding unskilled workers from other countries. Increasing reliance on technology means employers will struggle to find workers with technologically up-to-date skills.

The good news, Styring says, is that boomers who can read, write, do math and think will be okay in this Future World of graying workers. On the other hand, workers young and old who lack these skills will create unemployment problems "as far as the eye can see."

The challenge for today's aging workers is to save, save, save, he says. And "it becomes even more important for the school systems to make our kids knowledgeable and adaptable in the future. The school systems must deliver because the barriers of space and distance that once protected our workers no longer exist in the high-tech age."

Monday, August 4, 1997

Years ago, a college history professor told me people destroy their own good life. He pointed to the Romans, who conquered their world, got rich and lazy, hired mercenaries to protect them and eventually lost the empire. He said plagues are nature's way of thinning urban populations. He waved his arms toward the West Coast and predicted environmental gloom from the westward migration. But from his cramped Jesse Hall office at the University of Missouri, Dr. Leroy Spitz—who was tenured—never envisioned that the culture would turn against older people and force them into years of low-pay servitude.

That sounds extreme. But 40 years after rejecting his pessimistic view of history, I'm reluctantly embracing it. The latest chunk of evidence: a California Court of Appeal has ruled that California employers can fire people not for age but for wage.

In other words, if a business can prove that it's cheaper to get rid of someone who's 40 or older and has hung around long enough to get the top pay scale plus benefits such as three or four weeks vacation, then the business can say, "Sayonara. Don't let the door hit your backside on the way out."

Show me a company that can't prove younger workers will reduce overhead.

Play this scenario out with me: you go to work, stick around long enough to know something and make some money, then you get dumped and you start again. Often at the bottom.

Boomers around 40 know they're going to have to work until age 70 to collect Social Security. That's a lot of years to survive repeated downsizing. Social Security is structured to pay benefits based to a large extent on your last five wage-earning years, which are usually your highest. What if your highest wage years come in midlife?

Ask Billy Blanton. At 54, he lost his computer engineering job in aerospace downsizing and ended up as a security guard. The Garden Grove professional is in the ranks of 35 percent of the older workers downsized in the last recession. They're working, sure. They're also working for about the same wages they earned at 20.

"This decision is very troubling because the clock is ticking for all of us," says James Guziak, attorney for the plaintiff in the case in which the state court made its ruling, involving an aerospace account-ant who got caught in corporate restructuring and was fired, although younger workers stayed. Guziak says the court's argument that busi-nesspeople rather than judges know what's best for their own businesses doesn't mean business knows what's best for people. "If companies could really be trusted to do what's right, we wouldn't need child-labor laws or a minimum wage."

Organized labor takes a similar view. "It's a big step backward for everyone," says Judith Barish, spokeswoman for the California Labor Federation in San Francisco. She says union workers are protected on seniority issues, but "this opens the door to further discrimination— although it also opens a door for union revival."

The societal trend is clear, says Edward Lawler, research professor of business organization at the Marshall School of Business at the University of Southern California. "Companies are constantly looking at workers in terms of skills, performance and cost. They are always looking for a better buy. The old norm of 'seniority counts and loyalty is rewarded' is out the window. Every worker is a free agent today."

Lawler acknowledges this is a macro-social change. Older workers are at high risk because their skills can get outdated in a constantly changing market. They're also at risk because they work under out-dated psychological rules that expect some sort of tenure for loyalty. "It's a different game," he says. "In the old game, the winners were people who stuck around, who had longevity. In the new game, the winners may end up changing jobs many times but do well because they know how to market their skills."

Blame the global economy or shiftless workers or UFOs. The message is clear: you can't count on anybody except yourself anymore.

I keep remembering the old tale about the little girl who said, "Me first, me first." When she and her friends were surrounded by lions, the friends indeed let her be first. And the lions ate her right up.

*Group Members Dominate a National Conference with Concerns
from Social Security to Prejudices about "Longevity"*

Sunday, March 29, 1998

The boomer generation—a wave of people who have changed U.S. culture through every decade of their existence—is starting to shake up the nation's attitude toward old age.

Next on the agenda: a political action committee to represent boomer interests. And while they're at it, how about throwing out that word "aging"? The 76 million boomers, who start turning 65 in 2011, dominated the weeklong American Society on Aging conference, which drew 3,000 professionals and ended Saturday.

The society usually focuses on the concerns of four generations of Americans, including those old enough to have fought in World War I and those edging close to retirement. This time, the emphasis shifted from social-service needs such as nursing homes and senior centers to conversations about saving Social Security, changes in Medicare, age discrimination in the workplace and myths about the boomer generation's future.

The nomenclature of advancing years already is changing under pressure from boomers who do not want to be labeled the way their parents were. "I prefer to call the years after 65 the time of longevity, not aging," said Jeanette C. Takamura, assistant secretary for aging in the Clinton administration. "Aging brings up negative images and stereotypes. Longevity is more appealing to younger people."

BOOMER LOBBY EMERGING

"What boomers need is a voice to speak for them," said Robert Blancato, a Washington-based lobbyist and executive director of the 1996 White House Conference on Aging. Blancato will launch The

Boomer Agenda—a PAC [political action committee] that will contribute to Congressional candidates who support boomer causes—on April 7, coinciding with the first White House–sponsored regional forum on Social Security, in Kansas City, Missouri.

Organizations that address issues of aging, such as the American Association of Retired Persons, do not focus on boomer issues, Blancato said. What are those issues? Social Security and Medicare, of course. But also maintaining or reducing inheritance taxes. "We'll poll the grass roots for causes," he said. And he pledged to have delegates representing boomer attitudes at the national White House Conference on Social Security, scheduled for December.

Dispelling Boomer Myths

A boomer lobby might find itself dealing with conflicting issues. So says Steven Devlin, acting director of the Boettner Center of Financial Gerontology at the University of Pennsylvania. Boomers don't have a clear definition of themselves and their needs.

Devlin defines three myths that make knee-jerk conclusions about the postwar generation risky. First is the size of the boomer group. "All 76 million will not retire at the same time," he said. The generation includes people born from 1946 through 1964. Rather than an age wave, Devlin says, it will be "an age ripple."

Then, too, various experts tend to ignore the group's diversity—including a large immigrant population, he said. "To be a member of the boomer generation means to be born between certain years, not necessarily to be born in America. Not all boomers watched *Leave It to Beaver* and *Ozzie and Harriet.*"

His biggest concern is the way financial experts define boomer wealth. Experts at the conference decried what they consider the boomers' tendency not to save enough money. Devlin insists that boomers are saving but that the savings primarily are invested in their homes. Boomers are living on their means, not within them, he said, buying expensive houses without considering that they'll be followed by a smaller generation—which means fewer potential buyers.

"Boomers expect their housing asset will grow at the same rate as their parents' housing asset, and they are wrong," he said.

THE NEW RETIREMENT

If boomers cannot count on wealth from their homes, if Social Security is doubtful, if less than 50 percent of the boomer work force can look forward to company pensions, how will they finance their longevity? By redefining retirement, the experts said. And that redefinition means continuing with some income-producing work, either in the same field or in new endeavors.

Older workers are in greater demand because the "baby bust" generation currently entering the work force is small. That leads Nancy Platt, associate director of training and work-life initiatives at Time Warner Inc. in New York, to conclude that a "new retirement paradigm" is evolving.

Harking back to the farm-based economy, before the Industrial Revolution, Platt invoked a "farm family" concept, in which children took over more and more of the chores as they matured and their parents aged. But the parents aged in place, on the farm, and continued working. This could be the workplace of the future, she said. "People have a tremendous need to feel productive at all ages, and that needs to be honored."

Her suggestion: instead of sudden retirement, people would gradually reduce their work hours as they age.

There's a difference between *needing* to feel productive and *having* to be productive, however. Joseph D. Winger, administrator of Work/Family Programs for General Motors in Royal Oak, Michigan, said projections indicate that 75 percent of boomers will need to augment their retirement income. General Motors and other major corporations, including Time Warner and CIGNA, offer various worker programs to promote health—and hence longevity and employability.

The technological revolution will let more people work longer because they will be sitting at computer keyboards instead of doing physical labor. That trend also could benefit the disabled, said Eileen Crimmins of the Andrus Gerontology Center at the University of Southern California.

WORKPLACE CHALLENGES

Sheldon Steinhauser threw cold water on the assumption that older boomers will find jobs. They might be able to work longer, but they will have to overcome a bias against older workers, said Steinhauser, a Denver-based business consultant. "There is still a pervasive culture of age bias in business. Boomers are feisty and aggressive and more demanding, but they will have a lot to overcome."

Older workers are consistently frozen out of the job market, he said. Often, they lose positions in late years because they have not been given retraining opportunities. "Business has turned the older workers into invisible people."

Steinhauser is hopeful that the major advocacy organizations for older people will form a coalition "and take on 50 to 100 of the major corporations, force them to examine their attitudes toward older workers and make them get rid of age bias. By improving the environment for older workers at these companies, it would sound a bell to get others to deal with this issue."

If that doesn't happen, Steinhauser expects aging boomers will join together in class-action lawsuits to demand workplace rights. "But lawsuits take time," he said.

A SHORTAGE OF SUPPORT

If they can't get jobs and have insufficient retirement savings, will boomers eventually turn to government to solve their problems? Boomers don't trust government, said Fernando Torres-Gil, former assistant secretary for aging in the Clinton administration. Because of that lack of trust, he expects Washington gridlock in dealing with Social Security reforms, at least in the near future. Congress doesn't have the will, and the boomers aren't pushing the issue.

Torres-Gil predicts a social or political crisis before significant changes are made in Social Security.

Who will the boomers turn to?

Fewer will turn to family, said Robert H. Binstock, professor of aging, health and society at Case Western Reserve University in Cleveland. The preboomer elderly could count on family support. At least 80 percent of long-term care, for example, was informal and at home. "But that will erode in the future because of the women in the labor force, high divorce rates and the number of boomers who did not marry. That has weakened family ties. In the decades ahead, this will show up in caregiving," Binstock said.

He envisions communities segregated by age and other market innovations that will help boomers afford long-term care.

In the end, as now, the burdens of aging will fall on the shoulders of women, said Carroll Estes, director of the Institute of Health and Aging in San Francisco. Women form the bulk of the aging population and traditionally live at least seven years longer than men.

Estes expects a strong grass-roots movement will develop if government fails to provide sufficient services for aging boomer women. The seeds for a social movement will galvanize a rising feminist majority, she said.

AARP? AARTH! SOMETIME AROUND A BOOMER'S 50TH BIRTHDAY, IT COMES LIKE A CALLING CARD FROM THE GRIM REAPER

Monday, June 15, 1998

The letter salutes you as "Dear Friend." Friend? What kind of a friend reminds you that you're 50 years old?

The American Association of Retired Persons, of course. Thinking about ducking that half-century celebration? The nation's major "voice for seniors" is determined to light your candles.

"Life is just beginning at age 50," writes Horace Deets, executive director, in his "Dear Friend" invitation to join. For just $8 a year ($20 for three years), you can get hotel and rental-car savings, health-insurance options, annuity and investment programs, the AARP pharmacy service, credit cards and a "voice in Washington."

That's what Deets writes. But the message most boomers read is, You are aging. Time to worry about Social Security, Medicare, arthritis pain and Alzheimer's because you are a *senior citizen.*

"Oh, no," says Wayne Brown, 48. "That's the last thing I want to be. I grew up in the era when 'senior citizen' was created. They were poor, labeled as people who were no longer productive. I don't consider myself ready in any way to enter that particular group. I can't imagine AARP has anything to provide me that I can't provide myself," the Tustin-based television executive says. That's exactly what Deets and AARP's 1,100 employees, unpaid board of directors and thousands of volunteers don't want to hear.

MIDLIFERS VERSUS SENIOR CITIZENS

With a boomer turning 50 every 7 1/2 seconds, America's most powerful lobbying organization—known as the "800-pound gorilla" in Washington—is struggling to find ways to serve two masters: its key constituency of people 65 or older and midlifers 50–64. At its recent biennial convention in Minneapolis, for example, presentations by

Deets and others focused on "selling" AARP's benefits to the midlife crowd. But the conventioneers were people older than 65, queuing up for tickets to see Debbie Reynolds kick up her heels or kicking the tires of GM cars prominently featured in the exhibit hall.

These aging retirees are AARP's core members. They buy AARP's supplemental Medicare insurance, auto policies for older drivers, drugs through the mail-order pharmacy. AARP lobbies for them on Capitol Hill to maintain Social Security and Medicare benefits.

Boomers, AARP is learning, are a different breed. They are self-reliant, don't necessarily trust government or institutions, do not fit into a single category, expect to work after age 65 and will fight the image that they are aging, according to an AARP-sponsored Roper Starch survey released at the convention. It should surprise no one, then, that boomers are not embracing AARP the way previous generations did. While the population older than 50 continues to grow, AARP membership—32 million—has declined slightly in the past five years.

AARP is signing up about 25 percent of the boomers when they turn 50, says Melinda Halpert, director of membership development. Many have seen their parents take advantage of what AARP offers. "My parents really used AARP's insurance and stuff like that," says Virginia Clemmons, 43, of Irvine. "I'd probably try it to see if there's anything there for me."

A characteristic of the younger seniors is a willingness to question, to shop around, and that could turn them away from AARP. "I tried it," says Lynne Lawrence, 53, of Irvine. "I asked for an auto insurance quote, and they came in $400 over my existing policy. Where's the discount?"

An internal memo, "AARP's Vision of the Future: Into the 21st Century," tracks a decline from a high of 22.7 million member households in 1992 to 20.2 million households in 1997. At the same time, the pool of people eligible for membership has increased from 66 million to 71 million. Bottom line: six years ago, AARP captured 52 percent of the market, and now it attracts 45 percent. But politicians can't ignore AARP, the "voice" of retirees in Washington. President Clinton invited the organization to co-host Social Security forums this year. The nation's loudest voice for aging issues is far from losing its timbre.

To AARP or Not to AARP

"AARP is a great political force, and I count on them taking care of the over-50 population issues because they have more time than I do to study the issues," says Jackie Brodsky, 55, of Orange, a nurse practitioner. Brodsky signed up for a three-year membership because she has a vested interest in a key AARP program: improving the rights of grandparents raising grandchildren. Brodsky is legal guardian of twin grandchildren, 3 1/2. AARP is a leading source of information for boomers and others needing caregiving, grandparenting and other social-issues information. But will this draw the younger seniors?

AARP says 26 percent of its members are ages 50–59, 17 percent are 60–64 and 57 percent are 65 or older. In some states, AARP has kiosks in shopping malls touting its services and information. In Orange County, "we have a booth at the fair to reach people locally," says Joe Drlik, 80, of Buena Park, volunteer regional coordinator for AARP/Vote. Drlik is chairman of monthly meetings with AARP volunteers interested in political issues.

While midlifers might shy away from attending most AARP events because they are held in senior centers—such as the "55 Alive" driver training courses—"They go after the insurances, the auto, life and health, and the Visa card," Drlik says. "The young people are after the Visa card." But again, the boomer tendency to shop around could work against AARP. The AARP Visa card, offered in conjunction with Bank One, has a five-month introductory interest rate of 4.9 percent and a monthly rate of 13.9 percent. Bank One also offers a Visa card not tied to AARP with a monthly interest rate of 9.9 percent.

"AARP has the wrong mentality," says Nona Bear Wegner, vice president of the Virginia-based Seniors Coalition, a conservative organization that competes with AARP and has 3 million members. "AARP is product-driven, and I think they should be focusing on the enhancement and rising esteem of aging."

What about the senior discounts? "I am never, ever going to flash an AARP card and ask for a discount," says Toni Bush, 47, owner of Clinical Skin Care in Orange. Bush works out two hours daily, often makes lunch out of whipped egg whites and is an avid movie fan. "I can't imagine asking for a senior ticket. I'd rather skip the show."

The truth is that AARP's touted discounts—with the possible exception of rental cars—are no better than discounts offered through an auto-club membership, says Dale Van Atta, author of *Trust Betrayed: Inside the AARP* (Regnery, 1998).

What AARP Says

John Rother, AARP's chief Washington lobbyist and head of the Younger Member Breakthrough Team planning for the 21st century, acknowledges AARP has to broaden its appeal. "Basically, we are trying to respond to the perception that 'AARP was a good organization for my parents, but . . . ,'" he says. That perception is known inside AARP as "the big shrug." To turn around the association, "we are trying to develop an equal range of products and services that are immediately relevant to people 50 to 64," Rother says. "They want things that are useful right now, not just material that is relevant only to people 65 and older."

What kind of products? "We are trying to see if we can twist the arm of the insurance industry to develop health-insurance products for people under 65," he says. He also talks about health-promotion and disease-prevention services and workplace and finance issues such as lobbying Congress for consumer protections for managed care. "This will not just be about hearing aids and nursing homes," Rother says. The rollout of new services will be gradual over the next few months, he says. And then he adds, "Actually, no other organization in the world can claim 25 percent of the 50 year olds as members, so we are starting from a strong base."

So-called versioning of the AARP magazine, *Modern Maturity,* already has started. Older members get a magazine geared for retirement, while younger members get one supposedly geared for those in the workplace. How do you know the difference? Check the table of contents, says *Modern Maturity* editor Henry Fenwick. At the top, either an "R" or a "W" appears. In the future, expect to get one of three versions: for preretirees, new retirees and older members, he says. What's different in the editions? Advertisements for arthritis drugs and hearing aids in the "retirement" issue show up as heart-healthy oatmeal and mutual-fund ads in the "working" version. Sometimes, an article is switched or the crossword puzzle is different, Fenwick says.

Tailoring the magazine is not the only way AARP tries to reach younger members. In Orange County, AARP expects the younger crowd to show up for specific programs, says Ed Wolfe, 78, of Newport Beach, AARP's volunteer media representative. He points to a daylong computer seminar Microsoft and AARP will offer at the Irvine Holiday Inn on Saturday. "Younger people can come in," Wolfe says. "Of course, the younger people are just not joiners. They aren't joining the VFW or the American Legion, either."

Gerontologist Ken Dychtwald, 48, who identified the boomer trend in his book *Age Wave*, contends that AARP is stodgy and doomed to a declining membership. Unlike their parents, who felt security in being part of a larger group, "boomers want networks, facilitation, to be part of the game," he says. "We don't view ourselves as poor underdogs. . . . We don't join big organizations to have a pater-nalistic leader speak for us. One size does not fit all.

"What AARP has to come to grips with is that its views and solu-tions are embarrassingly outdated."

In interviews, AARP leader Deets admits the organization's future depends on being relevant to boomers. "Size," he likes to say, "didn't save the dinosaurs."

AARP hired Roper Starch Worldwide Inc. to survey 2,001 people ages 33–52 about their attitudes. The results were released at AARP's biennial convention on June 2 in Minneapolis. Forty-two percent are concerned about growing old, a 7 percent increase in four years.

Thirty-nine percent say aging means poor health; 27 percent say it means losing mental faculties. Sixty-seven percent are saving money for retirement; 44 percent think they will have enough to retire. Eighty-four percent say they need more money than their parents did to retire. Seventy-nine percent expect to work during retirement, including 41 percent who will work mainly for interest and enjoyment.

Part 14—Sex—What Else Is There to Say?

History will call us the "V Generation," the first Viagra-fortified couples. Forget the alluring whiff of his aftershave. Pay no attention to her fancy scanties. This is the era of Performance Art in the Bedroom.

Monday, October 21, 1996

Do you guys ever stop thinking about sex?

Last week, I quoted Wendy Reid Crisp about the way retirement can redefine marriage. The point: togetherness sometimes falters in the so-called Golden Years.

"If you never really liked each other or have nothing to share, you have to basically reach agreements that a significant portion of your time will be spent doing separate things," says Crisp, spokeswoman for the National Association of Female Executives. Separate things could mean separate bedrooms. But don't get divorced. Move to another room.

Wow! Dave English e-mailed a complaint that I was trying to "end the mutual pleasure of sex." Other men wrote and phoned less-printable comments. Someone named Jim insisted the Bible says wives owe sex to their husbands at every age.

Fellas, fellas, fellas. Did I suggest hanging a "do not disturb" sign on that separate bedroom? Did Wendy Crisp? But there are reasons—even Ann Landers agrees—for separate beds or bedrooms. Snoring. Hot flashes. Insomnia. Health concerns.

Some experts say keep it burning. "I believe people have 'skin hunger,'" says Ellen Kreidman, author of *Light His Fire* and *Light Her Fire*. You can separate for sleeping, but, she insists, "Bodies should be touching at some point during the night."

Work on the connection: living with someone as only a roommate "erodes the soul," says Dr. Irene Goldenberg, professor with the Neuropsychiatric Institute at the University of California, Los Angeles. "As long as people are living together, they need to be trying to have an intimate relationship," she says.

Some space is okay: there's nothing wrong with wanting psychological space, even a room of your own to read or work in, says Myrna I. Lewis, co-author of *Love and Sex after 60* (Ballantine, 1993). But she likes couples sharing a bedroom. Still, Lewis is pragmatic. Separation could be a solution for some people, she says. "I can understand two people who don't want intimacy but don't want to leave each other," she says. "In fact, I think we'd be surprised if we ever fully understood relationships couples have. People don't admit to different behavior because they think it's not acceptable."

Well, I'll admit I sleep in a separate bedroom from my husband, Bob. His workday starts at 3 P.M. and brings him home about 1 A.M. My day starts at 5:15 A.M. and ends about 10 P.M. Our separate bedrooms are just for sleeping, if you know what I mean.

Granted, separate bedrooms are a step beyond the separate beds demanded by television censors in the 1950s. Not that separate beds kept Lucy and Ricky from producing Little Ricky.

Let's do an unscientific survey. Separate beds? Separate bedrooms? Togetherness at all costs?

Monday, February 9, 1998

Looking for a quickie? A fast way to put sizzle into a ho-hum marriage? Try this trick from Ellen Kreidman, known as the "Fairy Godmother of Relationships":

Grab your partner. Pucker. Merge and count. One thousand one. One thousand two. One thousand three. . . . Hold that kiss for 10 seconds. "And when your mate says, 'What has gotten into you?' " Kreidman advises, "say, 'I don't want to be just roommates anymore.' "

It won't take years. It won't take months or weeks or even days. In 24 hours, you and your mate can be the couple everyone envies, Kreidman says in her new book, *The 10 Second Kiss* (Renaissance Books, 1998). It's true even for couples in their 60s, 70s and 80s, because age is not bound by passion, she tells me.

Kreidman, 54, talks rapidly, with a sense of urgency about the "5-second compliment" and the "30-minute talk" and the "20-second hug." Once, she took a pyromaniac approach. Her earlier books, *Light His Fire* and *Light Her Fire*, sold a couple of million copies. Her audio and video programs, hawked on TV infomercials, have more than a million couples listening.

Why is she in a big hurry? "I am here to tell you to stop putting off for a future day the passion and relationship you want. That future day may never come. Be grateful you have lips for kissing, arms for holding, a body to make love." She calls it "the meaning of life—to love somebody and to receive love."

Kreidman, a Lake Forest resident, is married to her high-school sweetheart. In 1991, she was diagnosed with breast cancer. In 1995, the cancer returned. She had a bone-marrow transplant, a procedure that requires three weeks of total isolation.

"When you're hooked up to life support, when you have no hair, well, that's when you begin to know the meaning of life," she says.

Now she wants all married couples to share her passion for passion. At her seminars, she tells them to pretend they are madly in love with each other. To touch and talk and share like lovers. "Cause the feelings to come back," she says.

She tells couples to listen, to walk and talk, to share frustrations, dreams, hopes and emotions. "Go back to the beginning when you first fell in love. I believe opposites attract. Know why you really fell in love. Then compliment your mate."

She's realistic. "What you are really in love with is the way you feel about yourself when you're with another person." So do a better job of loving yourself.

Kreidman says when she was diagnosed with breast cancer, she realized, "No one knows if they will have tomorrow. Every day, we start out the day with 24 hours. Use that day to show your care and concern for another person."

Set your mind at "sizzle" and change your life.

VIAGRA AND THE MACHO MAN: A WOMAN'S VIEW

Monday, June 15, 1998

It took Viagra for many men to acknowledge what they really think of women. While many relationships undoubtedly benefit from the impotency drug, Viagra-fortified "randy roosters" are even less amusing than in the days before the blue pills.

Listen to Ann, a widow, 68: "I'm afraid to go on a date. There's a lot of pressure. I mean, at the end of dinner, a guy takes out the blue pill, looks at you and, you know, acts like a panting dog wagging his tail." This, Ann concludes, "is not love or affection." There was a comfort in growing older, she notes. Guys who "acted like hungry apes years ago with hands all over you" mellowed. "Now we're back to all that again," she says.

(Do I hear the guys saying, "There's love and then there's pleasure"?)

Prostitutes in Nevada's legal brothels claim men in their 70s and 80s are cashing Social Security checks, buying little blue pills and paying a visit. Suzette Gwin, manager of the Moonlight Bunny Ranch near Carson City, says Viagra is the "best thing (for business) since prostitution was legalized in 1970."

(Maybe they have wives who think Viagra is for the birds. Or whatever.)

Dr. Hal Shimazu, a family practitioner in Orange, says he spent days just writing Viagra prescriptions for guys over 60. "They didn't care what the drug cost," he told me. "And a lot of them said they were really doing this for their wives."

(Wives, do you believe that? Shimazu doesn't.)

John, a widower, 73, says Viagra makes sex four to five times better than his relationships before the pill. "It's absolutely amazing," he says. His girlfriend, he adds, is in her 50s. His sex life, John says, is "very very—probably the most—important thing to me."

(Try visualizing world peace, John.)

Viagra is doing more than altering relationships or bolstering macho attitudes. It's changing how we talk to each other. Jeremy Laurence, writing for the *London Independent,* says, "Critics say it has provided . . . the license to talk dirty in a culture that has become oversexualized, overdemanding and where millions have been made to feel that without the drug, they may be missing out."

Gentlemen, gentlemen, turn off your engines.

Romance novelist Barbara Cartland says, "If you read newspapers today . . . it is sex, sex, sex all the time, and it is not what we want." Women want tenderness, she says.

(Of course, Barbara is 94 and probably living on memories.)

Will Viagra prove it's a man's world, after all?

"Antibiotics changed our world," says Alan Savitz, psychiatrist with Secure Horizons, a Medicare HMO.

"Suddenly, we don't know what is normal for a man at age 70 or 80 anymore."

CHEMISTRY KEEPS THOSE OLD BEAUS FROM FADING AWAY

Monday, September 7, 1998

It was a "Set 'Em Up, Joe" kind of evening. Girl talk over the Merlot. An upscale hotel cocktail lounge. The topic: guys, of course.

Over in a corner of the room, a trio played old standards. At the bar, men and women were doing what they always do—trying to pick up each other. The only difference between this scene, this conversation, and similar evenings in my youth was the age of the crowd. Let's just say, only our hairdressers know for sure what we really look like today.

"There's another woman," I told Barbara. "I got an e-mail from her today. She asked me to join them for dinner next week. Can you imagine trying to sit down to dinner with him—and her!"

"Your husband?" Barbara hissed.

"Oh, heck no," I replied. "I'm talking about a guy I dated and dumped 20 years ago, between husbands. He's in another relationship."

"That hurts," Barbara nodded. She passed the Pepperidge Farm fish crackers. As I scooped a handful, the trio launched into "Moonglow."

"That was our song," Barbara said. "Sam's and mine. Before our divorce. And look, it doesn't even bother me anymore."

"How long has it been?" I asked.

"Twenty-five years," she said.

We nursed our drinks and wondered why we even talk about guys long gone—guys we don't care about at all, at all. The sun slid into the Pacific, the vocalist sang, "Maybe I'm right, and maybe I'm wrong . . . but nevertheless, I'm in love with you."

The next day I called therapist Pat Allen to ask why I care about this old beau. "I long ago stopped caring, so why do I care today what he does and with whom?"

"It's the 'my toy' attitude," said Allen, a marriage, family and children's counselor in Newport Beach. "It's the 'I don't care how old I am, I want my dolly.' We're all territorial. None of us wants to be replaced. That's an ego-breaker." Allen calls it the "Romeo and Juliet" reprise. "'If I can't have you, I die,' Romeo said. Only this guy didn't die."

So I want what I don't want to want me? Right. But divorced Barbara scores points from Allen for "desensitizing," so that old love song has no power over her anymore. "The only way to get over someone is to stick around until you're sick of them or stay away until your body forgets. We are more animals than you know," Allen said. A lot of people get "logically divorced" but not "animally divorced."

It takes a long time for lovers to forget each other's pheromones. Those are the chemical substances behavioral scientists say we secrete. My mother called it "chemistry." Allen agreed. "Chemistry is beyond comprehension. That's why we end up with jerks."

Of course, women have a more difficult time with fading pheromones than men. But you knew that, didn't you? "That's because women tend to remember physically and not mentally," Allen said. "Men are just the opposite. They remember mentally but forget physically, so they just replace us."

Should I be complimented he waited almost two decades to replace me? Or should I let sleeping pheromones lie? "If I were you," Barbara said, "I'd go meet them and knock him dead so he'll never be happy with old what's-her-name."

Ah, isn't this romantic?

Monday, November 16, 1998

Whoops!

There are single men and women around 50 out there who haven't had a date in six years or more. And, lo, they hear their age bell tolling the knell of romance in their lives. "I've been in Orange County for five years and have not met one *single,* fit, attractive, intelligent, employed 50-year-old man. Is there not one 50-year-old man with hair and teeth who is still able to see his own shoes?" asks Micki Lee of Newport Beach. She describes herself as hip and happening but won't expose herself to the dating-service mill. Still, "It's hard to live out the second half of your life alone," she writes.

Lee, 48, is looking for one good man. My friend, Paul, 50, of San Francisco, is looking for one good woman. "I did the coffeehouse thing, sitting there looking interested and interesting," he says. "I went to ballrooms that feature swing music. Finally I signed up for a dating service. I call a woman and ask, 'How was your day? I'm looking for someone to unwind with.' So far, I've found women who are very pleasant, but there's just no sizzle, nothing happening."

Well, "Our Time" is not a dating service. But who can be insensitive to the plight of aloneness—particularly when there are more boomers who are alone than any previous generation?

Talk about a generation that can't stomach the word "commitment." The U.S. Census says that 13.6 percent of the boomers never married. Compare that to 5.3 percent of those born in 1933–45 and 4.2 percent of those born in 1909–32. And not walking down the aisle is only half of it. A further 13.7 percent of the boomers are divorced, and 3.5 percent are separated.

"Why, oh, why?" thousands moan, along with Lyle Lovett, "By night's end it's night's abandon. You look across the floor, ain't anyone around."

Because they put themselves under house arrest, fantasize about the "perfect person" instead of pursuing reality, says Dr. Joy Browne, author of *The Nine Fantasies That Will Ruin Your Life (And the Eight Realities That Will Save You)* (Crown, 1998.) Browne, a nationally syndicated talk-show psychologist, can pin a relationship to the wall in seconds. "I've got three minutes," she said last week when I called to discuss Micki and Paul. She listened. She responded.

On Micki: "She's got an attitude. Before she leaves the house, she should take that chip off her shoulder. There are lots of 50-year-old men who are content to just date and have relationships. Find one of them instead of having such a narrow focus. Forget about age and looks. Look for a friend. Find someone to go to the movies with. So he has a little more girth. So he's not your one true love. So what?"

On Paul: "He can't find his soul mate in one telephone call? Piffle. He should get real. Get out there. Go out and meet people."

This is reality: "Life is not Noah's Ark. Everyone doesn't go through it two-by-two," Browne said. Lower your sights. Face the music. Put yourself in the line of fire. Take the time to let a relationship develop.

And stop humming that chestnut, "Some Enchanted Evening." Life is not a theatrical experience scored by Rodgers and Hammerstein.

ROMANCE IS ELUSIVE FOR MANY BOOMERS

Monday, November 30, 1998

Be honest, now. Is Iris Antin, 51, of San Juan Capistrano, asking too much from life? "I want a man with a certain awareness that matches mine . . . a man who eats and lives healthy, a man who takes care of himself financially . . . a man who has dealt with his issues in life. . . . I want a man who appreciates me for all I've been through and survived and wants a commitment. . . . *I have no more time for mistakes.*"

Or is Barry Segel, 47, of Laguna Niguel, off base when he writes, "What I encounter are selfish, whiny women who, in middle age, are chronologically adults but are emotionally children. I am sick and tired of meeting women who are drama queens with endless, never-to-be-resolved catastrophes . . . self-imposed hassles all caused by a failure to act responsibly. . . . I would never have guessed that middle-age women would have so many problems."

Antin and Segal are among the many singles stung by the glib way Dr. Joy Browne, psychologist with a national talk-radio program, dismissed the middle-age plight of loneliness in a recent "Our Time" column. To a large extent, Browne says, you make your own single bed. Get out and meet people; stop looking for perfection.

With more than 26 percent of the boomers nudging middle age either unmarried or divorced, simple answers are not providing simple solutions. They wrote, called and e-mailed to protest Browne's assumptions. Jon Walker, 43 and still dateless in Laguna, says getting out there is not all it's cracked up to be. Walker says he was the poster boy for Great Expectations dating service for three years, appearing on many local talk television and radio programs. He met 70 women. The ones he liked didn't like him and vice versa. There is a lack of understanding, compassion and forgiveness, he says. The North Carolina native dubs California women self-centered and untrusting.

And older women, Walker says, are more set in their ways. Walker says he is finding women 28–32 more open and eligible.

Antin wades in with a litany of her five-year effort, including spending $800 on a dating service, using personal ads, attending singles dances. She will not date older men, she says, because boomers have a problem with preboomers who tend to have backward attitudes about women. Why do older men get younger women? My feeling is, in most cases, it's security/money, Antin writes.

Segel says his own parents, married 52 years, should have divorced 35 years ago.

Maybe it is asking too much to find a life partner at any age. The only fella having a good time is Michael McMahon, who says he's 40-plus and has found joy in square-dancing, where there are usually five women to every man. McMahon says he has several dancing partners, all of them energetic high-steppers. You do have to get off your rear and want to find something that is lively and social, he writes.

Ah, where to go? What to do?

We understand the fear, especially at the end of a committed relationship. Suddenly, there is no one. What does one do? Ask Nancy Kirsch, senior vice president of the It's Just Lunch! dating service. We exist to put people in touch with people who fall into their own demographic groups, she says. Once you are out of college, you're out of the group pool. Her advice to singles: loosen up the laundry list. Realize everyone brings something to the table. Maybe he's a nice guy but not for you; well, who says every date should be a lifetime-commitment event? You might end up being friends, having someone to go to the movies or out to dinner with.

Kirsch quickly points out this singleness is not exclusively a California problem. It's Just Lunch! was founded seven years ago in Chicago and now has offices in 30 cities, including several in Southern California. The lunch-bunch charges $1,000 to sign up, guarantees 16 dates a year and boasts of 2,000 marriages among members.

You want a more relaxed approach? Bonnie Danielson, 54, of Anaheim Hills, checks out available guys in the produce sections of local supermarkets. A widow for two years, she says she's not going to singles bars, which she dubs meat markets where guys have white bands on their ring fingers because they took their wedding rings off at the door.

"I go to the grocery store on Sundays," she says. "I see the guys with the little baskets, not the carts, hanging around the produce section. You know, they've got a six-pack of beer, some frozen food and now they want something fresh." If she likes what she sees, Danielson follows them out of the market and copies their car license plates. She has a friend who's a private investigator and he checks them out, she says. "Then I call and say, 'I saw you in the grocery store,'" she says. She has had two dates using this approach. Danielson is looking for a guy who likes country-western music and wants to shop at swap meets. Meanwhile, she drives around Orange County in her cranberry Toyota pickup, the one with the license-plate frame that reads "The more I know men, the more I love my dog."

Sex after Menopause: Women Live by Their Own Assumptions

Monday, March 22, 1999

I have an aunt who couldn't wait for menopause. "That's when I can stop having sex," she always said.

Her attitude was either a comment on my uncle's lack of abilities—or his demands—or the result of some ingrained attitude that sex has only one purpose: children. Auntie is apparently not alone in her assumption that hot flashes signal an end to sexual desire. According to some gynecologists who study women's intimate habits, American women have widely believed that menopause spells the beginning of the end of sex.

The truth is a woman's libido can decline after menopause, says Dr. Jane Bening, a Newport Beach gynecologist. "Even with estrogen, some women need a little testosterone, they need a little extra help. Once they get going, everything can work again, but some are just placid and content to let sex pass." Pollsters say women may be demanding more, but Bening points out that their expectations may be limited by whether they have a partner.

A recent report says a majority of women 50–65 just told pollsters that their sexual desire is as robust as before menopause, and some say it's more so. The reasons, the women told pollsters, range from fewer child-rearing responsibilities to no worries about getting pregnant, a report says. Researcher Dr. Donnica L. Moore, a gynecologist in New Jersey who chairs an educational campaign that commissioned the survey, says it's the first study that really asked women their views about menopause and sex. "We want women to look forward to menopause," Moore says. "It's the beginning of the last third of their lives." A sexology expert and professor of psychology at California State University, Sacramento, says the effort women put into having an active sex life depends on where they are matewise in their 50s and 60s.

"A married woman or a woman in a relationship where there is psychological intimacy will say sex is important to her and will have great sex," Joanne Marrow says. "The end of worries about pregnancy really is a release." On the other hand, a woman who has to be dating to meet the man of her dreams late in life may decide it's not worth it, she says. "A lot of them feel the good ones are taken," Marrow says. Her book, *Changing Positions* (Adams Media, 1997), gives voice to women's attitudes toward sex and desire. Her Web site, www.jmarrow.com, includes a page for sex questions.

But we are the sexually liberated generation. Are we the first, then, looking forward to sexy 60s and sizzling 70s? I thought I'd better call another aunt, this one my mother's sister. Aunt Virginia, now 83, was widowed early in life and married again.

"We really liked doing it," she says.

I asked if she's slowed with age. "Well, maybe your desire lessens a bit," Aunt Virginia says. "But I can't remember that we slowed down that much." And then she adds: "My kids aren't going to read this, are they?

"Oh, heck, they should have as much fun as we did."

MIDLIFE CALLS FOR RENEGOTIATING RELATIONSHIPS

Monday, June 21, 1999

Apparently, middle-age wives who want to keep their husbands can do two things: stop using deodorant or drag him to marriage counseling.

Some scientists have promoted the theory that the reason older men are attracted to younger women is the pheromones the younger women emit, "odorless" scents that immediately promote changes in the physiology and behavior of potential opposite-sex mates. Think of dogs in heat. Need I say more?

And, yes, these same scientists have isolated the pheromones. Entrepreneurs who claim to use armpit perspiration from healthy people in their 20s are marketing pheromones as "nature's love secret." A few drops of "love secret" behind her ears could cheer up the middle-age woman I overheard at the gym. In a conversation with a sweet young thing in a leotard and tights, the older woman groaned, "I can't compete."

"Oh, I know what you mean," said the younger woman. "My dad is dating a girl, 28, at the same time my sister is dating a guy, 28. Isn't that a hoot!"

The older woman definitely was not laughing. What's funny about younger women scamming all the guys in our age bracket?

Increasing numbers of 20-year-plus marriages are hitting rocky forks in the road primarily because we all live longer. Eleven percent of all U.S. divorces take place in older marriages, and that number will increase dramatically as baby boomers enter midlife, relationship counselor Richard A. Osing says.

Midlife is a time when people yearn to express what they have suppressed, says Osing, a retired Episcopal priest and counselor living in Cedar Rapids, Iowa. His book *Love at Midlife* (Rudi Publishing, 1998), focuses on maintaining and building relationships. "There are two major arenas in life," Osing contends. "One arena is the achievement arena where a person, usually the husband, experiences a sense of fulfillment and meaning through work, for example. The second is a relationships and intimacy arena, where women usually excel."

Problems arise when men and women naturally "switch" arenas, usually when children are leaving home. Men start looking for relationships and go sniffing for pheromones. Women start going to college and upgrading achievement skills. "Older men, because they have achieved a certain level of success, are extremely attractive to women who are younger and turned off by men their own age who are struggling with financial problems," Osing says. "These women think, 'Wow, I've met this marvelous older man who is well off and son-of-a-gun, he wants intimacy.'" Osing, 66, wisely does not suggest older women achieve similar success in the relationships market. But they do achieve, particularly if they have advanced college degrees or small businesses. The rub comes when women achieve at the same time men want to stay home.

He does offer a solution: "It's important to start renegotiating your marriage. That has to start about the time the first child is launched from the family and should be completed by the time the last one is launched."

Dabbing each other with jugs of "nature's secret" probably can't hurt, either.

It's Never Too Late to Have Frank Talk about Good Sex

Monday, September 6, 1999

Let's talk about sex. Let's be frank. Let's admit we need it for all the reasons that fill the novels and how-to books, the confessionals and the corners of our mind that won't go quiet in the middle of the night. Yes, let's talk about sex. But for heaven's sake, let's be grown up about it.

AARP (the new name of the old gang we used to call the American Association of Retired Persons) makes an honest effort to portray grown-up sex in its latest issue of *Modern Maturity* magazine, appropriately headlined "Great Sex—What's Age Got to Do with It?" Granted, AARP's leap between the sheets is motivated by a need to woo baby boomers, turning 50 at a clip of one every 7 1/2 seconds and bringing to their wrinkled years a more open attitude toward bedding with or without wedding.

Whatever it takes, AARP scores, if you'll excuse the pun, with articles that truly put an adult perspective on "great sex." One is a special report on an AARP survey of sexual attitudes and behavior. Among the findings: about half of 45- through 59-year-olds have sex once a week, but among the 60- to 74-year-olds, the percentage drops to 30 percent for men and 24 percent for women. Most people who have partners are satisfied with their sex life. With advancing aging, a partner gap leaves more than half without a mate and, presumably, without "great sex."

So much for the data. What struck me is the comment of Dr. Stephen B. Levine, author of *Sexuality in Midlife*. Noting that drugs, disease and relationship problems can slow late-life libidos, he adds, "We used to treat older people as though sex was not possible, but now we've flip-flopped and transmitted the message that everyone is supposed to be having fantastic sex forever." Quality of sex after 50 depends more on relationships than it does for younger couples, he notes.

Which reminds me of a situation a friend of mine found herself in after a recent date. The gentleman brought her home, stood at the door and asked, "Wanna mess around?" Surprise! She had a headache.

More vital, in my view, than the resurgent data on who's doing it and how often and where is Helen Joyce Harris admitting her "Silent Craving for Body Contact," one of the articles in *Modern Maturity*. Harris, a widow at 50, lets us breathe her air of loneliness and shuddering reaction to her desperate longing for some sort of touch. "I'm ready to be peeled like a grape," she writes, "peeled back until there's no skin at all, just pulsing, urgent need."

Men might relate to Robert W. Stock's candid observations about his impotent moments. "Most of us," he writes, "have known that desperate, humiliating moment when our sexual machinery fails to operate—and some of us have known it more often than others."

Oh, yes, let's be honest about sex—about as honest as the late-60s receptionist in a Los Angeles law office was in a conversation with a young lawyer friend of mine. He complimented her on her hairdo one morning.

"Oh, does it still look good?" she said. "It usually gets messed up when I have sex. Nothing ruins a hairdo like great sex."

Part 15—No-Geezer, Over-50, Light-Verse Contests

OLD, SCHMOLD—PROCLAIM THE NAME AND HONOR THE PERSON.
AMONG THE BEST AT LONGEVITY VERSIN'.

Winners of the First No-Geezer, Over-50, Light-Verse Contest

Tuesday, September 8, 1998

Who knew that in hamlet and on hillock, from city to cyberspace, from sea to shining whatever, older Americans by the score yearn—nay, pine—to versify upon the impact of passing years?

What we need is a little "light verse" about the passage of time, I wrote in my "Our Time" column July 13. You know, a few funny lines in the style of Ogden Nash, famed light versifier in the 1940s and 1950s. That's what I said. What I got was mail from a dozen states with more than 1,000 poems from writers 50 and older, doggedly rhyming lines about sex, age, creaky joints, crepey skin, birthday candles and age spots.

As in

> Becuz I've aged
> I'm a golden oldie
> Wots got mottled skin
> And lots of foldy
> —Dale K. Goodman, Placentia, California

Or

> I'm old
> So's mold
> —Larry V. Luebbe, Cypress, California

You ask for doggerel and what do you get? What Webster defined as "trivial, poorly constructed verse usually of a burlesque or comic sort." In other words, doggerel.

This was the First International Longevity Light-Verse Contest. It had simple rules: be 50 or older, try to stay to four lines, don't use the word "geezer." The prize? A $25 gift certificate to Barnes & Noble bookstore. And in the end, we had so many poems we couldn't pick just one. So we have four first-prize winners:

Thoughts on Contemplating a Bronze Bust of Imhotep
(architect of the Step Pyramid near Memphis, Egypt, 2630
B.C.)

What old prince
Could be meana?
I got age spots
You got patina
        —Mary Edwards, Granada Hills, California

Elder Hostile

Though as I age, I can't expect
A flood of adulation,
I'd like a trickle of respect
From the next generation!
        —Doris O'Brien, Vandenberg Village, California

A Point of View

A lady who's an octogenarian
Said, "It's not that I'm yet antiquarian.
Though my birthday comes yearly
I don't love it dearly.
It simply is necessitarian.
        —Lucille Hutton, Dana Point, California

Longevity a la Ogden Nash

Life's a continuum
From birth to invaliduum.
        —Barbara Jean Hall, Encino, California

And a special salute to Vernon Haverstick, El Paso, Texas, who
cleverly avoided "geezer" in his entry:

Cantankerous Older Person

If you're old as Julius Caesar,
And you ought to use a tweezer,

On the hairs upon your beezer,
And you think a joke's a wheezer
And you're ready for the freezer,
Then you really are a Cantankerous Older Person.

But there are more! Hundreds and hundreds more. The oldest
entrant was a woman, 99, who wrote about flirting on the telephone
late at night. The youngest also was a woman, 49, who sent in her
poem despite being a year shy. And, of course, a few went over the
four-line limit, and then some. Here are some of our other favorites,
for which we

Proclaim the Name! Honor the Person! Among the Best
At Longevity Versin'!
   You've now gotten older,
   Just tally the votes.
   You now feel your corns,
   Far more than your oats.
         —David Orr, North Hills, California

Crinkley, wrinkley
Aging is stinkley!
         —Virginia B. Harchol, Irvine, California

My youthful skin was peaches and cream,
A virtual cosmetologist's dream.
Now crow's feet, prune lip, cow's throat, turkey neck and
chinny-chin hair:
Nightmare.
         —Helen Ward Gall, Wayne, New Jersey

She moved into the old folks home
He fell in love at sight
"Because," he said, "she's what I need
"She can drive a car at night!"
   —Nora G. Hecker, 89, Van Nuys, California

The question I'm asked:
"Do you still have sex?"
And I never mind to say,
"Being now as we're both seventy-two
"It's only once a day."
   —Eunice White, Rosamond, California

Old Age has waged a war with me
For nigh two decades now.
And though I know he'll win the war
I fight him anyhow.
I fight him in the hair salon
And in the dentist's chair.
I fight him with my pots and paints
And in the doctor's care.
I fight him on the treadmill
And with a hearing aid.
I fight him with the glasses
My new technician made.
And when at last he thinks he's won
And I can fight no more,
I'll smooth my hair, put on a smile,
And trip him at the door.
   —Charlene Garoutte, Santa Ana, California

Midnight, and I just can't slumber
Dialed the phone and got a wrong number,
A man who answered said, "Hello."
And I said, "May I talk to Joe?"

"There's no Joe here, but carry on,
"You're talking to a man named John.
"I like your voice and this is true
"It's pleasant just to talk to you."
"Now, John," said I, "that's very sweet."
And he suggested that we meet.
When I said, "John, how old are you?"
Our talk was over, that I knew.
"Last April I was twenty-three."
"Well, that's a bit too young for me.
"But sometime when I'm all alone
"I'll call you on the telephone."
   —Beatrice Segar, 99, Indianapolis, Indiana

"You haven't changed a bit," they said,
"You look just like you used to."
It must have been a scary sight
If I looked this way in youth, too!
   —Viola Vomhof, 88, Eau Claire, Wisconsin

I've grown old before my time
Can't do what I used to
At eighty-two
Now that I'm eighty-nine.
   —Rosemary Hetfield, Goleta, California

Aging brings two major troubles:
Time halves, gravity doubles.
   —Robert J. Eichenberg, Newport Beach,
    California

My old age is filled with excitement
Dull days I can't endure.
I'm off to the park rose garden
To watch them spread manure.
   —James D. Ochs, Santa Barbara, California

You know youth has deserted you, surely,
And your memory has flown out the door
As with purpose you climb up your stairway
To get—who knows what, and what for?
            —Dorothy Sutherland, Santa Ana, California

Generation X tends to perplex
They pierce their tongues, they pierce their pecs.
Now how in all humility,
Can we be accused of senility?
            —Beverly Gillespie, Garden Grove, California

And finally, who knew that more than 50 people would be compelled to rhyme "Niagara" and "Viagra?" Creatively. As in

For older women it's called Niagara.
June Allyson helps us cope.
For older men it's called Viagra
But who helps when the mate says "nope!"
            —Joan A. Wragg, Anaheim, California

Or that another 37 could not resist linking "adventure" and "denture?" As in

My old age is never dull;
In fact, it has great adventures.
Like trying to remember now and then,
Where the heck I left my dentures.
            —Ken Bonnell, Greenville, Michigan

Our Bodies in Their 50s
Women's cease their ovulations;
Men's begin their prostations.

LONG LIFE SHORT VERSE

*Here They Are—The Best of Our Second Annual International
Longevity Light-Verse Contest*

Monday, September 13, 1999

From hamlet and glen, from nook and cranny, more than 800 muse-struck—or is it muse-stricken?—poets bared their aging souls for our contest.

They wrote with passion, never mind the meter. They followed our rules prohibiting the word "geezer" or rhyming "Niagara" and "Viagra" and instead focused their creative might on flatulence, incontinence, creaky joints and achy bodies. The poems came from all over: Orange County. San Fernando Valley. Wisconsin. Texas. New Jersey. New York. Georgia. Illinois. Florida.

Some pouted:

Your roses are dead
Your violets are, too.
That's what getting old
Did for you!
—Thora Framsted, 81, Amery, Wisconsin

Others soared

My hair may be gray
My gait may be slower.
But now my grandson
Has to push that damned mower.
—Michael R. Taylor, 52, Corpus Christi, Texas

To all, our annual salute:
Proclaim the Name, Honor the Person, Among the Best At Longevity Versin'. And the winners are . . .

(After Kilmer's poem "Trees")

> I thought that I should never be
> So old that I would do tai chi
> In groups at dawn in public places
> With no expressions on our faces.
> This dance is done by fools like me
> In hopes of immortality.
>> —Victor and Virginia Dale, both 60-plus, Buena
>> Park, California

> Don't call me "senior citizen,"
> That dreary euphemism.
> I greet the image—and the term—
> With senior cynicism.
> Call me "older," say "mature."
> Perhaps it's egotism,
> But I won't answer to the call of "senior citiz-ism."
>> —Leone C. Anderson, 76, Stockton, Illinois

> As I face new horizons
> I've come to understand:
> My "used to be" was younger
> But my "gonna be" is grand.
>> —Anita Mari, 53, Burbank, California

> She was lovely and young, and one-third my age,
> So I naturally tried to romance her;
> But alas, I discovered, when push came to shove,
> I could not accept "yes" for an answer.
>> —Jim Woolf, 75, Fullerton, California

> Old Age Attitude Adjustment
> While looking for tweezers, my chin hair to pluck,
> I interpret my plight as a stroke of good luck,

For, though I am older, and no springtime chicken
I still FEEL pretty good ... and, at least I'm still kickin'.

My bounty of wisdom's quadrupled so far—
Although I've misplaced both my keys AND my car.
It now comes to mind youth is way overrated;
I'm old, but I'm stylin', and far from outdated.
I still can remember more than I forget—
I've got (fill in blank—be optimistic) more years
So I won't give up yet!
    —Ricki Mandeville, 53, Huntington Beach,
       California

Big Game
  In Africa they hunt the lion
  In Aussie-land, the dingo
  OUR danger and excite comes
  From senior citizens bingo!
    —Pamela Gilmore, 70, Burbank, California

Maturity's Prayer
  Dear Lord, as I grow older
  Please let me skip the phase
  That somehow makes me glorify
  The good-old-bad-old-daze.
    —Terri McDaniel, North Hollywood, California

Surfin' Years
  I'm past 88 and feelin' just great
  Though modest, I do get the raves
  I'm not for "pretentia," but my old age dementia
  Keeps me ridin' the crest of the waves!
    —Grace Mitchell, 88, Freeport, Illinois

Easy Does It
> "Light and easy" is my motto.
> Here today, gone to matto.
>> —Kathy Lomardo, 58, Oak Park, Illinois

No Fear
> Growing old has a few problems
> But you really have nothing to fear,
> Till your hearing aid goes in the Polident
> And your denture won't fit in your ear.
>> —Quinton Duke, 80, Woodland Hills, California

Good as Gold
> Oh how I love this being old,
> I'm happy beyond measure.
> Why? Because I've just been told
> That I'm the family treasure!
>> —Christine S. McMillan, 88, Eau Claire, Wisconsin

Lament for the Departed
> It's very strange, my husband said,
> You see, my love, I fear,
> The hair that once was on my head
> Is growing in my ear.
>> —Mary Edwards, Granada Hills, California

Bright Side
> Crepe-y neck?
> Wot the heck!
> Liver spots?
> Old age dots!
> Saggy tush?
> Much less cush!
> Walks a creep?
> Don't lose sleep!

Shrunk a bit?
Stand less, sit!
Can't recall?
Walk the mall!
Aging blues?
Lifetime dues!
  —Dale K. Goodman, Fullerton, California

Six vs. Fifty
"Snap, Crackle & Pop!" went my cereal.
At 6 I thought it was nifty.
"Snap, Crackle & Pop" go my bones
Since turning the age of 50!
  —Patricia Trudeau, 51, Corpus Christi, Texas

Migration
I knew I was getting older,
When my hair began to thin
I used to tweeze my eyebrows,
And now I tweeze my chin.
  —Betty Million, 66, Mission Viejo, California

A Good Man Is Not Confused
When I was young I was very fussy
About the man I chose.
Now it doesn't matter
As long as he is not confused.
  —Marion Smith, 87, Santa Ana, California

Positively 50
If you want to be remembered
As a person very nifty

Remember to be positive
When you hit the age of 50.
—Charlene Garoutte, Santa Ana, California

Big Bang
My ashes scattered on the sea
This formerly appealed to me.
Now: By rocket blast them skyward!
Big Bang Farewell is my new "die-word."
—Shirley Shaver, Huntington Beach, California

What Inheritance?
We're no longer chickens, turkeys or ducks,
Just a couple of old folks who've run out of bucks.
But heirs who expect we will leave fortune royal
Best keep their day jobs and continue to toil.
—Robert McNiel, 80, Santa Ana, California

Wishful Thinking
You're not old when your hair turns gray
And you're not old when you lose your way
But, brother, you're old and it's time to weep
When your mind makes a date that your body can't keep.
—Frank Kauzlaric, 78, North Hollywood,
California

Old Is Just a Word
All my little rainbows
Have turned to pots of gold
For I'm alive at 85
And still not growing old!
—Lois Stene, 83, Fullerton, California

It's a Verb (in response to rules that said no use of the word
"geezer")
 Here I am out in the sun,
 My elbows on my knees,
 With not a single thing to do
 But sit around and geez!
                —Dean A. Grennell, 75, Mission Viejo, California

Advice and Consent
 One of the rewards of age
 Is being taken for a sage.
 That's when your word of wise advice
 Is taken once, but never twice.
                —Wayne S. Cody, 70, Westminster, California

Part 16—And Other Stuff

AND FURTHERMORE . . .

Monday, May 20, 1996

Listen up, Yahoo, get outta my face.

On second thought, get back in. Give me a chance to fire back. Turkey. Toad. Tumescent tub of treacle. Truncated Tarzan-wannabe. Let me get off an invective or two.

"Two wrongs make a blight," says Miss Manners in her *Guide to Excruciatingly Correct Behavior.* But she never ran into you, you bilious blob of rancid butterfat. There I was, minding my business and sitting near the horse book at the Golden Nugget in Las Vegas. I was waiting for a friend and reading the morning paper.

"They taking bets on California tracks yet?" you asked me.

"I'm sorry, I don't know," I replied pleasantly.

"Don't know?" you yelled. "What the (bleep!). You're sitting here. What a dumb (bleep!) broad. All you (bleep!) broads are the same. (Bleep!) am I glad I'm not married."

Wow! I'm looking at you—a short man with gray hair and a belly bulging over your Sans-A-Belt polyesters—and I'm speechless. Worse, I couldn't respond if I wanted to. I was raised to believe ladies ignore rudeness. Of course, that attitude did the women working in the Mitsubishi plant in Normal, Illinois, a lot of good. That's the place where managers left explicit graffiti on the bathroom walls. Where the U.S. government has levied sexual harassment fines.

The thing is, Mr. Cheese Mold, ignoring your behavior does nothing to alter it. Nor does it relieve my frustration. If incivility is where it's at today, maybe I should go with the here's-a-finger flow. I'm not talking about funny stuff like the bumper sticker that reads "Your wheels are turning but the hamster died." I'm talking about provocative behavior. Nine out of 10 Americans think rudeness is a problem;

78 percent say the problem has gotten worse in the past 10 years; and more than 90 percent think it contributes to the nation's violence. That's according to a poll by U.S. News and Bozell Worldwide.

Most people just won't take it. Caroline Wilson, 27, the physical-therapy aide helping me get rid of a shoulder problem, says enough is already too much. She wouldn't tolerate you, ghastly geezer. "I would have said, 'Excuse me? Do you have a problem?' And then added a couple of comments."

Even Miss Manners agrees that the rudeness of others "arouses that bestial desire" to respond. She overcomes it. "If rudeness begets rudeness, which begets more rudeness, where will it all end?" she rightly asks.

But at a recent luncheon for "Possibility Thinkers" at the Crystal Cathedral, the Reverend Robert H. Schuller encouraged a take-charge attitude. His motivating slogan: "If it's going to be, it's up to me!"

So since it's up to me, I have a question, Boar Breath: did it hurt when your brains slid to your lower extremities?

FICTIONAL BRAND-NAME PEOPLE PERSONIFY
OUR EVERYDAY REALITY

Monday, June 3, 1996

The white-haired woman sitting across the aisle from me on the flight from St. Louis to Phoenix to Los Angeles struggled in vain with the plastic-wrapped snack pack served in lieu of a meal. "I can't rip it open," she said to me.

"A 900-pound gorilla couldn't rip it open," I assured her, pulling the hidden tab that opened the package.

Ah, what a treat awaited her! A low-fat cake bar to go with the peanuts just dispensed by the flight attendant.

"I've never had one of these," said the lady from Webster Groves, Missouri, opening the cake bar. "But Betty Crocker made it. She always bakes such good things, don't you think?" She bit into the bar. "I was right. Betty's done it again. She's the best."

So I'm asking myself if this woman really believes there is a Betty Crocker shoving sheets of cakes into ovens. I ask if she's read the stories about the '90s makeover for Betty, a 75-year-old trademark.

"Of course," she said. "Don't you wish you could stay young like her?"

Betty, Betty, Betty. It takes a staff of 60 to answer her letters, calls and e-mails. General Mills encourages the fiction, printing Betty's addresses and toll-free numbers on product packages, product spokesman Barry Wegener says.

Betty always has the answer. During World War II, she had tips for wives trying to extend rationed flour and sugar. In 1954, she shared flour-grinding suggestions with Mrs. Ernest Hemingway, who wrote from Kimana Swamp, Kenya, while on safari. The native women try to bake between lions and locusts and so on, she wrote, but they yearn for a flour light in texture, like Gold Medal.

Betty Crocker succeeds, says Frank Conaway, president of PrimeLife, an Orange-based ad agency, because, as a brand, her trademark is used on products that deliver value, service and convenience. Betty also reminds everyone of home.

Aunt Jemima—she's 107, by the way—encourages the same loyalty. "People view her as a person," says Quaker Oats spokesman Ron Bottrell. "They tell us they see her as a working mother, a churchwoman, whatever experiences mirror their own growing-up experiences."

Because that's what these brand-ladies are: mirrors of our lives. They offer a sense of stability—a nostalgic, sugarcoated view of the past. Sure, Betty probably has cooked up her batches of bombs. General Mills isn't talking about them. Agreed, Aunt Jemima went through a major makeover in the 1960s. But it worked. She's now the favored brand in the African-American community.

As Wallace Stevens wrote: "The final belief is to believe in a fiction, which you know to be a fiction, there being nothing else. The exquisite truth is to know that it is a fiction and that you believe in it willingly."

And if you want to message Betty for some recipe tips, you can reach her at Bettycrocker@cis.CompuServe.com. Tell her I said hello.

Monday, December 16, 1996

Lady Winifred, Duchess of Orange, has her nose out of joint—which is a singular feat for a Boston terrier, since their noses are squashed into their faces. Because God squashed their noses, their eyes pop. But that has nothing to do with this column. Winnie, as her intimates call her, resents not being a Dalmatian, this year's official cutest dog in America.

I've told her she's full of okay cuteness, but her kind are, regrettably, past their prime. Back in the 1920s and 1930s, Bostons were so popular they were turned into cast-iron doorstops. But that was then, and now the demand for Bostons is less than intense.

Actually, that's why Bostons make excellent pets and are valued visitors at nursing homes, says Linda Trader, head of the national Boston Terrier Club rescue effort. Bostons are not overbred, yappy or difficult to control. "Dog popularity goes in cycles. Poodles and cockers and, now, Dalmatians get popular, and the result is, they get overbred."

Trader knows her Boston business. She has 11 adult Bostons and routinely takes them to visit convalescent patients near her Pennsylvania home. "Lots of old people remember when they were the most popular breed," she says. "These dogs are so friendly. They love everybody."

Which is the point of this column. Dogs and love and sharing.

Lots of love is about the best Christmas present we can give the elderly at Christmas. And there's increasing evidence that pets contribute substantially to improving the quality of life for many. Some people like goldfish. Others favor birds. There are even cat lovers in the world. But the American Kennel Club says dogs are one of the best ways we can give and share love with the old.

Dean Leo Bustad of the College of Veterinary Medicine, Washington State University, said it at a Toronto meeting on Pets in

Society: "One of the big rewards of having loved dogs all your life is the fact that you will be spared a lonely old age as the result of your continuing affection."

Dogs are so important in California that the state has a law forbidding discrimination against elderly pet owners in government-subsidized housing. Increasingly, nursing homes have volunteers bring their dogs in to visit residents. Actually, sharing your dog's love with another person might be the best Christmas present you can give yourself this year. Winnie and I are sharing hers with relatives in Oregon, which prompted a trip to the pet store to buy a winter coat.

"Is this your little girl?" the clerk said as he fitted the sweater.

"No," I responded. "My little girl lives in Oregon. This is my little dog."

You can carry this dog-doration too far.

STEREOTYPES HAVE GROWN TOO OLD TO USE

—

Monday, April 14, 1997

"Nothing will change the world like who we are."

Marketing consultant Maddy Kent Dychtwald chants that boomer mantra with conviction. But while American business listens, it hasn't implemented many of the "mature marketing" techniques trumpeted by Dychtwald and others who study the 50-plus set. Oh, everyone knows the data: some boomer turns 50 every 7.5 seconds for the next 20 years. But what does that mean, to "turn" 50? Trade in the sports car for a sedate sedan? Give up briefs and buy Depends? Stop having sex, learn nothing new, tumble off the shelf of youth into the muck of *old age?*

Somebody please get a grip and drop the stereotypes! Even the Huntington Beach Chamber of Commerce, which brought Dychtwald to town to advise businesses, can't avoid clichés. The chamber titled her seminar "The Graying of America."

Boomers will not stereotype as they age, says Dychtwald, a partner in Age Wave in San Francisco. Indeed, they've spent years avoiding stereotyping of any kind. Savvy businesses will figure this out: the so-called youth culture of 18- to 34-year-olds is yesterday's market.

When people lived short lives, it made sense to market to youth, Dychtwald says. It made sense when people worried about dying young. It doesn't make sense when people are worried about outliving their financial resources. Today, people older than 65 outnumber teenagers. And those older people have more money than the kids, too.

Being 50 means different things to different people, depending on their health, goals and education, Dychtwald says. She talks about the 50-year-old who wants to retire and travel; the 50-year-old who quits a nine-to-five job to become an entrepreneur, the 50-year-old who gets remarried and starts a second family. Each represents a different "mature" market opportunity. And that disparate market frustrates businesses used to selling things to clumps of people based on age: condoms at 25, anti-aging creams at 35, burial plots at 55.

"It's hard for business, because they can't figure out how to market to people based on life stages," Dychtwald says. She suggests marketing to empty nesters, to single women, to retirees as groups of people, not necessarily by age. "We are at the early stages of a long revolution in age," Dychtwald says. "We are re-imaging age, changing the chronic markers of age." She laughs about a Lou Harris survey that asked boomers when their parents turned old. The reply was 51. When the pollster asked the boomers when they would be old, the average response was 79. Aging, it seems, is for everyone else.

Dychtwald and others who advise business are correct when they say the sheer number of aging boomers will change attitudes toward aging. But business doesn't have to wait for boomers to tell them what to do. The market's already out there. "Get rid of age," Dychtwald says. "It's not working. Health tells you more about a person's life stage than chronological years." And then she speaks a great truth: "Our task must be to get the generations working together."

SOME WORDS OF ADVICE FOR THE CLASS OF '98

Monday, June 1, 1998

This is the season when young graduates sit on hard seats in the hot sun and suffer through boring commencement speeches by older people. The theory is that these older folk have the answers to life simply because they have lived so long. Which caused me to ponder: what would I say to the Class of 1998?

You lucky ducks! The economy is robust; there's spell-check on your computers and Viagra in your future. How can you fail?

But remember, life is not like a box of chocolates. Sometimes you reach for nougat and get a mouthful of peanut brittle. That, as they say, is the way the cookie crumbles, for it is only by surviving the crummy parts of life that we achieve wisdom.

I am older than you are and have had plenty of crummy days, which makes me wise enough to stand here this afternoon and tell you what to do.

Be brave; have the courage to take risks, but never forget the only winners in Las Vegas are the casino owners. The only thing you have to fear is fear itself—and going outside without sunblock.

Have an escape route; don't paint yourself into a corner or max out your credit card. Remember the story of the Nobel-winning scientist and his chauffeur. "I can give your speech as good as you can," the chauffeur boasted. So the scientist switched places with him at his next presentation. Everything went fine through the speech until one question from a woman in the audience stumped the chauffeur. Then he came up with this escape route: "That question is dumb. It's so dumb, even the man who drove me here and is standing at the back of the room can answer it, can't you?"

Keep learning; you never know when you will be replaced by a robot. Think of all the buggy-whip manufacturers who laughed at the first automobiles.

Like yourself; "No one can make you feel inferior without your consent," Eleanor Roosevelt said. This truly is the land of opportunity—the opportunity to succeed and the opportunity to file a lawsuit to get the chance to play on a level field.

Have ethics. Recycle. Take the time to learn who is running for public office and vote. Then you have a right to complain when you pay your income taxes.

Be versatile; accept fresh ideas. Think of the future as a bunch of career choices, not just a single stairway to paradise. And we all know the *Titanic* sank, so let's get over it, please.

Turn off your computer; don't believe everything you read on the Internet. No one can sue the Internet for slander. Get out of those chat rooms and connect with real people. It's important to understand what others think and feel, although you don't have to pierce your own body parts to share humanity's pain.

Discover your own frontiers—it's every generation's challenge. Take what we pass on to you—opportunity, peace, freedom—maintain the best of it and do better. The American Dream is alive and well.

Be a "Trekkie"; honor the motto to "Live Long and Prosper." Chances are most of you will see your 100th birthday. Medical science virtually guarantees it. So you can look forward to long life, and if you prosper, I can look forward to you paying taxes so I can retire and collect Social Security.

Graduates, you not only get the future, you get a new millennium! Just remember to duck for asteroids.

Monday, March 15, 1999

Pogo said it best: "We has met the enemy and he is us."

We are all living too long. And because we are living long, we threaten the economic well-being of our children and our grandchildren. That's one strong message of 1999, officially the International Year of Older Persons.

"There's an iceberg dead ahead. It's called global aging, and it threatens to bankrupt the great powers. As the populations of the world's leading economies age and shrink, we will face unprecedented political, economic and moral challenges." So writes Peter G. Peterson in his new book, *Gray Dawn* (Times Books). His treatise is an important, albeit depressing, read.

By 2040, America's elderly will outnumber college-age youth by four to one. By 2030, the developed world will gain nearly 100 million elders—while the number of working-age adults shrinks. For the sake of our children and grandchildren, the time is coming when the "current affluent," as he calls them, will have to give up something. No, not tomorrow. But soon.

"By 2030 the entire federal budget will be earmarked to finance entitlements," Peterson told me. Peterson, 72, has been labeled the Paul Revere of a graying world, sounding the alarm about the economic impact of age. Part of his agenda—allowing private investment for Social Security—could benefit some boomers. But there are honest differences about the depth of the problem. "The elder population has doubled since 1960 and we have survived that," Robert Friedland, deputy director of the National Academy on an Aging Society, says. Friedland points out this is a remarkable century, the most significant in terms of longevity. "We are either at the beginning of a remarkable trend in aging or, at the least, at a shift, a demarcation," he says. And while he is concerned, he is not hysteric.

Economic growth matters a lot, he points out. An annual 2.8 percent growth in our gross domestic product will keep the system on course. Maybe slowing the cost-of-living adjustments, maybe raising the retirement age could make a huge difference. But, he adds, "There is no question if we continue to finance Social Security on a pay-as-you-go policy, the burden on future workers will grow disproportionately."

Still looking at the doughnut and not the hole, Friedland emphasizes that people do change. They change their attitudes, how they form families, how they raise children. The labor force is already changing. In the last three years, the rate of early retirement has slowed and the percentage of workers over 65 has increased. "Demography is not destiny," Friedland says. The old will never "take it all" because "most people who have had children focus on children. That focus may move to grandchildren, but the simplistic attitude that once a parent, always a parent, keeps people connected." We will change.

Most change occurs gradually. So gradually, we don't notice it—like the frog in the old proverb who jumps out of a pot of boiling water but doesn't notice if he's plopped into a vat of room-temperature water and the heat is gradually turned up.

I vote we go ahead and live longer.

Like those critters that shared the Okefenokee Swamp with Pogo were wont to say, "Don't take life so seriously folks—it ain't no-hows permanent."

GRADUATION IS KNOWLEDGE, ON THE WAY TO GREATNESS

Monday, May 31, 1999

Once again we have reached that time of year when graduates sit on hard seats in the hot sun and listen to boring talks from older people like me who supposedly know everything because we have lived so long.

Well, I don't know everything. If I did, I could program my VCR. But I do have words of advice to pass along to the Class of '99.

Proud family will tell you that today you have achieved greatness. Don't believe them. What you have achieved is knowledge. How you apply that knowledge will determine your greatness.

To put your achievement in perspective, consider a message bouncing around on the Internet. Like most of these Internet messages, no one knows exactly where the information comes from or how accurate it is, but it illustrates the challenge your generation faces.

If we could shrink the Earth's population to a village of precisely 100 people, with all the existing human ratios remaining the same, it would look something like the following:

There would be 57 Asians; 21 Europeans, 14 from the Western Hemisphere, both north and south; 8 Africans; 52 would be female, 48 would be male; 70 would be nonwhite, 30 would be white; 70 would be non-Christian, 30 would be Christian; 89 would be heterosexual, 11 would be homosexual; 6 people would possess 59 percent of the entire world's wealth and they would all be from the United States.

Eighty would live in substandard housing; 70 would be unable to read; 50 would suffer from malnutrition; 1 would be near death, 1 would be near birth; 1 (yes, only 1) would have a college education; 1 (yes, only 1) would own a computer.

What's your challenge in that message? Clearly, you have not only achieved knowledge today, you also have won the advantage. Unlike 99 percent of the others in this global village, you graduates have education. I expect most of you also have a computer.

You control—or will control—almost 60 percent of the world's wealth. Burdened with debt from college loans, you may not feel rich today. But put your wealth in perspective: you and a date can spend $80 or more for tickets to a Backstreet Boys concert. A rural family in Vietnam needs only $100 a year to buy the food they cannot grow, the clothing they need and a few luxuries.

All parents want their children to live a better life. Getting you this far is part of the way we reach that goal. Now you have an opportunity to live—and flourish—like few who have come before you. Celebrate the knowledge you have achieved. Recognize that you have the advantage. And expect to have that advantage challenged in your lifetime by those who haven't got it.

Realize that your responsibility is twofold: to preserve the present and to expand the future. Now, go reach for greatness!

Part 17—In the End

SOONER OR LATER, I ALWAYS GET THE LAST WORD.

CHOOSING DEATH IS EASY; ALL YOU NEED IS NOBILITY

Monday, July 8, 1996

We are such a nation of wimps. On the one hand, we fear death is not going to be the exclamation point of our lives. On the other, we really want to believe that death is an okay way to put people out of their misery. Provided they go out in style, of course. Performance dying, I call it. It looks so easy, why don't all those old, sick people do it?

The best performance opened last week. It's by John Travolta in *Phenomenon*. Sans blood, whimper or Dr. Jack Kevorkian, John goes sweetly into that great good night wrapped in the arms of his lover.

Isn't death a whiz if you have the right attitude? We know Travolta does because he talks enthusiastically about the vigor of the human spirit. Truly, it's the human spirit that turns death into a performance. Timothy Leary not only knew that, he raised it to a higher level, spreading his Be-All-You-Can-Be spirit across his Internet home page. John Wayne did it on celluloid and remains an American hero.

Kevorkian taps into that life force. If reports are true, Dr. Jack's patients are fearless in the finale. In May, he assisted Austin Bastable, a Canadian multiple-sclerosis patient, in ending his life. Before he died, Bastable gathered his family for one last portrait. Later, they ate pizza. After he died, his son-in-law told a *Detroit Free Press* reporter, "We're happy and we're proud. He's in a much better place." What a performance!

Last week, Kevorkian attended another suicide, that of a 63-year-old Oceanside woman suffering from bowel cancer. The woman, Shirley Kline, reportedly died in the presence of Kevorkian, her son and two friends. Her performance gets less attention only because Kevorkian's "off-helpings" are becoming common. So far, Dr. Jack has helped 32 people, usually by having them inhale deadly carbon monoxide gas through a mask attached to a canister.

Kevorkian has assisted more women than men. Women seem to prefer pills and gas, suicide experts say. Men use guns and create a mess. But it's not Dr. Jack that worries me. It's our Hollywoodesque version of death that has me concerned. If sick people in extreme pain opt to die, you've got to hope they have made an honest appraisal of the situation. But we have to ask ourselves if we are setting unrealistic deathbed standards for the old, the sick, the weak.

Even the doctors in the forefront of the Hemlock Society movement to allow assisted death recognize that taking one's life is not a "natural" act. "There's a lot of agonizing during the dying process," says Dr. Ronald Koons, a Hemlock member and retired Laguna Beach oncologist. "Who wants to lose a loved one? And who wants to just turn over and have life be over? As prepared as you are, the last breath of life is difficult for everyone to accept."

Unless, of course, you regard it as your last performance. Performance dying takes away the sting. Instead of concentrating on what's happening, you focus on the folks around your bed. Like Violetta in *La Traviata,* you can sing loudly and die of consumption at the same time.

Can't you hear the kids now: "Way to go, Mom!"

Monday, September 16, 1996

How do you prepare for the moment when your parent demands your permission to die?

"I've got to believe we're the first generation facing this," says Mae, 46. "Our parents are living longer. Doctors and medicines can keep them going longer. And suddenly, we are the only ones who can let them die. They end up begging us."

Mae let her mother, Laura, 79, die a few weeks ago. Her father, brother and sister still don't understand or forgive. Their rejection leaves her alone in grief. "Is this what you get for being the responsible child?" she asks in bitterness. "That's another problem a lot of people in my generation are going to face. Being responsible. Responsible for death."

The saga began several months ago when Laura's sister, Mae's aunt, suffered a stroke. Paralyzed and unable to speak, the sister's condition declined. Doctors recommended no feeding tubes, but her husband insisted. The shell-person left drained the family's resolve. The questioning—leave the tubes in? take the tubes out?—was almost too much for them to bear.

"My mother watched her sister suffer and made me promise that wouldn't happen to her. She begged me to make sure. She wanted to be certain," Mae says.

Mae is a single woman with her own business. She knows where to go for answers. She got a Durable Power of Attorney for Health Care form for Laura. When Laura signed the document, she specified no life-sustaining care and made Mae her health-care agent. Two weeks later, a stroke felled Laura. "It was like a storybook event. The timing," Mae says. "Until I brought Mom's wishes up with Dad."

Others in the family rallied to keep Laura alive. After treatment, she was partially paralyzed and sent to a rehabilitation hospital. "She asked me, 'Is this it?' I had to be honest with her. I told her yes, that's what the doctor says. 'I want to die,' she said. 'Let me die.'"

Three times, Laura's doctor sat with his patient and listened to her plead. Finally, reluctantly, he asked Mae what she wanted him to do. "I had to tell him to stop everything. He gave her water and morphine. I sat with her, reaffirmed that we were doing what she wanted. I stroked her face," Mae says. "And she said, 'I am okay.'"

It took Laura three days to die. Most of that time she was in a coma. "I know I did what she wanted. I know she picked me to do it because she knew I am strong, like she was strong," Mae says. "She knew I would not waver. My family is still upset with me, but I am telling you this story because people have to know what to do. They have to be ready when these moments come. They have to help their parents."

Then Mae looks away so a stranger won't see the pain in her eyes. "I realized 10 years ago how much my mother loved me. No one loved me so much. No one ever will.

"I had to do it. It was what she wanted."

Monday, December 9, 1996

A friend sat by her mother's hospital bed recently, holding her hand in her final moments. "Go to the light," she urged. "Go to the light." Her intentions were loving. But since hearing is believed to be the last sense to go, my friend's voice might have been thundering in her mother's ears as the old woman groped for her final thoughts. No chance to pray with all that chatter going on. Or maybe she didn't see any light. What a sense of panic!

Lord, when my moment comes, spare me—from bores and boors, from well-meaning but intrusive people, from those who want to drain me of my last personal energy. Plenty of time, after I'm gone, for the survivors to take over. And Lord knows what creative plans they harbor!

For the past 25 years, there's been a trend to deny death, says Bill Bates, president of Life Appreciation Training Seminars Inc. in North Bay Village, Florida. Bates trains funeral directors to help consumers through their grief. He argues that seeing a body, looking at death, helps with closure.

Bates lived in the Los Angeles area for 20 years before moving to Florida in 1994. "In the whole time I was in Southern California," he says, "I never went to a service where a body was present." Bodies are rushed to crematoriums so no one has to look the dead in the face. Memorial services are held when everyone has pulled themselves together.

A few months ago, I was invited to a wine-and-cheese party "celebrating" the life of a woman who had died suddenly. The talk was crisp and sophisticated. We extolled her virtues and never shed a tear. We were all very modern, and I left feeling strangely empty, yearning for a grieving ritual.

Bates explains: "Active participation rather than passive observation is much healthier for the bereaved. People in mourning can only heal if they acknowledge their grief." He hopes that mourning—old-fashioned grief—is creeping back in style. That's why he is endorsing the Expressions casket produced by the York Group Inc. Expressions (retail about $3,000) is made of solid ash hardwood and features a glossy, pearlescent finish with a choice of several interior colors. It is shipped with a set of permanent markers. Mourners are encouraged to grab a marker and scribble a parting thought on the dearly dead's resting box.

Final shots—such as "This end up"—are discouraged.

Grieving is well and good, but don't look for Expressions at Fairhaven Memorial Park & Mortuary in Santa Ana. The casket is not part of the inventory. Not that Fairhaven doesn't go with the flow. "Sometimes families build their own caskets and bring them in," says John Gettys, preparation-room coordinator. "Anymore, there's not too much that shocks or surprises me."

So far, however, no one has asked for a post-a-note-style casket. Probably because no one has thought of it until now. York's publicity for the casket cites a 1994 study commissioned by the Jewish Funeral Directors Association that polled more than 300 psychologists to conclude the obvious—funerals are for the living. The most important value of the service is to enable the mourners, friends and associates to participate in the grieving process. Scribbling on a casket is a "therapeutic release necessary for full emotional healing," the casket company's publicity says. Instead of tucking photographs and trinkets around a corpse, surround the body with graffiti.

I can see it now: "Way to go, Jane."

"Bye, bye, Blondie."

"Happy Trails to You."

Is that the real meaning of grateful dead?

Death Is Less Terrifying If We Don't Have to Face It Alone

Monday, January 20, 1997

Jim Jeffrey was a very scheduled man. When he was diagnosed with prostate cancer, he set up a financial plan and brought his wife, Nancy, into his Ontario real-estate business so she would understand the operation. He made a video with his adult children, regaling them with tales of his childhood. Then, as the cancer progressed, Jeffrey, 62, visited John Colombe, pastor to senior adults at First Evangelical Free Church in Fullerton. He felt he wanted to do more to bring his life to closure. Colombe had an inspiration: Why not "attend" his own funeral by creating a living eulogy?

The pastor offered to guide a family session in which everyone—down to the youngest grandchild—talked about the value of their years with Jeffrey. "It was hard because he knew he was going to die, but he didn't know when," Nancy Jeffrey says. "But the experience brought us all together to face death. We don't want to face it, but we all have to. This way, we all shared our love for each other."

The Jeffreys gathered as a family in November 1994. In January, Jim Jeffrey died. But their experience lives in a video Jeffrey authorized as a teaching tool, a road map for other families facing a death. Colombe will include parts of the video in a curriculum he is developing to help others create living eulogies.

Jim Jeffrey recognized that most people spend years preparing for life and little time readying themselves for their own death, Colombe says. "People think they know how they want to die, but they have rarely come to terms with their mortality," he says.

Families get involved, demanding treatments, refusing to let go. A study of 4,124 deaths, published this month in the *Annals of Internal Medicine,* determined that most elderly and seriously ill patients died in acute-care hospitals with severe pain, fatigue and other symptoms.

Most of these people had living wills—directives that authorized no heroic treatments.

The study says healthy people might say they do not want futile care, but it's often impossible to define when care becomes futile. And people who are seriously ill cling tenaciously to any shred of hope or sign of life. "Maybe if people believe they have life after death they can let go more easily," Colombe says. "Maybe they can go if they treat death with respect and talk about it and bring it into the open."

Nancy Jeffrey talks to people facing death when she volunteers as an assistant for Colombe two days a week. "So many people have told me they regret not having a chance to say goodbye, to say what a parent's life has meant. It's not easy, but it is important," she says.

Authors of the latest study on how people die say it is the first extensive report since one done 90 years ago by doctors at Johns Hopkins Hospital. At that time, death was found to be mostly quick and peaceful, they say. "Our society has not yet accepted the inevitability of death," says an editorial that accompanies the current study. "We must change our attitudes and accept death as a natural phenomenon. . . . We must provide our patients with a peaceful and dignified death, without pain and with as little anguish and anxiety as possible."

No one wants to let go. It helps to let go together.

PEOPLE'S WISHES FOR THEIR FINAL FAREWELL
AS VARIED AS THEY ARE

Monday, June 16, 1997

How do you want to go into that great good night?

Most of us don't give our own funeral ceremony much thought. Journalist Murray Kempton, who died in May at 79, did set out his wishes. For his last rites, Kempton asked for Order for the Burial of the Dead, prescribed by the 1559 *Book of Common Prayer,* no flowers, no speeches. The short list prompted *New Yorker* magazine to survey other notables, turning up exit expectations for everything from ribaldry to extensive public mourning.

I got the same mixed bag when I asked several people, "How would you design your own funeral?" Final bows, it appears, depend on how one struts across life's stage.

"I want a lot of open sobbing," says Liz Carpenter, 76, writer and former press secretary to Lady Bird Johnson. "I don't want them to say, 'She wouldn't want us to weep.'" She's asking the women in her Bay at the Moon senior club to fill the pews in the Methodist church to render a stirring "How Great Thou Art."

And then, the Austin, Texas, resident says, "I want to be cremated, mixed with wildflower seeds and strewn from a silver champagne holder in Salado, the home of my ancestors." Each "strewer" will get a pair of white gloves, she says, "because I've done some strewin' and you always end up with little bits of grit under your fingernails."

No such florid farewell for Orange County resident Van Arsdale France, 84, founder of the Disneyland University. Recalling his aunt's funeral at 92, France says, "The undertaker and I were the only ones there, so I figure I should go quietly. I hate to talk when there's no audience."

Lilias Folan, 61, who popularized yoga with her PBS series, was at her farm in Virginia when I reached her. She says she has thought about her funeral for years and has been collecting stories and sayings. "I want to put a booklet together. I want to give people something that is very personal from me. Everybody should think about their death every day and their life every day. If you look at things that make you feel uncomfortable and fearful, usually the fears will dissolve right away."

Then there's James Doti, president of Chapman University in Orange, who says, at 50, "I have no plans at all." He pauses, reconsiders. "I want to be cremated and my ashes scattered privately. A quiet event. No big deal. Something peaceful."

Or Dr. Max Schneider, director of education for Chapman General Hospital Positive Action Center in Orange: "I want Ronnie (Smelt), my life companion, to douse me with kerosene and light my left great toe.

"I picked the left toe because I don't do anything from the 'right' in Orange County."

Sick and Alone, Edith Palazzo Doesn't Want to Prolong Her Agony

Friday, June 27, 1997

Every day, Edith Palazzo dies a little.

It's not the "little dying" that worries the Leisure World Laguna Hills resident. It's the "big dying"—the pain and loneliness she expects in the final stages of her lung cancer—that Palazzo fears. "I want euthanasia," says the 84-year-old retired nurse, who has no living relatives.

On Thursday, the Supreme Court said she has no constitutional right to that option.

Palazzo says that leaves her two choices when her disease forces her to bed. She can die under hospice care, relying on a hired caretaker or nursing-home workers to join with hospice professionals to keep her pain-free. Or she can follow the "suicide recipe" outlined by Derek Humphrey in his book *Final Exit.*

Dying at home frightens her.

"I am very much afraid to be here alone," she says. Sweeping her arm to take in the one-bedroom retirement manor where she has lived for 16 years, Palazzo says, "There will be no professional care here. How will a caretaker know if I'm in pain?" She rejects hospice care in a nursing home for the same reasons.

Twice widowed, the native of Germany says she is a long way from requesting help. But, she says, "Now is the time to think things through."

"I still swim and do aerobics, clean and cook for myself. I am not ready to die," she says.

But her lonely life concerns her. The Hemlock Society's recipe for suicide advises having someone on hand to help. "I don't have anyone," she says.

People who have experienced hospice with a loved one say it is nothing to fear. "Hospice gave us a solid foundation for care," says Jim Conway, whose wife, Sally, was a hospice patient for eight months, until her death May 27. "They were always smiling and cheery."

Conway and his wife founded Midlife Dimensions, a Fullerton-based ministry that encourages lasting marriages. "We worked together for years, and so we faced her death together," he says. He turned down speaking engagements and other business ventures to care for his wife, a luxury he admits is not possible for many.

Conway says he was not aware of the breadth of hospice services until professionals from Hospice Care of California took over Sally Conway's care last August. Sally, dying of breast cancer that had spread to her spine, remained relatively pain-free through her decline, he says. "Sally and I talked very bluntly about suicide. We just wanted to stay connected as long as possible.

"I'm glad we made that choice."

Ever feel like you can't win for losing?

There you are, feeling pretty darn good about hitting 50 or 60 or even 70 birthdays, and along comes a whole party of poopers calling you nasty names.

No, I'm not talking about the gloom-siders who view your aging as yet another nail in the economic destruction of the American way to life because you leech tax dollars for Social Security and Medicare. I'm talking about confusion in everyday conversation over the right words to use to identify people over 50.

Ten years after "elderly" scared me into the crinkly-wrinklies, "aging issues" still is a lousy term to describe what I write about. In fact, there isn't a word that won't raise objections from somebody, which ought to tell us something about our diversity but only addles our attitude.

Are we geezers or geezerettes? Old people or mature adults? Seniors or retirees? Does it matter?

"There are so many of us, there is no good word to describe us all," says Theodore Roszak, author of *American the Wise* (Houghton Mifflin).

We span more than 50 years and four generations: the oldest boomers (born 1946–64) the Silent Generation (1930–45), the World War II Generation (1915–30) and the Depression Generation (1895–1915), celebrated today as centenarians.

And we don't know what to call ourselves. Truly. We are an army of people euphemistically challenged.

Well, who cares what people call us if we feel good and have money in the bank?

A study of 3,000 adults of all ages conducted by the National Council on the Aging and the International Longevity Center found that most Americans are pretty happy, even those in their 70s and 80s. The share of older Americans saying these are the best years increased substantially (44 percent versus 32 percent) compared with a similar survey in 1974.

When does old age begin? Not with birthdays but with declining functions, respondents said. Forty-one percent said a "decline in physical ability" and 32 percent a "decline in mental functioning" marked the beginning of old age.

Who is middle-aged? One-third of Americans in their 70s consider themselves middle-aged. Nearly half (45 percent) of people 65–69 call themselves middle-aged.

You are only as old as you think you are. You are as young as your body will let you be.

Bernard Baruch is right. Old age will always be 15 years older than I am.

Author's Note

Jane Glenn Haas is available for speaking engagements and workshops. You may contact her at (714) 997-0542, by e-mail at jghaas@aol.com or through her Web site, www.womansage.com.

WHAT IS WOMANSAGE?

- It's a Web site—www.womansage.com—launched by Jane Glenn Haas (in cooperation with the Women's Center at California State University, Fullerton) to provide a forum and information for women 50-plus. The site includes a lifestyle survey that is a part of book research.

- It's a 12-page newsletter to be published 12 times a year, dedicated to empowering and informing women 50-plus on their unique lifestyle issues. Edited by Jane Glenn Haas, the newsletter includes regular features by women experts on topics such as finance, caregiving, relationships, health and fitness, and leisure pursuits such as travel. Womansage is committed to providing the highest-quality information and resources possible in a format exclusive of paid advertising.

HOW TO SUBSCRIBE TO WOMANSAGE:

Send check or money order for $18 to:

Womansage

1450 N. Harding St., Suite E

Orange, CA 92867

Or check the Web site, www.womansage.com

Or call (714) 997-0542 for information.

SPECIAL OFFER

Enclose this charter subscriber coupon with your check or money order and your one-year subscription to Womansage will be automatically extended for an additional three months. That's 15 months for the price of 12!

YES, I WANT TO BE A CHARTER SUBSCRIBER
TO WOMANSAGE!